# AFTER THE TRAUMA

# AFTER THE TRAUMA

*Representative British Novelists Since 1920*

Harvey Curtis Webster

The University Press of Kentucky

*Lexington: 1970*

823.9
W379a

*"If way to the better there be, it exacts a full
look at the worst."*

THOMAS HARDY, "IN TENEBRIS."

*"For poetry makes nothing happen. . . . it
survives. . . . A way of happening, a mouth."*

W. H. AUDEN, "IN MEMORY OF W. B. YEATS."

# Contents

## Preface

In selecting the novelists I write about, I have been helped greatly by my English friends L. P. Hartley, Walter Allen, Lord and Lady Snow, and John and Veronica Kilgour. I am indebted also to Ivy Compton-Burnett and the late Rose Macaulay for the kindness of letters and interviews that have helped me to make up my mind about those I decided with difficulty to select as "representative." Granville Hicks helped me plan a far more comprehensive book than this one. He also helped me modify my too ambitious initial plan and has criticized many parts of this book. To him I owe an unpayable debt and none of my errors in selection, judgment, or writing.

Though this is not a "scholarly" book, the habit of "thoroughness" that infected me in graduate school compelled me to read dozens of novelists before excluding them, all the British Council pamphlets on contemporary novelists, the discriminating appraisals of the novels of the week that have appeared in the *New Statesman* and *Spectator* during the seventeen years I've worked on this book, the valuable critiques of contemporary literature by Sean O'Faolain, G. S. Fraser, J. K. Johnston, R. A. Scott-James, William Tyndall, D. S. Savage, John McCormick, Frank Swinnerton, Edmund Fuller, Anthony Burgess, Arnold Kettle, Frederick Karl, and Walter Allen—I'm sure I've forgotten others. To the writers of the pamphlets, the periodical reviewers, and the named critics I am indebted much more considerably than I have acknowledged specifically. I am aware, particularly, of my indebtedness to Walter Allen—whose *The Modern Novel in Britain and the United States* is definitive enough to assuage my guilt for not carrying out my initial intention to be comprehensive—with whom I have discussed my book often and recently.

An incomplete list of those who have helped me should include Professor Tom Ware of the University of Chattanooga, who made abstracts of reviews of English novels of the past forty years from all the important periodicals while he was my undergraduate assistant, and my wife, Lucille Jones Webster, who has heard and read all the many versions and treated them kindly. Without the grant of two Fulbright fellowships in England, four fellowships at Yaddo, a year's sabbatical leave from the University of Louisville, and several grants for books and travel by the University of Louisville Research Fund, I would have been unable to undertake this study. In earlier versions, chapters or large portions of chapters appeared in *Critique,* the *Saturday Review,* the *Sewanee Review,* the *Kenyon Review,* the *New Leader* (copyright © The American Labor Conference on International Affairs, Inc.), the *New Republic,* and in *Graham Greene: Some Critical Considerations* (University of Kentucky Press, 1963); they are reprinted by permission of the publishers. Of course, I assume the blame for mistakes of fact or judgment. And I extend my apologies to the gifted novelists my critics will regret my excluding.

## Introduction

Since neither I nor anyone else has read more than a small fraction of English novels published since World War I, it is with hesitance that I say the novelists I write about in this book represent the age they are unhappy with. I knew little about most of them when I taught American fiction and poetry at the University of Durham, England, in 1950 and 1951. I became aware then of the immense gaps in my knowledge of British fiction since Joyce, Forster, Lawrence, Woolf, and Dorothy Richardson, and I started (at first casually, later avidly) to read and write about the novelists usually excluded from "academic" respectability.

Human nature did not change in 1910, as Virginia Woolf suggested. But the conditions affecting the development of those who had not matured before 1914—including Rose Macaulay and Aldous Huxley, who matured late—did. The Wasteland is more than Eliot's metaphor and the Age of Anxiety more than the title of a book Auden wrote. Both terms legitimately symbolize part of the way sensitive and aware readers and writers have felt life for five decades. Of course, to use Horace Gregory's equally useful phrase, the anxious sufferers in the wasteland have been a chorus for survival, too.

All good writers, I presume to believe, are aware of the awfulness of our times and hope both to make the present endurable and to prepare for a future which will have a place for the traditions and the individual talents that recognize awfulness, tragic joy, and comedy. Such an anxious chorus for survival would have been out of place in the years before 1914. Joyce, Woolf, Richardson, Lawrence, Forster, all of them were aware of the horrors that made the 1914 war appear inevitable. But what they wrote about was what they considered to be the usual human condition and individual salvation. After writing *Ulysses,* in which social salvation seems both unthinkable and futile, Joyce became a great artificer excessively enchanted with verbal agility. Virginia Woolf beautifully caught the falling atoms; except in *Between the Acts* she did not make them cohere. Dorothy Richardson elevated the trivial into what many call aesthetic importance. Lawrence saw the connecting of individuals of unusual awareness as the chief—perhaps only—value. Forster believed we should connect the poetry and the prose but he published no novels after visiting the Marabar Caves. All of these older writers survived the trauma but none of them felt it unusual enough to affect their already chosen directions.

More popular but still good writers, whom we neglect currently, wrote about social survival and social improvement. Galsworthy and Wells and Bennett and Shaw and Chesterton and Hilaire Belloc—in a sense the progenitors of many of those I write about—wrote voluminously to improve "the age." But how idyllically muted or stridently "progressive" their protests now seem to us! They lived in and never totally grew away from an age in which there was always tea at Grantchester.

The novelists about whom I write more appreciatively than critically—though I try to discriminate among them and among their novels—probably are not great. In this year of good writing that is rarely more than that, I doubt that any twentieth-century writer in English except Yeats is, if one uses the word precisely, great. But all these novelists are gifted, and the best of their novels are more available to most intelligent readers' enjoyment, comprehension, and enlightenment than, say, what Joyce wrote after *Portrait of the Artist.* I believe that all of them are skillful in disparate ways much of the time and that they have much to say, in unconstraining voices, now and in any predictable future. This is, to a great degree, the consequence of their maturing during the years that included and followed World War I. No one and no thing, except essential human nature, has been the same since.

*Chapter One*

# The Trauma

THE LAST YEAR of an age golden enough to make us think it so opened quietly. The London *Times* for January 1, 1914, talked about the extreme cold, editorialized against pessimism, carried a leader in its literary supplement about Hans Christian Andersen, said in its special supplement about 1913: "We may surely . . . count among the securities for peace the existence of a better understanding between England and Germany." On the same January day in 1914, the *Daily Graphic* found nothing more sensational for its front page than pictures of those honored in the New Year's list: twenty-five new peers, six baronets, twenty-two knights, pictures of many of them. It also commented upon the extreme cold and, the next day, found Hobbs's just missing a hundred in cricket, the appearance of the "Divine Sarah" Bernhardt in a play, and Lloyd George's remarks about disarmament equally important. Lloyd George was quoted as saying, "This is a propitious moment for reconsidering the question of armaments."

As the year warmed, still no marked tension about international affairs was evident in either newspaper. The *Times* complained about Irish troubles, editorialized in favor of the protection of rare birds, favored being a gentleman, discoursed learnedly about the ways of rooks, noted (on July 1) with faint alarm German naval increases. The *Graphic* was indignant (March 11) about "one of the most disgraceful outrages of which the suffragettes have been guilty in a long series of crimes," the slashing with a hatchet of Velasquez's Venus. It also wrote about the "Magnetic Girl," about a bishop who praised advertising, a strike of 30,000 miners (March 31), about 84 degrees in the shade on July 1 and the delightful respite one might find in Wiesbaden.

If one turns to the weeklies, which had more time to think

things over, the difference is largely in subject matter and style. The *New Statesman* wrote interestingly of Shackleton's projected trip to the South Pole (the war prevented it), defended post-impressionism and feminism, advocated a supertax *if* the naval budget was increased, carried criticism of Walter Pater, of the correspondence of Marx and Engels, of Frank Swinnerton, Joseph Conrad, Frank Norris, and Saki. The *Spectator* wrote of international danger, perhaps because it intensely disliked Lloyd George ("the quick change artist of politics" who had suddenly gone over to the Little Navy Camp) and admired Winston Churchill, who advocated a strong navy. If the British navy is strong, the *Spectator* said on January 3, "There is a distinct possibility of German effort being relaxed as useless." The magazine's main concerns until late July were with Home Rule, labor troubles in South Africa, and a pernicious effort to democratize the army. Among the books it paid particular attention to were *The British Bird Book, Leonardo Da Vinci,* the poems of Carducci, Lord Curzon's *Modern Parliamentary Eloquence,* and F. H. Bradley's *Essays on Truth and Reality.* In addition to the concerns that mildly agitated the *Spectator,* the *Saturday Review* (also anti-Lloyd George and pro-Churchill) found time to write intelligently about Freud's second book to be translated into English, *The Psychopathology of Everyday Life,* about Matthew Arnold's *Essays,* and about the most widely read of contemporary poets, Ella Wheeler Wilcox, "the exact echo of the public voice." As late as August 1, 1914, the *Saturday Review* continued to publish a series of travel articles, "Motoring Routes in France," a series suspended in the issue of August 8.

Except for the very few who felt the coming of the war before it came, the mature and immature believed war an impossibility. As Gilbert Murray wrote in the *Twentieth Century* for March 1957, J. A. Spender, "the typical moderate liberal of the day," said, "It is unthinkable that we should have a war with our German cousins," a few days before war was declared. Even Thomas Hardy confessed after the outbreak of war, "If I had been told three months ago that any inhabitants of Europe would wilfully damage such a masterpiece as Rheims in any circumstance whatever, I should have thought it an

incredible statement." A little earlier he had written of "The
Sick Battle God," who "rarely gladdens champions now." As
G. F. Hudson remarked in the same issue of the *Twentieth
Century* for which Murray wrote, "War came swiftly and
suddenly to the European peoples in 1914; within a few days
of the first public awareness of the danger the armies of five
out of six Great Powers of Europe were launched into battle.
Today it is hard for us to imagine how strong was the sense of
stability and security in the world of 1914." Indeed it was hard.
On July 29, the *Daily Graphic* saw no reason "for enlarging
the area of the war" after Austria had marched on Serbia. On
August 1, the *Times* hoped there would not be a general war.
On July 25, the *New Statesman* urged its readers to disregard
"the more lurid telegrams . . . from Vienna"; on August 1 it
could still say, "As we write the worst has not happened."

The change from apparent stability to what seems like permanent insecurity strongly affected nearly all the writers who
matured after 1914, and a good many of those who "grew up"
earlier. The war and the impermanent peace caused a trauma
no other experience could have caused by itself. Before the
war, in an atmosphere in which it seemed perfectly natural to
write of leisure, of the delight of escape through books, of
"Milk for the Cat," of Eve "deep in the bells and grass," of the
power of imaginative sympathy to right everything, Siegfried
Sassoon wrote quiet, effective poetry about natural things,
Charles Sorley wrote of "the dear soft grasses under foot" and
of Beauty that "never can be mute," and Wilfred Owen wrote
of "Birds/Cheerily chirping in the early day." Before they died
in war, Sorley and Owen had subjects that seem natural to us
now, that would have seemed unnatural to them before August
1914. Sorley wrote of "millions of the mouthless dead" crossing
dreams "in pale battalions." Owen wrote of red lips not so red
"As the stained stones kissed by the English dead" and of "The
old lie: Dulce et decorum est/Pro patria mori." For a long
time after World War I was over, the only one of these
distinguished poets who survived, Sassoon, wrote bitter poems
about whether it mattered losing your leg and about "The
visionless officialized fatuity/That once kept Europe safe for

Perpetuity." Could even Yeats have written "The Second Coming" without experience of World War I?

> Mere anarchy is loosed upon the world
> The blood-dimmed tide is loosed, and everywhere
> The ceremony of innocence is drowned;
> The best lack all conviction, while the worst
> Are full of passionate intensity.

One may feel that the war was inherent in the hundred years' "peace," that war was a delayed manifestation of aggressive impulses the Victorians, Edwardians, and early Georgians almost suppressed. Even the most sensitive of them could not anticipate adequately its awfulness.

After more than fifty years of aftermath we incline to condescend to the gentlemanliness of Galsworthy, the provincial realism of Arnold Bennett, the Lamarckian optimism of Shaw, the patriotic pastoralism of Rupert Brooke. Yet to do so means that we have forgotten the stable world the Allies thought they fought for the return of, against unmitigatedly evil Germany. It was not only H. G. Wells who felt: "For this is now a war for peace. It aims at a settlement that shall stop this sort of thing forever." On August 8, 1914, the intelligent *Spectator* editorialized: "We are now embarked in a just and necessary war . . . a war . . . thrust upon Europe by . . . a power of brutal might." A poem in the same issue began, "This is our cause, the freedom of the World." On the same day the *New Statesman* declared, "We all feel that the greatest of all human victories will be the victory over war." The London *Times* for August 5 stated, "We have worked for peace. Now we must fight for it." With few exceptions the British and their allies believed that they were joining forces against the Devil and that their right would prevail, that after victory wars would end and the world would be made safe for democracy. World War I was both a trauma and a crusade. What C. E. Montague said of the group of which he was a part was true of nearly everyone at first:

> most . . . volunteers . . . were men of handsome and boundless illusions. Each of them quite seriously thought of himself as a molecule in the body of the nation that was "straining every

nerve" to discharge an obligation of honour. Honestly, there was about them as little as there humanly could be of the coxcombery of self-devotion.

As the war continued, as the soldiers came to see the mistakes of their own command, to observe the humanity of their enemies and the too comfortable belligerence of those who acted like E. E. Cummings's Aunt Lucy, disenchantment began. The development of this disenchantment can be read about in novels from all countries: Dos Passos's *Three Soldiers* and *1919*, Cummings's *The Enormous Room*, Hemingway's *Farewell to Arms*, H. M. Tomlinson's *All Our Yesterdays,* and Richard Aldington's *Death of a Hero*, Remarque's *All Quiet on the Western Front,* and Arnold Zweig's *The Case of Sergeant Grischa*, Henri Barbusse's *Under Fire,* Sholokhov's *And Quiet Flows the Don,* Ford Maddox Ford's *Parade's End*. But I doubt if there is a more accurate first-hand account than C. E. Montague's *Disenchantment* (1922), the record of what happened to him and the group he joined at the age of forty-seven.

Montague's chapter titles give an overview of the experience of the average and not-average man: "The Vision"; "Misgiving: At Agincourt and Ypres"; "Tedium"; "The Sheep That Were Not Fed" (about the chaplains); "'Ware Politicians"; "Can't Believe a Word" (the newspapers); "The Duty of Lying" (the propaganda machine); "Autumn Tints in Chivalry"; "The Old Age of the War"; "Our Modern Satirists" (the "peace" and its consequences).

Idealistic visions faded rapidly, despite the fact that most soldiers *had* taken their "pastors and masters" as trustfully as they had their parents:

> A century of almost unbroken European peace . . . had built up insensibly in men's minds a consciousness of an unbounded general stability in the political as well as in the physical world. The crust of the political globe . . . felt as if it were so firm that we would safely play the fool on it, as boys jump on the ice of a pond and defy it to break under them.

Montague's group soon discovered that the regular army sneered at the idealism of such volunteers as they were, that the officers were often incompetent. They learned also, particularly at

Ypres, that the courteous warfare they had read about in
Shakespeare had disappeared, that "To honour while you strike
him down/The foe who comes with eager eye" (Montague's
quotation from Sir Henry Newbolt), was considered a lack of
patriotism by chaplains, officers, and home front patriots. The
true Englishman should enjoy the cruelest possible use of the
bayonet. Despite censorship, too much leaked out to the soldiers
who were not enjoying the tedium of the trenches. Conscription,
so they heard, was cried for by "healthy young publicists who
then begged themselves off before tribunals"; conscientious
objectors, for whom the soldiers at the front were beginning
to feel respect, were mobbed by belligerent civilians. Profiteers
were having their safe fling and, as for the politicians, their talk
semed as obnoxious as their mismanagement of incompetent
generals. Worst of all was the growing distrust of Christianity.
The men could not agree with the bloodthirstiness of the
"virilist" chaplains who, even after the armistice, complained
because "the killing was not to go on until a few German towns
had been smashed and our last thing in gas had had a fair
innings."

The consequence was the angry disenchantment Montague
believed typical of the twenties:

> A child who has rashly taken parent on trust, and yet more
> rashly taken the parent's all-round perfection as some sort
> of . . . proof of a creditable government of the world, must
> have a good deal of mental re-arrangement to do the first time
> the parent comes home full of liquor and sells the furniture
> to get some more.

This mental rearrangement, particularly after peace was made
"with a vengeance" at Versailles, included a distrust of religion,
of politics, of newspapers, of conventional morality. Though
there remained a vague yearning to be fed by trustworthy
pastors and masters, it was difficult to find them. God had
advocated both the war and the peace, the Church seemed to
say. Yet the soldiers liked and felt sorry for the enemies they
had and had not killed, and gave survivors their rations after
the armistice, despite orders not to. And was not the Englishman's God supposed to be the God of all mankind? Yet it was

hard to distinguish between the stoking up of hate by the
Archbishop of Canterbury and that of the Archbishop of
Cologne. Neither they nor their followers seemed trustworthy
pastors. As for the masters, they had promised and not fulfilled;
not only had they blundered in the war; in the peace they were
quite as bad, disregarding Keynes's advice about its economic
consequences, the needs of the returning soldiers, and calls for
Christian charity with equal equanimity. The press had lied
during the war; why should it be believed afterwards? Indeed
it appeared that the plainest moral duty was the duty to lie.
"You need to have two gears to your morals, and drive on
one gear in war and on the other in peace" was the most
charitable interpretation of what the pastors and masters did
and said. Or, as another of Montague's comrades felt, "They
tell me we've pulled through at last all right because our propaganda dished out better lies than what the Germans did. So I
say to myself 'If tellin lies is all that bloody good in war, what
bloody good is tellin truth in peace?'"

What may someday be called the century of the common
lie, Montague makes clear, was off to a good start. The average
man ran "about looking for little pick-me-ups and nips of something mildly exciting to keep to par their sagging sense of the
adventuresomeness of life. Derby sweeps . . . every kind of
gamble . . . rawest sensationalism—anything that will give a
fillip, any poor new-whiskey fillip, to jaded nerves." Why not?
For to him and to the not-average man as well, it seemed that
an honest expression of those they thought responsible for
World War I would go something like this:

> Even amid the horrors of peace you will find little shoots
> of character fed by the gentle and timely rains of plague and
> famine, tempest and fire; simple lessons of patience and courage
> conned in the schools of typhus, and gout. . . . For remember
> that even these poor makeshift schools of character, these
> second-bests, these halting substitutes for war—remember that
> the efficiency of every one of them, be it hunger, accident,
> ignorance, sickness or pain, is menaced by the intolerable strain
> of its struggle with secular doctors, plumbers, inventors, school-
> masters, and policemen. . . . Every year thousands who would
> in nobler days have been braced and steeled by manly tussles

> with smallpox or diphtheria are robbed of that blessing by the
> great changes made in our drains. . . . I cannot help asking
> myself—whether we are not walking into a very slough of moral
> and spiritual squalor.
>
> Once more, I am no alarmist. As long as we have wars to
> stay our souls upon, the moral evil will not be grave; and, to
> do the Ministry justice, I see no risk of their drifting into any
> long or serious peace.

The bitter, obvious irony Montague puts into the phrasing of
this "honest" speech is a, almost *the,* tone of the twenties that
abated (partially) in the thirties and forties, that is still to be
heard in the writing of the Angry Young Men of England and
the "militants" in the United States, accentuated further by
bureaucratic and technological developments that appear to
make collective protest futile. It is an irony that followed,
naturally enough, the discovery that a century of progress had
led to what seems to be a century of regress in which, indeed,
no governments seem in danger of "drifting into any long or
serious peace." Whether man's condition, considered objectively,
justifies the tone or not, it is a tone founded upon substantial
happenings that most modern writers must recognize, whether
they write with bitter irony or against bitter irony. A background of shattering war and uncertain peace is the essential
social fact which, with its metaphysical implications, all good
writers deeply involved in the life of their times must face if
they are to show anything valuable to the contemporary reader.
The varieties of life, thought, and belief dramatized in the
stretch of modern novels from Rose Macaulay's and Aldous
Huxley's to C. P. Snow's and William Golding's have not solved
the social or the metaphysical problems that life since 1914
presents. But these deeply involved writers can, quite as much
as those who matured before 1914, help us to comprehend and
adjust—perhaps even to remake. Certainly they do not deserve
the neglect they have received since it has become convenient
to think of Joyce, Virginia Woolf, Dorothy Richardson, D. H.
Lawrence, and E. M. Forster as the only modern novelists worth
taking seriously. There is a great deal to be said (and most of
it has been) for the writer who imitates "The God of the creation . . . within or behind or beyond or above his handiwork,

invisible, refined out of existence, indifferent, paring his finger-nails." There is also a good deal to be said for the involved British writer who agrees with Hemingway in his preface to his short stories:

> In going where you have to go, and doing what you have to do, and seeing what you have to see, you dull and blunt the instrument you write with. But I would rather have it bent and dulled and know I had to put it on the grindstone again and hammer it into shape and put a whetstone to it, and know that I had something to write about, than to have it bright and shining and nothing to say, or smooth and well-oiled in the closet, but unused.

## Chapter Two

# Rose Macauley: A Christian a Little Agnostic

WHEN ROSE MACAULEY FIRST CAME to London (she tells us in the *London Magazine* for March 1957), it was from her home in Italy, where she spent most of her early childhood with her "never at all respectable" parents. Much of her childhood she spent reading omnivorously, learning Latin and math, going to a convent school, using Sunday "as a day for license and liberty and riotous living." London was the exciting place where books came from, where on their occasional visits, the Macaulay children could buy also "ships, magnets, pistols, cannons, knives . . . and many other very useful things," where they could walk on stilts and play hide and seek around St. Mary Abbot's Church, go to the zoo and the Natural History Museum, behave in a "most uncultured way."

When the Macaulays left Italy and settled in Cambridge, where the father lectured on English literature, Rose began going to London frequently, lunching with a friend of the family, Rupert Brooke, going to dinner or to plays with him and with Edward Thomas, Wilfred Gibson, Ralph Hudgson, others. Sometime between 1910 and 1912 she met Naomi Royde-Smith and "was dazzled," Walter de la Mare, who "was very beautiful and had a fantastic wit and funniness and his poetry . . . blurred the frontiers of reality and dream, which is what poetry ought to do." Being friendly with writers and civil servants and journalists, "the contemporary literary, political and social scene became," to her inexperienced eyes, "very amusing and alive." As, intermittently, it continued to be until her death in 1958.

But never quite as much as then, especially when "then" was 1913 and she had a flat in London where she could come part of each week. She rushed about with friends, went to the readings at the Poetry Bookshop, where Brooke or Gibson or de la Mare read his most recent work. She devoured the new books by Hardy, James, Shaw, Wells, Conrad, Beerbohm, Bennett, Maugham, Galsworthy, Saki, Elizabeth Russell ("some are famous today, others almost forgotten, for oblivion scattereth her poppies and some are quite covered up by them and some not, and it seems largely chance"). She was excited or angered by the new magazines: *Blast* (BLAST . . . SENTIMENTAL HYGIENICS ROUSSEAUISMS FRATERNIZING WITH MONKEYS DIABOLIC—raptures and roses . . . in PURGATORY OF PUTNEY), Middleton Murry's and Katherine Mansfield's *Blue Review*, where one read D. H. Lawrence, Ford Madox Ford's *English Review*, where E. M. Forster, "the most distinguished of the younger novelists before 1914," appeared. She went to the Russian ballet "about which we all went mad in those years," saw Diaghilev and Massine and Nijinsky and Pavlova, to the opera to hear Chaliapin, Caruso, and Melba, to the theatre for Granville Barker's Shakespeare, for Shaw's and Ibsen's plays. It was all

> great fun at the time, and part of the sociable London life which seemed so happy, clever, exciting and good. . . . Because in my world young men and women shared work and amusements, played games together, went out together in the evenings, went country walking together (we did not call it hiking, but we did more of it), discussed everything together, and, in fact, behaved much as they do now, except that there was rather less going to bed together, for sex, although always of course quite prevalent, has come on a good way since then.
>
> Then came the loudest and most uncivilized of the noises off, a chapter was closed with a bang, and the world ran amok like a herd of wild elephants.
>
> That golden age will not return; and anyhow one has grown too old for it.

But she did not, even in her seventies, grow too old to enjoy our ungolden age, and, though she grew up only a little later than Joyce and his contemporaries, she seems quite unlike all of them in her personality, her capacity to hope and be disillusioned, to find a reasonably firm faith eventually.

Perhaps "personality" should be stressed above all. "You can't 'interview' Rose Macaulay," John Davenport wrote in the *New York Times Book Review* for April 21, 1957.

> She interviews you. You can tease her up all sorts of metaphysical heights . . . and always get left behind by those long Cambridge legs of hers. She is the hopeless answer to the problem of how to be good and clever. Hopeless, because although she is as amiable as she is witty, you can't really be expected to emulate her. . . . Not, of course, that she is dispiriting; on the contrary she is the best company alive, especially when on her bony own, . . . [talking] of the advantages and disadvantages of polygamy, Greek lyric poetry, Stubbs' paintings . . . Gerald Hanley's new novel *Without Love*, the consciousness of sin as a 'prerogative of Roman Catholics.'
>
> A typically brisk preprandial chat. "Have something more to drink? What about the interview? Shall we pretend this *was* an interview? Right, then, I'll drop you." And off she goes, this Litt.D . . . at about eight miles an hour, like an animated broomstick, to her car. The passenger needs nerves of steel, for the talk never ceases and other drivers have to take their chance. You are dropped. "I'll see you when I get back from Venice. I'm taking some Americans *who've never been there.* Incredible. Fun, showing them everything don't you think?" The car zigzags into the darkness, bearing away one of England's most formidable and most endearing characters.

In the Davenport interview, in her account of her early years in London, in her *Letters to a Friend* (1961), *Last Letters to a Friend* (1962), and her letters to her sister, Dame Rose Macaulay (for she received that honor in the year of her death) reminds the reader of Laurie, admittedly based upon herself "at one remove," her most fully presented character in *The Towers of Trebizond* (1956). In her person, gaiety and pathos, learnedness carried lightly, formidable seriousness, and a keen sense of the ridiculous blended beautifully. One guesses she was always like that, though sometimes for a whole book she is entirely serious, though sometimes she spoils a gay book by intruding seriousness inappropriately, though occasionally she displays her learning too obviously.

In her book on E. M. Forster, Rose Macaulay quotes approvingly a passage about Cambridge discussion societies from his *G. Lowes Dickinson:*

> The young men seek truth rather than victory, they are willing to abjure an opinion when it is proved untenable, they do not try to score off one another, they do not feel diffidence too high a price to pay for integrity; and according to some observers that is why Cambridge has played, comparatively speaking, so small a part in the control of world affairs. Their influence, when it goes wrong, leads to self-consciousness and superciliousness; when it goes right, the mind is sharpened, the judgment is strengthened, and the heart becomes less selfish.

Clearly, Rose Macaulay was influenced by these or similar groups a little later than Forster and the Bloomsbury group and it did not go wrong. Possibly in her first novel, *Abbots Vernay* (1906), there is, as Frank Swinnerton says in *The Georgian Literary Scene,* "the strongest possible air of grown-upness and knowing better than others." However, it scarcely seems valid to say this on the basis of the sane remark of the heroine of the novel: "It always rather riles me to see people behaving in what strikes me—well, as a foolish manner of behaving, you know." This sounds like the spirit of G. E. Moore, the mentor of the Bloomsbury group, and of E. M. Forster, and is no more priggish than the conversations of Forster's almost contemporaneous characters. The whole series of novels that followed her prize-winning *The Lee Shores* (1912) does not show, to quote Swinnerton again, that Rose Macaulay "always felt herself to be fully adult in a world of children." She does not suffer foolishness gladly—who should?—but her novels, with few exceptions, dramatize an unending search for truth rather than victory. They celebrate seriocomically modern man's errant and formidable effort to find and maintain his own integrity while avoiding muddle, a favorite word of deprecation with Forster and the Bloomsburg group. Indeed it might be claimed that her early novels are farcical counterparts of the four novels Forster published before World War I.

In the two novels she wrote shortly before World War I,

one finds already the gay seriousness that characterized all her best work. *Views and Vagabonds* (1912) appropriately takes as its epigraph G. Lowes Dickinson's remark about the emptiness of abstract ideals of progress that take all the value out of "the past and present, in order to put it into the future." Though *Views and Vagabonds* does not come up to the level of her novels published after World War I, it is still good sense and good reading. Benjamin Bunter, the chief character, is evidently one of those Cambridge products who have become self-conscious to the point of superciliousness, though he is not aware of it. When he becomes a blacksmith-socialist, determined to live with and marry into the working class, he believes he acts with the utmost sincerity, just as he later does when he travels about the countryside trying to convince the middle and lower classes of the ugliness of the houses in which they live their too-ordinary lives. His trouble, one gradually sees, is that his obsession with the ideal of socialist progress blinds him to the realities of himself and others. He does not realize that he wants to marry Louie, the working girl, more to live consistently with his abstractions than to live lovingly with her, nor does he understand that "people are happier with the things they like than with the things you think they ought to like." He is, as Hugh Bunter tells him, "making the only hopeless mistake—putting individuality underneath a cause; doing a thing not because he wants to but because he thinks he ought to want to; trying to bring a particular case under the laws that in his opinion . . . govern the universe."

This is the serious point, rather implausibly resolved when Benjie settles down to have an ordinary good time, but the implausible resolution does not matter greatly in a novel that is, at its best, a comic vehicle for a serious idea. There is a lot else that it would be pleasant to dwell on in a longer study. Mrs. Venables, the lady novelist who thinks Benjie's wife "magnificently uncouth"; Lady Lettice who tells Louie "the poor do get along fairly well, after all, I mean, and don't feel things quite like—well, like that, you know?"; and the dedicately feckless Crevequers who give "beautifully disreputable" parties —all are good figures of fun and foreshadow kinds of people

Rose Macaulay continued to caricature with merciful wit. And it is interesting to note that the Crevequers who do what they please, no matter how silly, come off best, as do many of the most engaging characters in the mature novels that followed the war.

The Making of a Bigot (1914) satirically reverses the values of Views and Vagabonds, though it is also concerned with the absurdity of ideas held too abstractly. Eddy Oliver objects to those who draw any kind of lines, believes in accepting every thing, idea, and body as equally valuable. On the first page he is met by Miss Jamison, a propagandist bearing pamphlets:

> "Of course," she said, with decision, "You've got to join too."
> "Rather," he said. "Tell me what it is. I'm sure it's full of truth."

As the novel goes on, Eddy finds many things full of truth— settlement work, the latest most fashionable plays, all the books he reviews for the Daily Post, a working-class club, an association for better conditions in agriculture, and a magazine to unite all people of all opposing views. (This last he undertakes most enthusiastically with his co-editor, Arnold Dennison, who dislikes everything). Eddy is similarly eclectic in his relations with people. Besides the omnivorously dissident Arnold, he likes Cecil Le Moine, the "advanced" playwright whose parents "not only wrote for the Yellow Book, but gave it him to read in the nursery," the Christian socialist Bob Traherne (one of those who tried to save the doctrinaire Benjie in Views and Vagabonds), Ellen Le Moine and Datcherd, a divorcée and an agnostic who live together out of wedlock, Sally Peters, a Suffragist who might have enjoyed defacing Velasquez's nude, and Molly, a conventional girl who disapproves of all of Eddy's ideas and friends. Before the end, when Eddy, overwhelmed by the difficulties his universal tolerance has led him into, tries to transform himself into a "complete Bigot," there is a lot of serious amusement and, regrettably, somewhat too much unrelieved seriousness.

This conflict between the serious (almost the solemn) and the light-minded keeps these early novels from being more than intermittently pleasurable. As long as the characters are figures of fun, expressions of an excess that is delightfully personalized, all goes well. But when Rose Macaulay says of Eddy that he "had the gift of sympathy largely developed—the quality of his defect of impressionability," or when she makes Arnold say, "I see no place for this thing called love in a reasonable life," the reader feels that she has spoiled the unity of tone by asking us to believe amusing puppets are real people. This inconsistency of treatment diminishes, even after her post-war maturity, the pleasure with which one reads all but the very best of her novels. Fortunately it is an inconsistency that appeared less frequently as Rose Macaulay's command of her material increased, as she learned to make the serious and the comic complementary rather than contradictory.

For Rose Macaulay, as for all but the fully mature, such as Lawrence and Joyce, and the exceedingly young, "the loudest and most uncivilized of the noises off," was a trauma. Since the war, none of her characters feel that "joy is the great thing" as Benjie did. The two books she published during the war, *The Two Blind Countries* (1914) and *Non-Combatants and Others* (1916), show neither bland patriotism nor bland hopefulness. The poems in *The Two Blind Countries* deplore the cruelty of the opposite but equally abstract idealisms of Germany and England. *Non-Combatants and Others,* though it is not a particularly good novel, amply substantiates its epigraph from Reginald Bliss's *Boon:* "War is just the killing of things and the smashing of things," though the novel shows also that there is sensitive intelligence to be found among both those who went to war and those who chose to stay at home. The trouble is that the sensitive intelligences seem unable to cope with the leaders and the led who lump "other people together in masses and groups, setting one group against another, when really people are individual temperaments and brains and souls and unclassifiable." Looking back in *Potterism* (1920), she has Juke, the character who resembles herself most, write:

> Those of us who are old enough will remember that in June and July 1914 the conversation turned largely and tediously

on militant suffragists, Irish rebels and strikers. It was the beginning of the age of violent enforcements of decisions by physical actions which has lasted ever since and shows as yet no sign of passing. . . . It was a curious age, so near and yet so far, when the ordered frame of things was still unbroken, and violence a child's dream, and poetry and art were taken with immense seriousness. Those of us who can remember it should do so, for it will not return. It has given place to the age of melodrama, when nothing is too strange to happen, and no one is ever surprised.

Without doubt she agreed with Gideon in the same novel when he wondered why people were not honest enough to say that the war was fought "mainly to win the war—to be a conquering nation, not a conquered one," a remark very like Hemingway's in his preface to *Men at War* (1942). With Gideon again (and with the poets of World Wars I and II), she loathed the "eloquence and frills" that were used to disguise low aims and dishonest pretensions. Life had become "a little strip of pavement over an abyss," as Virginia Woolf wrote in her diary, where, as Stephen Spender said later, "People resembled dancers suspended in mid-air yet miraculously able to pretend that they were still dancing."

For the peace was altogether too much like the war. The only "lesson" a good many learned was Mrs. Potter's: "I do hope . . . that after this war we English will never again forget that we hate all foreigners," words that might have served as the coda for the treaty makers of Versailles who, as Gideon showed in "a cheery series of articles," had constructed a group of clauses every one of which "was bound to lead, immediately or ultimately, to war with someone or other." As the *New Statesman* editorialized in the year *Potterism* was published, "At the present moment we are living amid the ruins of a world of promises. . . . It seems like something happening in a far-off world when the democracies went to war merely because a great nation had broken a pledge." At home there was the Railroad Strike, where one heard "the same old cries again—carrying on, doing one's bit, seeing it through, fighting to a finish, enemy atrocities (only now they were called sabotage), starving them out, gallant volunteers, the indomitable

Britisher, cheeriest always in disaster (what a hideous slander!), innocent women and children." So Katherine Varick, like Gideon and Juke and Rose Macaulay, saw the peace at home.

But there was always another side of Rose Macaulay that hoped, that could be gay, that would like to "voyage . . . all oceans, peregrinate all lands, taste all foods, meet all people, enjoy all pleasures," as she wrote in *Personal Pleasures* (1936). Always in her, as in Juke of *Potterism,* there was "an odd tide of hope surging through the sickness, because of human nature, which is so mixed that natural cowards will sometimes take a steep and hard way where they might take an easy one, and because we all, in the middle of our egotism and vanity and self-seeking, are often sorry for what we have done." This odd tide of hope enabled her to escape Maugham's and Coward's fashionable futilitarianism, Huxley's sometimes angry pettishness, and Wyndham Lewis's manic compulsion to remain forever the Enemy. She was always aware, as Rome Garden was in *Told by an Idiot* (1923), that the "tiny squalid story of life upon earth, has been lit, among the squalor and the greed, by amazing flashes of intelligence, of valor, of beauty, of sacrifice, of love." Without this awareness of the post-war world as both a "silly story" and a "somewhat remarkable one," her fiction would lack both drama and consequence. As it is, even her least remarkable novels escape the monotony of an uninterrupted dirge, while her best books present a still relevant dramatization of the perpetual conflict between sense and stupidity, between hope for the better and despair at the worst.

The writers about contemporary fiction who have dismissed Rose Macaulay's novels with a few unkind words or none at all, cannot be blamed altogether. She is her own severest critic and may have been taken at her word:

> Heaven never, I think, destined me for a story-teller, and stories are the form of literary activity which give me the least pleasure. I am one of the world's least efficient novelists; I cannot invent good stories, or care what becomes of the people of whom I write. . . . My passengers know their places, and that they are there to afford me the art and pleasure of driving. . . . No: my people are retiring, elusive, and apt not

to come even when I require them. I do not blame them. They no doubt wish that they were the slaves of a more ardent novelist, who would permit them to live with her.

There is some truth in this misevaluation. In the books that precede *They Were Defeated* (1932), she is no more the "congenital novelist" than Aldous Huxley. Most of her novels apparently start with ideas rather than with people. Sometimes the course of the story and its resolution can be predicted by reading the epigraph. With notable but few exceptions, her characters are ideas and attitudes that talk, rather than round characters in Forster's sense, and there are few of her stories that do not stumble away from verisimilitude at some time or another. Most of her novels published before 1932 are novels of ideas in which the characters are driven by their author rather than allowed freedom of their own. Yet it is both pleasant and illuminating to observe their conflicting acts and antics when they serve an important insight. Then her part-people become more interesting than the round characters of less intelligent authors and, for those who are not hamstrung by *a priori* ideas of what *the* novel must be, delightful and plausible creations.

Her first good and typical novel is *Potterism* (1920). It starts with the introduction of Johnny and Jane Potter, "ordinary enough young people . . . linked by a deep and bitter distaste for their father's newspapers, which were many, and for their mother's novels, which were more." With Gideon, who resembles Rose Macaulay very closely, Katherine Varick, a research chemist who finds people, unlike the elements, "odd, unreliable, and irregular in their actions," and Juke, a Radical and a Christian, they form the Anti-Potter League. They do not aim at the Potters personally (the target of Rose Macaulay's characters is usually an attitude or idea), but at the "great mass of thought—or of incoherent, muddled emotion that passed for thought," which they agree to call Potterism. It isn't long, however, before the young Potters semidesert the League's organ, *The Fact* (a "scientific, not a sentimental paper") that makes post-war muddle seem very muddled indeed. Johnny transfers his attention to the current fashion of writing antiwar verse, Jane marries Hobart, the editor of her father's *Daily Haste*. But Juke, Gideon, and Katherine continue to fight "the welcoming of ugliness and prosperity," the "going for things for what they'll bring you . . . instead of for the thing-in-itself." Before they are finally defeated and *The Fact* becomes almost as lively a liar as the *Daily Haste,* they devastate amusingly the exalters of Red Flaggery and of over-and-under-dogs and leave standing (without a leg to do it on) the well-intentioned Potters and their like who "gently and unsurprisingly" please the "majority who are always wrong." Perhaps the tone is sometimes too bitter, particularly in the section told by Gideon, and the action sometimes more convenient than probable (the deaths of Hobart and Gideon), yet the over-all effect is a convincing coherence of the amusing and the caustic. It is as good an attack on the phony as anything Sinclair Lewis or H. L. Mencken ever wrote and is as valid today as it was the year it was written.

As much cannot be said for most of the other novels Rose Macaulay too swiftly published during the twenties. Delight and wisdom do not disappear, and there are still sections of these unsuccessful novels pleasant to read. But *Dangerous Ages* (1921), *Mystery at Geneva* (1922), *Orphan Island* (1924), *Crewe Train* (1926), and *Keeping Up Appearances* (1928) are not the superior novels one expects after *Potterism. Dangerous Ages* comes alive only when Mrs. Hillary, a not over-bright woman of 63, is suffering through her attempts to adjust to her dangerous age. *Keeping Up Appearances* starts as an interesting fantasy about a young woman who splits her personality but the book descends, half-way through, to the level of an inferior Galsworthy novel about why marriages between members of different classes are difficult. Read as amusement, the others can still charm most of the way. *Mystery at Geneva* is a burlesque mystery story (as good as Elliot Paul's *The Mysterious Mickey Finn*) not altogether successfully combined with a disenchanted parable of how all the nations still suspect each other. *Orphan Island* is a frequently delightful parody of English history since 1855, set on a desert island well provided with foodstuff, where Miss Smith brings up her shipwrecked orphans to become good and bad Victorians. It is not as good a novel, though, as Richard Hughes's *A High Wind in Jamaica* or William Golding's *Lord of the Flies,* both of which may owe a debt to *Orphan Island. Crewe Train* winningly develops the misadventures of a woman of twenty-one who continues to act with the wilfull independence of a child of twelve—very good for the first two-thirds, very trite for the remainder. But only one novel published by Rose Macaulay in the twenties equals *Potterism—Told by an Idiot* (1923).

On one level, *Told by an Idiot* is a terse and penetrating telling of what happened to a typical upper middle-class family between 1879 and 1923. There is a good deal of gentle and illuminated fun in watching the Gardens go through the motions the different periods require. Mr. Garden, with sincere instability, runs the gamut of most of the religions of the world before he decides that all of them are right. (How Ecumenical— and true.) With rather more constancy, his daughter Vicky follows the fashions of High Church sophistication and upperclass marriage. Irving Garden follows material conventions with no doubts at all and ends up wealthy, Conservative, and a patron of expensive "machinery." His brother Maurice does everything Irving wouldn't do, successively opposing all the movements the majority supports. Una Garden marries beneath her and is contentedly uninformed about everything except farming and motherhood. Among them, these "flat" and interesting characters represent the fads, ideas, and attitudes that typified England for some forty years and are still unsurprisingly with us.

On a more profound level, Rome Garden, Stanley Garden, and Vicky's Imogen represent conflicting attitudes toward the nature of man and the universe. Stanley is "an ardent hunter of the Idea." Though she reflects her time by becoming in succession Imperialist, Socialist, aesthete, pro-Boer, somewhat for the war to end war, and a worker for the labor department of the League of Nations, her activities are at worst hopeful mistakes, at best acts that make or may make history's idiotic tale less so. She represents an aspect of Rose Macaulay, who herself joined the League of Nations Union and became one of the leaders of the Peace Pledge Movement in the thirties and of the movement in the fifties to abolish nuclear armaments.

But undoubtedly Rome Garden, the most fully developed character in the novel, represents that side of Rose Macaulay that was dominant during the twenties. Rome joins no church, participates in no movement, writes no book (though, in her private journal, she amuses herself, as Rose Macaulay more publicly did, by tracing the queer connections between such things as dissent and little Englandism, socialism and queer clothes). Until the "comic show" becomes a bitterness in 1914, she is cheered by the "spectacle of human absurdity." Still, even when she is dying of cancer, she thinks life "well enough," and admires "the queer enduring spirit of enterprise which animates the dust we are." Vicky's Imogen, who is almost Rose Macaulay's age throughout the book, connects and transcends Stanley's wise heart and Rome's wise mind. Though, as she partially outgrows her love of travel and of islands (Rose Macaulay never did), she finds she has a "hampering and rather pedantic sense of logic, that prevents her from flinging herself into movements with sentimental ardour," still loveliness shakes her and she cannot think of life as less than a hopeful "mess." Like her creator, she could not belong to "the Continue-the-War party" that rises and falls as every war runs its course, but she does belong to "the Continue-the-World party" which has a kind "of solid permanency." It is to the conflict among these three characters who care and think deeply that the novel owes its claim to permanence. Granted that the point of view shifts with unfashionable frequency, that few scenes are fully dramatized, that the plot is not especially ingenious, that the minor characters are talking attitudes, that even the major characters are penetrated better as minds than as hearts, nevertheless *Told by an Idiot* is rewarding. The manipulation of recurrent types of mind as they embrace and reject ideas that continue to recur in the 1960s forms a significant philosophical pattern adequately embodied in characters in action. Nothing like it exists anywhere else, even in Rose Macaulay's other novels, though a family resemblance may be discerned.

*Staying with Relations* (1930) is nearly on a level with

*Potterism* and *Told by an Idiot*. Indeed, since it is most deeply concerned with the impossibility of typing human beings and the dangerous ways novelists have of doing so, it can be considered the most adequate statement of an idea Rose Macaulay was always worried about and a fine exercise in self-criticism.

Catherine Gray, a novelist who thinks she understands people at first sight, visits Sir Richmond and his entourage at the Hacienda del Capitan, Perdido, Guatemala. She thinks Claudia "ironic, amused, passionless, detached, elegantly celibate"; Julia, a "lounging girl of twenty-one"; Benet, a fastidious "mincing young gentleman"; Isis, a primitive; Meg, the twelve-year-old, "just a jolly tom-boy." The disclosure of Catherine's mistakes about all of them is as plausibly amusing as our learning that Meg, mildly ill, murmurs to herself:

> And so it was to end here, her brief inglorious career. . . . Let this be her epitaph, for she has no other: here lies one whose name was writ in water. She might have been a great poet if she had lived, but fever took her in a Central American forest, and only a few brief lines from her pen are left us. They are strangely good lines, some of them. . . .

Certainly the novel "proves" entertainingly that "there are no types, no groups," a conviction Rose Macaulay had had always, but had put too rarely into practice in her fiction. That she had learned as well as said this lesson becomes evident when we read *They Were Defeated* (1932), *The World My Wilderness* (1950), and *The Towers of Trebizond* (1956). (Though she reverted to the presentation of clichés as characters in *Going Abroad* [1934], an occasionally amusing satire of the Oxford Groupers among Englishmen abroad, and in *And No Man's Wit* [1940], a knowledgeable essay on the Spanish character and what made it so, spoken at too great length by characters who never come alive.)

While Rose Macaulay was writing the novels before *The Towers of Trebizond*, she was technically an agnostic. But agnostics, like other people, come in many varieties. Rose Macaulay was never a smug agnostic, she was not even a contented one; even her early novels show that she felt the pull of the religious community she grew up in and admired the most—Anglo-Catholicism.[1] Bob Traherne, the Christian socialist she sympathetically portrays in *Views and Vagabonds* and *The Making of a Bigot*, says in the former book, "God is bound to know that personality is the source of all life, the keystone of all systems." Though the aesthetic requirements of the novels of ideas that preceded *They Were Defeated* usually demanded that she make her characters personified ideas and attitudes, she was sufficiently aware of the sacredness of the human personality never to pillory any of them, though she did satirize their stupidities with severe amusement. Her rejection of religion was never "the modern way" she refers to in *The Making of a Bigot* (1914), to let it alone "as an irrelevant thing, a thing known (and perhaps cared) too little about to pronounce upon." In nearly every novel there is a religious person, an Anglican generally, who believes devoutly in both the importance of the individual personality and God. (Though he is also, as Rose Macaulay continued to be after entering the Anglican community, "a little agnostic." Surely "one must always be this, however much 'in' the Church," Rose Macaulay wrote me in 1957.) One remembers also the fine sympathetic knowledge of Christianity Rose Macaulay shows in her *Milton* (1934, revised 1957) and in *Some Religious Elements in English Literature* (1931), where she speaks of Anglicanism as "a more or less intelligent, perhaps a rather secular compromise" that "has always lacked some of the negations, the doctrinal austerities, and the excesses of Roman Catholicism and dissenting Protestantism." Her posthumously published letters show that she would not have modified any part of this statement later. One is tempted to argue that she was an unconscious Anglican throughout her life though she did not rejoin the Church as a regular communicant until 1952, after her lover's death.[2]

In *Some Religious Elements in English Literature*, Rose Macaulay describes Robert Herrick, almost the main character in *They Were Defeated* (American title, *The Shadow Flies*):

> The Reverend Robert Herrick must be nearly the only seventeenth-century clergyman who continued to write love poems

[1] See *Letters to a Friend* (1961), and *Last Letters to a Friend* (1962), passim.
[2] See the letters.

and light odes after his ordination, and lightened the cares of his incumbency by maying-songs and uncivil lampoons upon the more irritating members of his flock.

It isn't difficult to see how this "pagan-Christian parson" particularly appealed to Rose Macaulay in 1932. He was the kind of Christian Rose Macaulay eventually became ("I have a passion for *mélange* and the fantastically impure . . . Apollo into Christ, Artemis into Madonna," she wrote Patrick Kinross in a Christmas card that arrived after her death;[3] Herrick lived in a century in which there was emotional, intellectual, and political turmoil comparable to ours. He was surrounded, he is surrounded in the novel, by characters who have modern analogues aplenty: Doctor Conybeare, a likeable, disputacious atheist; Sir John Suckling, elegant as Michael Arlen; John Cleveland, a brilliant and unprincipled man; Kit Conybeare, an Anglo-agnostic who becomes a Roman Catholic; numerous others who are placed accurately in the seventeenth century but seem to be our contemporaries.

The central character is Julian Conybeare, who resembles Rose Macaulay. With her father and Herrick, Julian tries to save Moll, an accused witch, from the mass of people who blindly follow conventions and keep "men's minds in swaddles and scholars groping beneath blankets of darkness." Unsuccessful, Julian goes to Cambridge with Herrick and her father, hoping to learn how to understand man and the universe more fully than her witch-burning community allows. Cambridge then seems as exciting and baffling as Cambridge now. She sees John Milton, "a very fine poet . . . but his blood runs too thin in his veins," Henry More, Abraham Cowley; she hears John Cleveland deliver a Latin oration, is present at a production of *Comus* and of a Latin play by Cowley, gets involved in her brother's attempt to conceal his papism, sees much of the political discord that prevailed in 1641. Until she becomes involved in a love affair with John Cleveland that makes Rose Macaulay pump her prose too hard, Julian is created in the round and enables us, through her ingenuous, ingenious eyes, to live in and comprehend a period that helps us to understand our own.

[3] "The Pleasures of Knowing Rose Macaulay," *Encounter,* March 1959.

What stands out, however, is the portrait of Herrick, a man of the "cheerful middle English way, hating Puritanism, heartily damning all extremes of piety." We see him first rusticating at Deancombe, preaching a Harvest sermon while a pig gravely eats the harvest fruits that surround the pulpit and the parishioners laugh more and more as he, not seeing the pig, becomes angrier and angrier. Later, we see him matching wits with Sir John Suckling, waiting at a Cambridge poetry reading while he wonders whether he is not too homely a poet to be appreciated by the fashionable metaphysicals. Finally, in the Epilogue, dated 1647, we find him preaching his last sermon at Deancombe to three people, despite the danger that Puritans may kill him. Throughout the novel, he is an individual seen in the round, with all his quiddities and virtues, as well as a convincing embodiment of the "cheerful middle English way." With Doctor Conybeare, for whom almost as much could be said, and Julian, he is largely responsible for making *They Were Defeated* a good novel that transcends the usual limitations of historical fiction. Less deft in execution than her own *Potterism* and *Told by an Idiot,* not as deeply conceived an historical novel as Mann's Joseph series, Wilder's *The Ides of March,* or Lagerkvist's *Barrabas,* still *They Were Defeated* excels and points toward the superior virtues of *The World My Wilderness* and *The Towers of Trebizond.*

The epigraph from *The Waste Land*—"There is the empty chapel, only the wind's home"—announces the serious theme of *The World My Wilderness.* There is little humor and very little pillorying of stupidities in this novel of the time immediately following World War II. It makes one feel that the Second World War very nearly brought Rose Macaulay to the despair that made Virginia Woolf commit suicide, that she felt with the French priest of the novel the awfulness of a world in which most people of good will have turned away from God, a world where everyone, almost, takes his wilderness with him so that ruins make "a lunatic sense, as the unshattered streets and squares" do not.

The story is a simple one. Barbary, the daughter of Sir Gulliver and Helen Denniston, has lived in France with her mother since the break-up of her parents' marriage, has joined the maquis during the war years, afterwards retains as her simple code, "Annoy the gendarmerie and the local authorities." When she returns to England to stay a while with her father, Barbary finds it impossible to live the respectable life Sir Gulliver and his second wife, Pamela, wish of her. She spends most of her time putting the maquis's code into practice and feels most at home in the bomb-sites with her half-brother Raoul and some young Englishmen who rebel against British civilization as the maquis did against the Nazi occupiers. Trying to escape arrest after one of her escapades, she falls and is injured seriously. Her mother returns to England and takes her back to France, where, with her nonconforming mother, it seems she will have some chance to rehabilitate herself.

It is the characters in *The World My Wilderness* who make powerful Rose Macaulay's representation of the postwar world. Helen, who resembles the detached Rome of *Told by an Idiot* except that she takes sex as a "pleasure by the way" and believes in snatching what good she can on the way "down into catastrophe and the abyss," is a good pagan who can like people without trusting them. Sir Gulliver is a respectable, ironic sceptic, incapable of understanding either Helen's paganism or his daughter's wildness. Barbary, who was raped by a Nazi and cannot understand either the muddled moral universe of her mother or the tidiness of her father's world, is thoroughly lost, thoroughly pathetic, and very much worth saving. She hopes "God's not like the law, to destroy a man that confesses," but she feels certain only of the existence of Hell. Somewhere in between Helen and Barbary is Ritchie, her elder brother and apparently the spokesman for Rose Macaulay's best insight at this time. As he observes the ruins that symbolize the moral destruction of a world that prefers to live without God, he thinks, "So men's will to recovery strove against the drifting wilderness to halt and tame it, but the wilderness . . . might slip darkly away from them, seeking the primeval chaos and old night which had been before Londinium was, which would be when cities were ghosts haunting the ancestral dreams of memory." And on the concluding page he thinks "we are in rat's alleys, where the dead men lost their bones." This somber close to her most somber book points up the despair Rose Macaulay herself must have felt, for her way to religion resembles T. S. Eliot's—modified, of course, by the individuality that makes her an important writer in her own right.

*The Towers of Trebizond,* the only novel Rose Macaulay wrote after becoming an Anglican, is a picaresque *Pilgrim's Progress* that leaves the pilgrim outside the gates of Heaven.[4] It is a serious, unsolemn novel that is frequently beautiful comedy, ultimately purging tragedy. It unites in one book all the Rose Macaulays her novels, and books of travel, of criticism, and of essays have represented partially. In it one finds the perpetual seeker after truth side by side with the mocker of absolutes, the traveller to strange places and strange people who does not try to escape herself, the despairer and hoper, the mocker and praiser of life, the Christian who must always be a little agnostic. Few novelists have united more discordant complexities into a more harmonious whole.

Formally her last novel is as difficult to categorize as *Ulysses* or *Tristram Shandy.* The plot is a ramble that is always going straight to the heart of her matter. The texture is finely thick. The characters other than Laurie are alternatingly caricatures and real human beings because that is the way Laurie, who *is* Rose Macaulay in everything but age, perceives them. It is Laurie, Rose Macaulay's most fully conceived and moving character, who makes all the seeming discords cohere into a work of art that will be remembered.

As Laurie travels about in Turkey with Father Hugh Chantrey-Pigg, a stupid and devout man, and Aunt Dot, who would like to convert the Turks and Russians to Feminism and Anglo-Catholicism, we identify with her so completely that everything that occurs seems at the same time strange and believable. We identify with her urbane amusement at Turkish music "which goes on and on like crooning and which Turks love so much that western music is hateful to them and Mozart just a noise to be turned off," with her meditation about the dead at Gallipoli

---

[4] Intentionally, as she says in her letter to Father Hamilton Johnson of October 1, 1956, *Last Letters to a Friend,* p. 233.

("it seemed too soon for them to be lying dead, in their sixties, though it was all right for Hector and Achilles and Patroclus . . . for they would have been several thousand years old. Death is awful, and one hates to think about it, but I suppose after all those years of it the dead take it for granted"), with her thoughts about the Church which is "very wonderful and comprehensive, and no other church, it is said, is quite like it, and this variety that it has is one of its glories, and not one of its scandals at all, though there are plenty of these," with her perplexity at American sects that proliferate "like rabbits in Australia," with her sympathy for the camel which was in love and "could not get over it either," with her experiments at making human an ape who comes about as close to humanity as many people do, with her sorrow that "neither Islam nor Christianity has exercised a very moderating influence on cruelty down the ages," with her gay recollections of the ambiguity of English drug prescriptions, with the discord in her mind excited by her will to love God truly and Vere adulterously ("the happiness and the guilt and the remorse pulling in opposite ways so that the mind and soul are torn in two, and if it goes on for years and years the discord becomes permanent, so that it will never stop, and even if one goes on living after death, as some people think, there will still be this deep discord that nothing can heal, because of the great meanness and selfishness that caused such a deep joy"), with her sadness at the failure of the Christian Church "of every branch in every country. . . . But it is what happens when a magnificent idea has to be worked out by human beings who do not understand much of it but interpret it in their own way and think they are guided by God, whom they have not yet grasped," with her feeling that "Churches are wonderful and beautiful, and they are vehicles for religion, but no Church can have more than a very little of the truth . . . and we have to grope our way through a mist that keeps being lit by shafts of light, so that exploration tends to be patchy and we can never sit back and say, we have the truth, this is it, for discovering the truth, if it ever is discovered, means a long journey through a difficult jungle, with clearings every now and then, and paths that have to be hacked out as one walks," with her sorrow that even after Vere's death God comes second to her adulterous love, with her faith that Christianity, like the Towers of Trebizond, will always continue as "the pattern and the hard core," though "these I can never make my own: they are too far outside my range."

*The Towers of Trebizond* spiritually and aesthetically recapitulates Rose Macaulay's own difficult and happy life. It recapitulates dramatically the almost comfortable assurance that she knew the ways things are in the books before the twenties, the sad and witty and gaily disenchanted novels of the twenties, the mostly sober searchings of the thirties, the near despair beneath the surface gaiety of the forties and early fifties, the faith that was a little agnostic that characterized her last years. Possibly, as it sometimes seemed to her, her survival as a novelist depends, as it seems to with so many others, on chance. One does not like to think so, for it would be a badly improverished world in which the pleasures of knowing Rose Macaulay and her books did not survive. There will never be again any one like her nor any books with the special sad-gaiety that the best of hers admirably communicate.

## Chapter Three

# Aldous Huxley: Sceptical Mystic

IT IS TEMPTING TO SUGGEST that Aldous Huxley felt the impact of World War I more than the disenchanted combatants. Kept from participation by bad eyesight and perhaps, like his character Richard Greenow, a conscientious objector who did not object actively, he did not see war as a noble crusade against Hunnishness. He wrote no war novels, and after the books published in 1920, said little directly about it, yet his books show the effect of the physical and psychical disgust he felt for its presumed consequences to a fuller extent than anything Rose Macaulay wrote. Possibly this was because Rose Macaulay was thirty-three and he was twenty when World War I began.

In the two books he published in 1920, he had a good deal to say about the war directly. In "Soles Occidere Et Redire Possunt," a poem about a friend who *did* fight and die in battle, he castigates those who talk patriotism in comfortable homes, the unspeakableness of the human situation exposed by the war, and the efficient officers who do not question the end for which they use men and machines, quite as bitterly as did C. E. Montague, the actual participant. "The Farcical History of Richard Greenow" and "Happily Ever After" (both in *Limbo*, 1920) displays the stupidities of women who make war behind their typewriters, of clerks safe in the Army Service Corps, of clergymen who embellish religion with the old lie, *dulce et decorum est*, of women who secure the vote by distributing white feathers and organizing the bureaucracy essential to slaughter. Huxley's own summation at this time was very near to Jacobsen's in "Happily Ever After": "I think you can take it that a world which has let itself be dragooned into this criminal folly is pretty hopeless." Huxley became, like the "I" of "The Bookshop," a "deteriorationist," who felt devolution a more accurate term for what has happened to the species than the evolution his grandfather almost bulldogged a century into cheering.

The poems Huxley published in 1916 and what one can gather about the twenty years he lived before 1914, show that he became a "deteriorationist" reluctantly. A good many of the early poems are unabashedly romantic. He wished to be "like a pure angel," to "live in beauty, free from self and pain." Like Wordsworth, whom he continued to like, "Robbed of all speech and thought and act," he saw "God in the cataract/ In falling water and in flame/ Never at rest, yet still the same." He even felt a Shelleyean fondness for "a phrase, a melody/ Like a fair woman, worshipped and possessed." Romantic wishfulness is never altogether absent in his later work. Indeed it could be said that his last work, *Island* (1962), both affirmed and dramatized the unlikelihood of a modified realization of what his romantic hopes matured into before his death in 1963. Ambivalently he makes absurd and sympathizes with the youths some critics have seen as caustic portraits of ineffectuality: Richard Greenow, who has "all the feelings of Bunyan without his religion"; Guy (of "Happily Ever After") who "intellectually . . . was a Voltairean, emotionally a Bunyanite"; Denis of *Crome Yellow* (1921), an ineffective writer of "beautiful" poetry and a reluctant imitator of Scogan's cynicism; Gumbril Jr. of *Antic Hay* (1923) who cannot avoid shame-making speculation "about the existence and nature of God"; Calamy of *Those Barren Leaves* (1925), who deserts the discomforts of hedonism to meditate upon ultimates, who believes "Perhaps he [is] a fool. . . . But . . . [is] somehow reassured." In their emotions and attempts at action, all these characters predict the firmer believers of the later books: the Savage in *Brave New World* (1932), Beavis of *Eyeless in Gaza* (1936), Jeremy of *After Many a Summer Dies the Swan* (1939), Sebastian in *Time Must Have a Stop* (1944), Dr. Poole of *Ape and Essence* (1949), Rivers in *The Genius and the Goddess* (1955), Dr. Robert of *Island* (1962). Of course those who hope or believe are always counterpointed by "reasonable" scoffers. In Huxley's best fiction, there is always a Jacobsen, a Eustace Barnack, or a Maartens to try to make silly any transcending faith. These were a part of Huxley, too. Without their resistance Huxley's novels would be as undramatic as something by Lloyd Douglas.

By chance, heredity and environment, Huxley was doomed to too much knowledge and too many conflicts within himself. His grandfather, Thomas Henry Huxley, brought him the dichotomy of ethical idealism and biological naturalism; his great-uncle, Matthew Arnold, a worry about wandering between two worlds and a wish for sweetness and light; his aunt, Mrs. Humphrey Ward, more worry, including one about the high moral seriousness she represented more fully than his great-uncle. By example, genes, or contact, they added to the disorientation of too great height, near-blindness, too much knowledge, too little ability to mix with or feel for the common man. Though he *felt* for and with naïve romantics like Denis, he *thought* with what John Atkins has called his *personae:* Scogan, Cardan, the rest, men who did not need World War I to disenchant them.

In the early novels these brilliant scoffers (who resemble the sceptic Huxley never was but wished often he had been) have the best of it. To them World War I was merely an obvious suppuration that should have been predictable by anyone who knows human nature and human history: Waterloo, 1830, 1848, 1870, the Boer War; Shelley, Tennyson, Swinburne, the ethereal, respectable, and disreputable angels; Wilde, Ellis, Freud, Norman Douglas, Somerset Maugham, the masters of those in the know; evolution, agnosticism, scepticism, atheism, cynicism, deteriorationism, the successive failures in man's wearisome search for a law that does not bind him. To these *personae* Oscar Wilde's life as a bad quarter of an hour is as platitudinous as his homosexuality, only less boring than the over-seriousness of *The Ballad of Reading Gaol,* Norman Douglas's outmoded portrayal of amorality in Nepenthe, Maugham's figures in the carpet who say "Life is short, nature is hostile, and man is ridiculous"—all this much too obvious. As to Noel Coward and Richard Aldington, the one brightly bitter and the other verbosely pejorative, who could disagree with anything but their style and their lowering of fastidious deprecation to a level suited to readers of *The Green Hat?* I do not paraphrase what Huxley's Cardans and Scogans said. I represent what they would have said, had Huxley felt it desirable to make them talk about their contemporaries and the past that conditioned them.

What I am trying to show is that Huxley's early books were a battlefield, a contention between persons he wished to be and *personae* he thought were all he reasonably could be. He was attracted by religion (or religions) he could not believe in; he hated bogus spirituality, yet trusted, half-consciously, that there is a faith that comprehends and transcends dogma. The puritanism of D. H. Lawrence that made sexuality pure and monogamous, the sensibility of Virginia Woolf and Edith Sitwell that translated the disconnections of consciousness into something luminously aesthetic, he approved. Joyce's acceptance of Molly Bloom's delight in both sex and menstruation, he could not (though he did not approve altogether of his rejection). Like his earliest alter ego, Richard Greenow, "he felt in himself the desire to search for truth and the ability—who knows?—to find it. On the other hand, the horrors of the world about him seemed to call on him to put forth all his strength in an effort to ameliorate what was so patently and repulsively bad." He knew about the physiological functions Freud accepted and Lawrence celebrated. Yet, like Swift (and for some traumatic reason that we don't know and don't need to know about), he came close to hating concrete humanity that stank, even when he became eloquent about humanity abstracted and justice abstract. He approved democracy, internationalism, the oppressed whom he often found disgusting individually. In the twenties (and to an extent until his death) he was a snob who thought "only one in a million can think," but a snob with a social conscience that kept trying to force him into action against the insensitivity of the upper-middle class he belonged to.

I emphasize the division of Huxley's thought because it is a major source of the validity of both his earlier and his later novels. From the early poems on through the middle and late fiction, it is the tension between temperamental disgust and intellectual acceptance that makes his best work substantially and artistically important. Limitations he has, congenital novelist he is not, but he presents the twenties, the times that have followed, and what *may* underlie any time, with an insight you will seldom find in his more frequently praised contemporaries. If Huxley is often regarded as only good (though at times he is as "interesting" as Joyce), he is nearly always better than Dorothy Richardson, and in content is as relevant to what we are now as Virginia Woolf. In the novels his essays illuminate, illustrate, and do not destroy, Huxley is a more significant novelist than most critics or the common reader realizes.

The veering and interesting development of a world-view that made Huxley's novels significant can be traced with reasonable accuracy. At first, Huxley was a romantic idealist, a dubious Platonist who preferred what books predicated to what living elicited. By the time he published his earliest verses (1916), twenty-two years of living with earnest and disenchanted intellectuals had combined with two years of war to make him a reluctant and sceptical "deteriorationist." The closing poem of his first book, entitled "Philosophy,"[1] epitomizes the attitude that underlies his writing in the twenties:

> "God needs no christening,"
> Pantheist mutters,
> "Love opens shutters
> On heaven's glistening,
> Flesh, key-hole listening,
> Hear what God utters. . . ."
> Yes, but God stutters.

That God's apersonal equivalent *seems* to stutter is fundamental in the "Perennial Philosophy" Huxley ultimately accepted, but the dramatic consequences of the stutter sound loudest in the books that precede *Eyeless in Gaza* (1936) and *Ends and Means* (1937).

The novels and essays and poems from *Limbo* (1920) to *Eyeless in Gaza* can be seen *now* as Huxley's faltering attempts to arrive at Anthony Beavis's acceptance of the divine ground;

[1] Quoted from *Verses and a Comedy* by permission of the publisher, Chatto and Windus, London.

*then* they did not seem so to those who talked and wrote of Huxley as a futilitarian who had become (half-heartedly and full-mindedly) a Lawrencian humanist in *Point Counter Point* (1928) and its immediate successors. The dancing of the Antic Hay, the reluctant recognition of the barrenness of science, the inconsequent actions of most of the characters in *Point Counter Point* (1928), *Brief Candles* (1930), and *Brave New World* (1932), the observations about other cultures in *Jesting Pilate* (1926) and *Beyond the Mexique Bay* (1934), the essays that show this world's contradictory fiction—all these emphasize the unlikelihood of even the exceptional individual finding more than an all-too-human ground to stand upon.

In these books, particularly in the novels, poets are as ineffective as Denis or Shelley; the religious end up, like Burlap and Beatrice, discovering their divinity in a bathtub large enough for two; the philosophers are as unable as Cardan and Scogan to find a meaning that goes beyond the orderliness of Pavlov's salivating dogs; the scientists exhaust their kidneys pedalling bicycles; the hedonists anxiously savor moments that lead to satiety that is followed by desires that lead to satiety. It is the Satanists, Coleman and Spandrell, who seem to state the pointless point of existence:

> Thousands of women are now in the throes of parturition, and of both sexes, thousands are dying of the most diverse and appalling diseases, or simply because they have lived too long. Thousands are drunk, thousands have over-eaten, thousands have not had enough to eat. And they are all alive, all unique and separate, like you and me. It's a horrible thought. . . .

Our brief candles only flicker, for tomorrow will be as awful as today.

Still, when we reread *Point Counter Point,* it becomes clear that Huxley did not or did not continue to sympathize with either the Satanists or those who made Satanism plausible. Rampion, a representation of both D. H. Lawrence and what Huxley himself wished to be, sees Spandrell as a "morality-philosophy pervert," Burlap as a "pure little Jesus pervert." Hedonists, such as Lucy Tantamount, are sex perverts, a scientist

like her father is an "intellectual-scientific pervert," Quarles—
Huxley as he fictionalized himself—is a "barbarian of the
intellect." By action and by words, Rampion routs the rest and
states the philosophy Huxley-Quarles would like to live by. He
says, "To be a perfect animal and a perfect human—that was the
ideal"; "Civilization is harmony and completeness. Reason,
feeling, instinct, the life of the body—Barbarism is being lop-
sided." The essays that appeared at about this time prove that
Huxley deprecated, as he had since the early portrait of Richard
Greenow, what he conceived himself to be. In these essays,
he calls for a new humanism that rejects both the romanticism
of "the hour of glory in the flower" and that of the "hour of
glory in the machine," an avoidance of extremes, the maintenance
of a "realistic golden mean." Here he says also that the only
reading of life "which has any prospect of being permanently
valuable is a philosophy which takes in all the facts—the facts
of mind *and* the facts of matter, of instinct and intellect, of
individualism *and* of sociableness." This philosophy is far
removed from both the early naïve romanticism and the sad
"deteriorationism" that succeeded it, yet it does not satisfy
Huxley for long. Consciously or subconsciously, he wished to
go beyond Lawrence's and his own views. He hoped for something that might combine the Lawrencian assertion of the flesh
as spirit, his own disgust with the normal equation of war and
uplift, and his retained hope for something more deeply inter-
fused in the nature of things than angry idealism solidified into
sectarianism.

In *Eyeless in Gaza* and its successors, Huxley uncovers ends
that are not incompatible with means he had always approved
and preferred to utilize. Aesthetically it is fortunate that his
uncoverings remain tentative, that ambivalence does not disappear totally. Whether or not one likes what coalesces, in
these books there is an order by which the disorder that still
appears can be judged. The reversal of convictions, though it
includes as well as transcends the earlier attitudes, is almost
complete. Mass-man is actually bad; however, as an individual
who could help the perennial mess if he realized his potentiali-
ties, he could become good. Hedonism is a deadend, here and

hereafter, as Eustace Barnack's life and afterlife demonstrate. Practically and theoretically, science digs its own grave and ours. The religious who smother truth and the search for it are as bad as atom-bombers. No religion is an empire unto itself, no man other than an island that could become a continent (though *Island* [1962] makes this appear a dim possibility), no intelligence more than a limited perceiver of the imperceivable. The willful man, like power, corrupts himself and others. Only by accepting the God that inheres and gentles, by recognizing that God is gods, oneself, and no person, by "seeing" the divine ground within that also contains all without, by losing ourselves to save ourselves, can we reach the blessedness of unselfness that is union with the spirit which lies *very far* under ourselves and everything.

What I have just written is, of course, a truncation of many hundreds of pages. Huxley did believe before his death in the divine ground which he did not believe his many pages could make clear; particularly in his last years he acted and wrote knowing that neither action nor words can make known totally or clearly, what no man's acts or words made clear to him, for the personal experiences Huxley describes in *The Art of Seeing* (1943) and in *The Doors of Perception* (1954) he knew were to a great degree incommunicable. Nor did he have the illusion that he followed his belief any more adequately than he expressed it. He says in *Adonis and the Alphabet* (1956):

> As a self-centered ego, I do my best to interfere with the beneficent workings of this not-I. But in spite of my likes and dislikes, in spite of my malice, my infatuations, my gnawing anxieties, in spite of all my over-stultifying insistence on living, not in present reality, but in memory and anticipations, this not-I, with whom I am associated, sustains me, preserves me, gives me a long succession of second chances.

The qualifications that surround this passage and Huxley's own life may hurt his opportunities for immediate union with the not-I. But without these qualifications (perhaps one could say more accurately, doubts) or that inside of Huxley which made him make them, his novels would be as close to tracts for the converted as are his account of his experience with Dr. Bates and mescalin. Huxley's earlier novels are saved from the easy sophistication one finds in the books Maugham and Coward published in the twenties by his only partially suppressed longing to believe in the not-I; his later novels are saved from deadening laxity by his malice, likes, and anxieties, and by his realization that words cannot convey the reality nobody knows. Without the conflict between what Huxley is and what he wants to be, his early novels would be period trash, his later novels an undramatic monologue.

Reading again Huxley's fiction, most of it after many years, I am surprised a little by how much I admire and enjoy it. This surprise, I suppose, owes something to a half-conscious desire to agree with the current fashion of deprecating it: *Crome Yellow* was mildly amusing, a few passages that preceded *Eyeless in Gaza*, not bad; since then, highly intellectual awfulness or boring repetitiveness or unskillfully disguised propaganda for the Perennial Philosophy. Not that there are no other reasons for my mild surprise. Sometimes it seems as though Huxley would deprecate his own fiction, especially if it is pleasant reading. Men, their own termites, write art mostly about "immediate animal experiences," Propter-Huxley says, and create usually the mental equivalent "of alcohol and cantharides." He told John Atkins that he continued to write largely so that he could continue to live until he could consummate his wish to become one with the divine ground. Unable to agree more than partially with Huxley's world-view, I continue to find his best fiction very satisfying, and am compelled to accuse him of an artistry he himself would have claimed with great diffidence.

Huxley himself put the case against his artistry aptly. In *Point Counter Point,* Huxley-Quarles admits he is not a congenital novelist, agrees with his wife that he is trying to feel down with his intellect, wishes as she does that he "could break his habit of impersonality and learn to live with the intuitions and feelings and instincts" so that he could be better as both man and novelist. Other correlative limits are clear enough to both himself and his readers. Huxley could not identify adequately with the acts and feelings of any but the upper-middle class; characters from other social strata are often brilliant examples of psycho-sociological analysis, never people. Even when he presents characters from the class he knew intimately, he tends, as Virginia Woolf has said, to make "people into ideas," to make "his characters dangle rather too jangily"; as though they were "morality characters with horrified puppet-faces," as Elizabeth Bowen has said. Granting all this and, even further, Hemingway's accusation that Huxley's characters say essays that would reach fewer readers without the disguise of fiction, a reasonable case can be made for Huxley's virtues as a novelist.

There is, first of all, the superficial but compelling attraction of his fictional portrait of the life of the mind in our times. Since he does not avoid awareness of even the fashions he despises, he gives us the feel of our modern over-intellectualized medley of sophistications. From books and from observation at home and when he travelled, he knew about carnivorous plants, Jacobsen's method of scientific relaxation, Heard's pacifism, the physiological basis for aesthetics, the muscular accompaniments of passion, the upper-class compulsions that require an equal knowledge of Bartok, Picasso, Dada, Jung, nonrepresentational art, Leninism, and the psychogenic roots of fascism. Probably he was the most widely informed man of our time. If you want to know what was worst and best said, what was thought most widely or known only to the few, Huxley's novels are a more comprehensive, felt guide to the sense and no-sense of our time than any historian's panorama. Nor has his omnivorousness obscured his ability to see truly; rarely in his novels do you find facile sophistication or evident exhibitionism. Even the early novels present judgments dramatically; only if one equates knowledge of decadence with decadence itself can one claim him as a member of the "deteriorationist" party longer than briefly. Despite the fact that in the early novels he accepts as inevitable what he feels to be bad, he does not commit the moral or aesthetic sin of prettification. Huxley shows and shows up Spandrell, Burlap, Webley, Lord Tantamount, Lucy; in dramatic exhibition he displays the horror of artists who make vision merely geometric, of musicians who exalt cacaphony, of writers who bleed Jesus shrewdly or pretend scatology is a fine art.

This showing and showing-up of the blatantly modern accounts for much of his popularity in the twenties, for his historical interest to us now. It does not account for the persisting interest of even his first fiction. Fortunately, he always searched insistently for truths that lie under appearances, and dramatized the conflict between appearance and reality that he found in himself and projected upon the world outside. Our time he saw as related to any time, related also to the "ground" that time and space express. He can seem superficial only to people so superficial that they read him as though he were the accumulated issues of *Reader's Digest.*

Huxley's novels—often remarkably good, rarely mediocre—are his best work. The essays are always readable, but, excepting *Ends and Means* (1937) and *Theme and Variations* (1950), they are no more than exceptionally intelligent journalism. His historical studies, *Grey Eminence* (1941) and *The Devils of Loudun* (1952) are admirable in their limited, slanted way. *Texts and Pretexts* (1932) is the only anthology of poetry satisfactorily devised to make the common reader want what he should, as he should. Huxley's plays are readable, his short stories expert, his accounts of travel more probing than those, say, of Peter Fleming or Maugham. But it is difficult to see most of these as more than that now; later generations will come to them as aids to understanding the novels. It is in the novels that Huxley, a better uncongenital novelist than Peacock or W. H. Mallock, surpassed his more explicit statements because his fortunately divided self is unified enough to assume dramatic control.

The best Huxley novels always represent a conflict between a seeker and impediments put between him and discovering a faith that transcends contemporary awfulness. The short stories in *Limbo* (1920) and the early poems that try unsuccessfully to escape clever sophistication, announce the theme and its discords, the point that is always counterpointed. *Crome Yellow*

(1921), his first and still good novel, represents the dramatic tensions which the later novels more or less adequately vary and aesthetically fulfill. With varying brilliance, all the novels follow a design the first novel pronounces, a design that would seem merely a formula in a lesser, more readily integrated writer.

In *Crome Yellow*, the naïve poet Denis tries to find a satisfactory way of life in a social vacuum that must resemble the one Huxley early condemned himself to. The vapid hostess, Mrs. Wimbush, surrounds Denis with sophisticated monstrosities: the rector Bodiham knows that *his* Anglicanism comprehends the universe; Mary tries to live her misconceptions of Freud and Havelock Ellis; Anne is *the* determined pagan; Nigel believes all impulses are equally sacred and tries to help her out; Barbecue-Smith hopes to literally pipeline the infinite; others as monstrous are as amusingly portrayed. The intelligently cynical Scogan sees through all this social vacuity and is the antagonist who demolishes Denis's illusions and prevents his "social adjustment." A prematurely grayed Huxley, Scogan sees no greater hope for mankind than education to healthy insanities such as one finds in *Brave New World*. He defeats Denis's hope for hope, but it is Denis, the ineffectual seeker, with whom the reader identifies, as Huxley partially did. In *Crome Yellow*, Huxley One is pitted against Huxley Two—wish against intellect, hope against despair. It would perhaps be cheering to say that the conflict was resolved in the later novels, that all became pleasant and undramatic. What actually happened was that Huxley developed, clarified, and partially transcended the war within that the war without represents. Sometimes the novels that do this are partial, dim successes; frequently they are very good novels of a kind that is unfashionable currently.

Take *Antic Hay* (1923), for example. It repeats the pattern: Gumbril Jr. approximates Denis; his father, Scogan; the other characters resemble those who people the vacuous social world of *Crome Yellow*. But there is improvement and variation, the conflict of antagonists is more equal. Though Coleman's diatribe about the masses' hideous way of existing, and Myra Viveash's living through stanchlessly-flowing time are more devastating summings-up of futility than anything in the earlier book, Gumbril Jr.'s gaiety enables him to cope with the most depressing realities. Indeed, he so enjoys the absurdity of his campaign for inflatable underwear to make pew-sitting comfortable that the reader often laughs aloud, a rarity while reading most of Huxley's novels. *Those Barren Leaves* (1925) is slightly a comedown because the clever spokesmen of stupid attitudes repeat too exactly what has been said before and Chellifer is a too-similar throwback to Denis and Gumbril Jr., as well as a first attempt to create a Phillip Quarles who will represent more successfully Huxley's candid portrayal of his own limits; Calamy suggests, but less convincingly, the Anthony Beavis of *Eyeless in Gaza* (what Huxley had been developing into, what he believed he must become); Cardan is the sceptic Huxley felt compelled to put in his novels since, as novelist and divided person, he felt compelled to present the truth about even that part of himself he was unhappy with. Had *Those Barren Leaves*, like the earlier, better, less promising novels, concentrated the conflict by making Calamy and Chellifer one character, it would have been more successful artistically, though it might not have led to the superior art of *Point Counter Point* (1928).

*Point Counter Point* is the outstanding novel the early stories and novels foreshadow. Granting that today they are interesting in themselves, someday Gumbril Jr. may seem interesting only as the more mature successor of Denis; Chellifer and Calamy as the predecessors of Phillip Quarles. Quarles, in Huxley's unsparing characterization of what Huxley feared himself to be in 1928, is as successful a portrait of intellectuality disliking itself as one can find in modern fiction. Understanding the perverse pseudo-Baudelaireanism of Spandrell, the pretentious Christianity of Burlap, the constricting belief in science of Lord Tantamount, the not-Utopianism of Illidge's communism and Webley's fascism, and agreeing with Rampion's evaluation of them all as perverts and with his ideal of civilization as "harmony and completeness," Quarles remains a poor father and husband, a mediocre novelist. But it is Quarles's persisting effort to understand himself and to get out from under the net he and society entangle him in that makes *Point Counter Point* nearly as good now as when it was published. Despite his indebtedness to the technique of Gide and the ideas of Lawrence, *Point Counter Point* still is Huxley's best novel that far. In it, Huxley not only created a cast of believable caricatures who represent modern and persistent attitudes; he also, for the first time, created in Quarles a character in the round, one who is more than intellectually involved in a quarrel with himself and others. *Point Counter Point* is one of the few novels that transcend the twenties while evaluating them accurately.

After *Brave New World* (1932), the most effective modern novel to contradict Wells's shape of things to come, *Eyeless in Gaza* (1936) and *The Genius and the Goddess* (1955) are the best of Huxley's novels published after 1928. Of course *Eyeless in Gaza* has faults. The book shuttles back and forth in time with too little artistic justification; the spokesman for the perennial philosophy, Miller, is far too much a gospel articulated, far too little a person. But Beavis's effort to defeat the self he grows gradually to hate and to recognize as only *a* self (as Denis, Gumbril Jr., Chellifer, Quarles, and the Savage do with less percipience) is more fully internalized and more adequately externalized than in similar characters of the earlier novels. Clever sophistication makes Beavis self-centered and spiritually impotent. His cynicism (in our world frequently a promise of health, Huxley declares repeatedly) keeps him from Hugh Staithes's communism. Less happily, it also prevents him from accepting Helen's love, helps him to help along Mary Amberley's psychotic will to destroy herself, drives towards death Brian Foxe, the first man of thorough (but naïve) good will Huxley has made plausible in his fiction. Since Beavis's release from tension by conversion to the philosophy of non-violence is too largely the consequence of Miller, an idea flatly posed as a character, there is some failure in credibility. But *Eyeless in Gaza* survives as a way of happening that no man can properly ignore.

Despite the brilliant opening pages that caricature Hollywood almost as well as Waugh's *The Loved One,* and the later pages that are a Swiftian reduction to absurdity of man's wish for longevity, *After Many a Summer Dies the Swan* (1939) is inferior Huxley. The middle-aged Jeremy and the juvenile Pete—the two to be converted to Huxley's Perennial Philosophy —are set against Doctor Obispo, Uncle Joe Stoyte, and Virginia Maunciple, crude (for Huxley) caricatures of the scientist, the capitalist, and the "ideal" woman Hollywood has made dimensionally famous. Huxley wisely does not permit the complete conversion of either Pete or Jeremy, but there is no one as human as Beavis to identify with, and the saviour, Propter, is so boringly reasonable one almost wishes himself back to the discomforts of barbarism.

Somewhat the same could be said of *Time Must Have a Stop* (1944), (possibly Huxley's best fiction for the first half of its way), and of *Ape and Essence* (1949). Good to read then, they have become novels one rereads with lessening appreciation. Both of them utilize the pattern Huxley has more effectively and less effectively used before—Thomas Mann's child of life beset by contemporary confusion, chided and confused by tutors whose insights are plausible but do not agree. The adolescent Sebastian, in *Time Must Have a Stop*, is Denis better portrayed and Beavis more plausibly converted, blocked by the brilliance of Eustace Barnack, Huxley's most convincing and many-sided hedonist. But everything becomes so tractlike towards the end that the reader resents Huxley's designs upon him. Loola in *Ape and Essence* is Huxley's first woman to apprehend the divine ground, but she is characterized meagerly and her conversion is as incidental as the Savage's in *Brave New World*. Brilliant and provoking exposition of what we and our world may become makes *Ape and Essence*, like the earlier not-Utopia, better than Orwell's soggy *1984*, but it does not excite our emotions as much as it does our intellectual apprehensions. Nor does it have the saving amplitude of *Island* (1962).

Though something of too explicit prophetic vision infects *The Genius and the Goddess,* it is a better novel than any other after *Eyeless in Gaza*. Not that one feels with most of the characters. Maartens, the physicist who enjoyed the innocence of his occupation before Hiroshima; his wife, who can live *this* life intensely though she does not see through it to the divine ground; Rivera, the first of Huxley's characters to come

to the Perennial Philosophy without the too-mechanical intervention of a Miller or a Propter—none of these can I identify
with emotionally as I could with the seekers from Denis to
Sebastian. Though there are the exceptions I have noted, as a
not-congenital novelist Huxley probably distrusted passionate
identification; probably he cared little about the aesthetic
imperative that characters must be involved in action that seems
inevitable. What makes his novels through *Eyeless in Gaza*
apparently superior is their effective externalization of the inner
conflict he himself could not escape or avoid. Fortunately, this
externalization of conflict does not disappear entirely in the
later novels (though it is more on an intellectual than an
emotional level most of the time). However, I think we value
what has succeeded *Eyeless in Gaza* largely for other (but
honorable) reasons. The characters are accurate abstract
analyses of forces that dominate or may dominate our world;
the style that is the man and the artist makes excrement and
spiritual ecstacy seem proper improprieties in a universe that
may be divinely grounded. The style and the accurate abstractions make us suspend disbelief and make us feel at one with
Huxley, who was himself never totally capable of suspending
disbelief, in what he willed himself to believe.

The good and bad of his last "manner" is found in his last
novel, *Island*. Only upon rare occasions is there felt life. The
characters are caricatures or names to which things happen.
What happens occurs because it illustrates—beautifully—Huxley's
view of what man could have made of man, probably won't,
still may. The devising is obvious. The talk is longer than most
classroom lectures. None of the ideas are new in Huxley nor
unfamiliar altogether to those who have read Norman Brown's
*Life Against Death* or Alan Watts's books about Zen. Still, a
reader would have to be immensely lucky to find, now or ever,
as palatable a synthesis of the best ideas that societies should
have but haven't practised as he can in Huxley's *Island*. And
if he looks back through the other Utopias from More's to
Bellamy's, he'll find the same faults (or necessary virtues) that
appear in Huxley's intensely interesting synthesis of what life
might become if political and social leaders had Huxley's

knowledge and intelligence. One goes to utopias for wished assumptions that avoid impossibilities (to paraphrase Huxley's epigraph from Aristotle), prepared to listen and to think, not to follow a Strethers through his felt life or a Jordan through his necessary and likely journey to disaster. If we survive, *Island* may rank with the best of utopias, possibly with the few books of our time that show both disaster and a way out, not just how to cope with awfulness.

The adequately interesting plot, at least as good as that of *Looking Backward* and as plausibly peopled, is intended, like the art of the island, to be palatable to all who read intelligently —not a complexity designed for the few by "a few gifted manipulators of artistic or philosophical symbols." Will Farnaby—"the man who won't take yes for an answer," a "Special Correspondent paid to . . . report on the current horrors," "too clever to believe in God or be convinced of his own mission"—is shipwrecked on the utopian Pala that he's supposed to corrupt enough so that Lord Aldehyde can profit from its valuable oil reserves. To accomplish this, he's allied with Colonel Dipa, dictator of adjoining Randang and creator of the Five Year Plan for Interisland Economic Coordination. Will, like the cynical but teachable heroes of all the novels that have followed *Point Counter Point,* scoffingly tries to disbelieve his eyes and starts along the way that may lead to Pala's becoming another exploited country. Covertly he cooperates with Rani, the Queen Mother who delights in the doctrine of original sin that makes misery and conversion easy, who believes "happy coincidence" has made her will and God's identical, and with the emperor-to-be, Murugan, totally mother-ridden and an exemplar of the Peter Pan variety of dictator Huxley dissects astutely. Before probable disaster falls on Pala, Will sees the island at its best, falls in love with Susila, sees a world Huxley persisted in believing in with dubious optimism.

Pala, it seems, originated early in the nineteenth century because of the happy accident of Dr. Andrew, "a Calvinist-turned-atheist" and the Raja, "a Mahayana Buddhist," combining to put into practice the best of Eastern and Western thought. Not wanted by the imperialist powers, aware of "good" Western

technology, never forgetting the spiritual wisdom of Zen
Buddhism enhanced by other Eastern and by Western wisdom,
Pala has become a Utopian island of a million or so inhabitants
"surrounded by twenty-nine hundred million mental cases."
After reading about it, one wishes it were not so surrounded,
so distant, and so incapable of accepting immigrants.

Pala is realistically based upon known and not practiced
wisdom available to all of us (though we might shudder it off
as "silly" or "impossible"). Children are educated to practise
and enjoy sex as sacred, to see people die and learn how to do
it themselves, to use muscles and brain, to respect and preserve
the ecology of Pala, to live in the present intensely, as the mynah
bird insistently reminds them with its call of "Attention! Attention!" or "Here and Now!" Delinquency rarely occurs because
children are sorted accurately so that they can develop their
individuality, even if they are potential "Muscle People" or
"Peter Pans," and their aggressions are sublimated in dangerous
work and pleasure, practical, pleasant outlets that Hitler and
Mussolini and Stalin did not have, regrettably. Their education
is everything related, leading to individual separateness. There
is no gap between theory and practice, between one's New
Year's resolutions and actual behavior, between remembering
and the tyranny of one's past, between the branches of knowledge:

> Science is not enough, religion is not enough, art is not enough,
> politics and economics are not enough, nor is love, nor is duty,
> nor is action however disinterested, nor, however sublime, is
> contemplation. Nothing short of everything will really do.

The Palinese system works plausibly enough to frighten any
fullblown Calvinist or true AMA believer (doctors are paid for
preserving life only). It eschews and understands the contradictory and similar extremes of capitalism and communism. Its
metaphysical basis includes Christian insights that have been
practised rarely and Buddhistic insights that remind one what a
bother Laos and a good many other countries are because they
won't change their cultures overnight to suit either Americans
or Russians. A "poem," towards the beginning of the novel,

gives the essence of a metaphysic that makes slow, unforgettable sense:

> All things, to all things
> perfectly indifferent,
> perfectly work together
> in discord for a good beyond
> good, for a Being more
> timeless in transience, more
> eternal in its dwindling than
> God there in heaven.

This poem and its explication and implementation throughout the book may make one doubt Huxley's sanity or look to one's own. It does (annoyingly?) make "the best of many more worlds than any merely prudent or sensible person would have dreamed of being able to reconcile and combine," as Dr. Robert, supersensibly says.

Perhaps the supersense, sometimes combined with a tone of superassurance that resembles arrogance trying (honestly) to be humble, is what set many reviewers against *Island,* rather than its failure to conform to easy dogmatisms about what a novel should be. Perhaps the animosity of some is accounted for by Huxley's failure, like Nehru's, to choose sides between "armaments, universal debt, and planned obsolescence," and "ignorance, militarism, and breeding," though Huxley dislikes the first set of evils least. Most legitimately, gratitude should outweigh carping about *Island.* Marred and blessed by the style that is the man, Huxley's dramatized talks about everything he has ever thought about make him unforgettable, despite the fact that he is an incorrigible, sometimes tedious, lecturer.

I honor Huxley's search, cannot believe he found *the* answer, wish unreasonably that he had been more the congenital novelist. Still, what other contemporary British novelist knew as much, hoped for more good, recognized as much bad, interests us so consistently? In 1923, young Gumbril speculated ramblingly about the meaning behind apparent nonsense. Old Rivers, sixtyish like Huxley when he wrote about him, and the younger Dr. Roberts of *Island* continue to hope and to wonder. They and

Huxley would have no truck with denominational *hubris*. What they settled for may seem shoddy (peyotl, extrasensory perception). This should not blind us to Huxley's very great virtues. The constant facts about Aldous Huxley remain his serious, sometimes too solemn, search for an answer for himself and for us and the limited but superior skill he had in communicating it.

## Chapter Four

# Ivy Compton-Burnett: Factualist

THOUGH IT WAS DIFFIDENTLY subtitled "A Study" when it first appeared, Ivy Compton-Burnett's first characteristic novel, *Pastors and Masters* (1925) reveals in small the attitudes, pre-occupations, and techniques she has modified and improved in the novels that have followed. It begins, typically, with a speech by a minor character:

> "Well, this is a nice thing! A nice thing this schoolmastering! Up at seven, and in a room with a black fire. . . . I should have thought it might have occurred to one out of forty boys to poke it. . . . And while you are about it, don't pile on as much coal as it would take the day's profits of the school to pay for. . . . Here is a thing to be degraded by, every morning when I come down to an honest day's work, a middle-aged man working to support his family! I am surprised to see people with such a want of self-respect. I admit that I am. I would rather see a boy come in roundly late, than slip in on the stroke, half-dressed and half-asleep, and pass as being in [*sic*] time. It is an ungentlemanly thing to do."
>
> Mr. Merry, a tall, thin man about fifty, leaned back in his chair, and fixed on his pupils his little, pale, screwed up eyes, to which he had the gift of imparting an alluring kindness. His feelings towards them, affection, disgust, pride and despair, seemed to oust each other over his face.

About this beginning, a good many sophisticated readers would find much to complain of. No one would really talk like this; in particular the obvious exposition that he is a middle-aged man working hard to support his family should not be part of the monologue. No good writer should introduce so much expository description at once, especially what is said of the varying feelings toward the pupils and of his alluring kindness. This is more like a play, not a very good one, with the stage directions following the speech they should have preceded.

But any reasonably sensitive reader who reads the rest of *Pastors and Masters* would withdraw his objections. Like the rest of her novels, it is more like a play than any contemporary fiction apart from Henry Green's, but it is like a very good one. Ivy Compton-Burnett is as exact and economical a writer as one can find in modern times. She expects her readers to be alert, to cooperate intelligently in making of her book a work of art. He who runs will misread her; he who reads her novels with the attentiveness one more usually gives to poetry will find great pleasure and great enlightenment.

In the quoted passage, for example, he *may* discover that the school is very casually run, that the boys are not all well disciplined, that Mr. Merry is not sure of himself and that that is why he imparts an air of alluring kindness even while he barks more loudly than he will bite. The passage is necessary preparation for the presentation of the atmosphere of the school —watered marmalade, inattentive, not unhappy boys unrigorously schooled—and of the minor characters who are necessary to our understanding of the major ones: Mrs. Merry, "a smooth-headed, mild-looking woman with a grieved expression"; Miss Basden, who speaks "in a tone in which equality, respect, and absorption in her duty" remarkably mingle; Mr. Burgess, who comes late to breakfast and simulates absorbed attention to his "elders and betters." Only one of the major characters, Mr. Herrick, appears in the first chapter and then very briefly. He does the ten-minute scripture reading that constitutes his day's work, but we get no real insight into him.

In the second chapter the major characters, Herrick and his sister, reveal themselves with engaging abruptness:

> "This is a good room to come back to," said Herrick. "That hall and the woman, and poor Merry shuffling up to do his duty. It made me shiver."
> "The sight of duty does make one shiver," said Miss Herrick. "The actual doing of it would kill one, I think."

These speeches give a good idea of what to expect from Nicholas and Emily Herrick. The sight of duty makes Nicholas shiver. Emily not only agrees; she unhesitatingly and wittily expresses what a more ordinary person would veil with hypocrisy. This she continues to do throughout *Pastors and Masters,* for she is both herself and the author's eye. Her conversation, as Robert Liddell puts it, "sometimes approximates to what one might actually say . . . but also to what one might think and conceal . . . to what one might afterwards wish one had said; to what one would like to think oneself." What Mr. Liddell says applies to all of Miss Compton-Burnett's characters who are wits rather than witwoulds. The conversation that carries the plot forward, about eighty percent of the whole in all the novels, is not, *fortunately,* at all like what people actually say to each other. It resembles the beautifully unnatural language we find in Restoration comedy and Greek tragedy. Consequently the reader must have all his faculties about him while he reads Miss Compton-Burnett. Either he gets her or he misses her entirely.

What the reader who gets her uncovers in *Pastors and Masters* is worth his while. Nicholas is one of Miss Compton-Burnett's more amiable exploiters. By assembling his group of incompetent and barely competent masters, he is left free to do what he wills. Up to the time when the novel begins, this has been writing criticism, "unkindness to other people's" work. But early in the novel, at the death bed of Crabbe, a ninety-year-old don who has been his friend, he is presumed to have discovered the material for a short novel. This comforts him, since he has the egotism of one "who is really God's equal," and has hitherto lived in "his disappointment that in letters he had done only critical work." As the reader discovers when Herrick is about to read his novel to a small writer's group, he has stolen the manuscript from the dead Crabbe, who had been given it to read by its actual author. To complicate matters further, the actual author, Bumpus, also intends to read it to the group. What happens at this private reading is good comedy and penetrating criticism of the pretensions of human beings. Nicholas, who does not think "it is incumbent upon a man to keep nothing of his secret doings to himself," continues his egocentric course, discovered only by his sister. She prefers not to tell because she has found that she prefers his "wickedness and penetration" to the naïvete of those whom Nicholas gulls and exploits. By the end of the novel, all the characters except Emily Herrick, the witty observer, stand implicitly condemned. And, as the reader thinks back over the book, he gets the uncomfortable feeling that he resembles the other characters more closely than he does Emily.

Perhaps it is because of her disturbing insights rather than because of her unusual technique that Miss Compton-Burnett has not become a widely popular novelist. It is a pity that this is so, for her novels can bring delight even when they are about the undelightful, and the truths she compels us to face about ourselves are as important as they are disconcerting. No contemporary novelist writes better or tells us more penetratingly what we should want to know and prefer to ignore.

At any rate, apparently, Ivy Compton-Burnett had no more than a chronological connection with the twenties in which she began her characteristic series of novels about the "great deal" that goes on "beneath the surface in a family." She has said that she does not feel that she has "any real or organic knowledge of life later than about 1910—I should not write of later times with enough grasp or confidence." Of her nineteen novels,[1] only *Pastors and Masters* is set in a time later than 1910 and it, except for a passing reference to the attainment of women's suffrage, could easily be taken as a novel about an earlier time. Her way of writing shows no resemblance to the manner of Proust, Joyce, Virginia Woolf, or any of the more frequently imitated moderns. She resembles most, I suppose, Jane Austen, because she limits her cast to "two or three families in a country town," because she writes so concentratedly, and because she neglects quite as totally the temporary contemporary. (In her work there is no mention of a political figure, no reference to wars, no allusion to any writer later than Shaw.) She is also somewhat like Aeschylus in the austerity of the philosophy that dominates the novels—though, as Pamela Hansford Johnson says, such a comparison requires that we conceive of Greek tragedy "with the Furies impotent or non-existent."

---

[1] A careful reader of my early manuscript said eighteen. He did not count *Dolores* (1911), a mistake Miss Compton-Burnett preferred that everyone make.

The polished wit one finds in all her books reminds one of that of Congreve and Etherege, but it is so consistently employed to annihilate the clichés we say and live that it has a character peculiarly her own. The over-all impression of her matter and method is that she is completely herself, that whatever tributaries she may have are not so much absorbed as overwhelmed by her own originality.

Still it seems likely, particularly since her conversation showed an intelligent interest in contemporary life and literature, that she did not escape the world that followed 1910. It is even possible to see contrasts between what she thought and felt before World War I and what she felt and thought afterwards that remind us of similar contrasts in the work of Rose Macaulay and Aldous Huxley. Her first novel, *Dolores* (1911) celebrates the beauty of sacrifice for the good of others. In the novels that follow World War I, as in *Pastors and Masters,* sacrifice of self seems nearly always to be bad for the sacrificer and for those for whom it is made. This complete turn-about reminds one of the distrust of paraded virtue found in writers as disparate as Cummings and Evelyn Waugh. It is true, further, that the view of life she had adopted by 1925 is not totally different from those one finds in the members of the "Lost Generation." Like Huxley and Rose Macaulay and Evelyn Waugh and H. M. Tomlinson and Hemingway, she appears to agree with Macbeth's speech about life being a tale told by an idiot (though she never shows quite the despair or the hope of any of these other writers nor is obvious enough to quote from the speech). It is possible that the shock of the war and the peace helps to account for her concentration upon the prewar period. One guesses that she felt that such a cataclysm had its roots in ordinary human nature as it underlay the surface of the Victorian and Edwardian times of hope. Certainly what she shows us of what goes on "beneath the surface in a family" should inoculate her readers against any surprise at the course of war and uneasy armistice that has absorbed the headlines ever since Versailles.

In fundamental assumptions, the world of Ivy Compton-Burnett, though it is more artfully presented, resembles the world of the twenties presented by Huxley and Rose Macaulay.

God is "one of the best drawn characters in fiction," the Bible an unsuitable book but one from which we can profitably gain a knowledge of the prevalence of wickedness. Nature, Miss Compton-Burnett's closest approximation to a first principle, is indifferent, quite as well pleased at the success of a tyrant, an exploiter, or a hypocrite as at the success of a model of self-sacrifice. Indeed, it appears that nature has one law only: that man cannot violate the nature given to him, whether it be good or bad. Man is naturally and therefore appropriately self-centered and egoistic. "We can't choose the pattern on which we are made," the words of Matty in *A Family and a Fortune* (1939), are so frequently echoed by sympathetic and unsympathetic characters in all the novels that it seems almost the *leitmotif* of her work. So does the counterpart to Matty's words, "We must not find fault with what is natural." For a very unbiblical reason, we must judge not lest we be judged.

It is fortunate for her art that Miss Compton-Burnett, the controller of her characters' destinies, has a nature of *her* own—otherwise, with all characters "naturally" faulty, there could be no conflict and the reader would be lost in a maze, unable to identify with anyone because he would identify with everyone. By her portrayal of those who are not kind, as well as those who are, it is clear that Miss Compton-Burnett prefers those who are mainly gentle and intelligent to those who are usually cruel and intelligent, that she admires characters like Miss Ridley in *The Present and the Past* (1953) who, though their life is "divided between . . . conscience and . . . inclinations," try to "strike the mean between them." This does not mean that Miss Compton-Burnett admires stupidity when it acts virtuously or that she sees any of her characters as good or bad enough for either God or the Devil to pay attention to. Although there are occasions, as we will see, when she presents absolute evil for aesthetic purposes, for the most part the drama in her novels is the consequence of pitting bad-and-good characters against characters who are good-and-bad.

It has become a commonplace of criticism to speak of Ivy Compton-Burnett's domestic tyrants as the centers of her books.

If one insists that a tyrant is not necessarily one who seizes power, for her tyrants are nearly always tyrants by descent, and that a tyrant is not necessarily one who exercises power cruelly, one must agree. But I wonder if the secondary meaning of tyrant, one who misuses power cruelly, has not, in much criticism, absorbed the meaning that is etymologically primary. There is too much of a tendency to view Miss Compton-Burnett's tyrants as personifications of evil unredeemed, a tendency that has led to oversimplification, sometimes even to what the author must have considered distortion. It is clear that Miss Compton-Burnett did not regard power that approaches the absolute as an ordained necessity and that none of her domestic tyrants are to be considered Hitlers with limited opportunities (though I am sure she was not as much surprised by Hitler as naïve liberals were). She accepted the necessity of a ruling power just as she accepted the necessity of a domestic hierarchy where children and servants and school mistresses are subordinate to their elders or betters. Frequently her characters agree with Cook in *Manservant and Maidservant* (1947) that "happiness is not the only thing in life . . . and laxness and liberty may not always be conducive to it," and that it is possible for the domestic despot to "stand for welfare in the true sense." Her novels show that she was quite as concerned with the use of power as with its misuse. And, it may be added, she usually saw the unhappiness of the tyrant as clearly as she did that of those he has power over.

Sophia Stace in *Brothers and Sisters* (1929), however, does approximate the critic's stereotype. She is not an engagingly negligent tyrant like Nicholas in *Pastors and Masters*. She approaches rather closely the despot with absolute power that corrupts absolutely. Sophia marvels "at the gulf between the average person" and herself and makes all of her children except Robin her slaves because "It had not occurred to them or to her, that they might not adapt their moods to her." Quite consistently she is adept at saying "just the thing at the moment, that a decent person would not say" and "blamelessly" wounds because it has never occurred to her that other people might have sensitivities of their own. Fortunately for the tension of the novel, however, she does not rule absolutely. At the worst, her other children, Dinah and Andrew, have the freedom to see through her, to laugh at or pity her, while Robin, the son who resembles her, is able to combat her openly and to escape into his own detachment. When Sophia dies, the author summarizes their views dispassionately: "It seemed that a weight had fallen, as a weight had lifted. The survey of Sophia's life flashed on them, the years of ruthlessness and tragedy, power and grief. Happiness, of which she was held to have so much, had never been real to Sophia." There can be little doubt that Miss Compton-Burnett agrees with what Dinah says of Sophia, "It is no good to charge people with their natures," a more devastating statement about human nature than we find in any of the work of Rose Macaulay or Aldous Huxley. Though *Brothers and Sisters* does not show Miss Compton-Burnett in full possession of her powers, it is a good novel that suggests what her later novels were to develop with greater subtlety and power.

Though its central core is a variation of domestic tyranny and its consequences, *Men and Wives* (1931) is not rigidly delimited and shows, for the first time, the richness of texture that characterizes Miss Compton-Burnett's novels at their best. The tragicomedy of Harriet Haslam, whose weapon is hypochondria caused by unlovableness caused by not being loved, is movingly and humorously drawn. While she lives, one is glad that the children and others can laugh at her determination to make them extensions of her will; when she dies, killed by the son she cannot dominate, one feels, with the children and her husband, the pitiableness of her not ahuman effort to make her will rather than God's prevail, the continuing tragedy of the sons who bow to her wishes when she is dead as they often did not while she lived. The richness of texture comes from the fuller development of related characters—the comically pathetic father who preens his importance and never gets away with it, the children who are nearly always witty about themselves and their difficulties, the pastor who is always doomed to act and be recognized as an actor, his silly emancipated wife who almost marries three other men, Rachel, old and wise and

witty, only a little unkind in her commentaries upon the stupidities and hypocrisies of the people she is kind to. Every character
and every event has its appropriate place in this complexly
plotted novel that careful reading alone can show the virtue of.

*More Women than Men* (1933), the best of the early novels,
opens with purposeful quietness. Josephine Napier, the head of
a large and successful girls' school, who has "a conscious sincerity and simplicity of mien," greets the mistresses who serve
under her upon their return from vacation. She is abrupt,
considerate, and enlightenedly in favor of self-interest: "There
is very little self-sacrifice in the life of my mistresses. . . . I see
to that." It is obvious that she has the respect and some of
the affection of both her teachers and her pupils, that her school
is a superior one that balances nicely freedom and responsibility.
But before long, the reader becomes aware that she is despotic
as well as benevolent. Her adopted son Gabriel is expected to
love her more than he (or anyone) reasonably can; her husband,
whom she won by deceiving a friend, is kept in his minor place
as totally as is her brother. When she gives a position to the
friend she deceived, she subconsciously betrays what she most
deeply is. "I am fond of Elizabeth," she says, "and shall enjoy
having her work under me; working with me, for there is no
question of top and bottom." It soon becomes clear that we
are meant to agree with Gabriel when he says, "Josephine is
built on a large scale. . . . She is powerful for both good and
bad." We agree also with the deceived friend who replies,
"Yes, she is destiny, and we are her sport."

When Gabriel, against her wishes, marries Elizabeth's daughter
Ruth, she becomes a more active destiny. She tries to make
husband and wife sleep separately; she invades their privacy;
she encourages Gabriel to go away while Ruth is suffering from
a mild chill; when it becomes severe, she does not call Gabriel
back but deliberately kills Ruth by exposing her to cold air
while extolling its ubiquitous healthfulness. She does not regain
Gabriel nor is she able to keep Rex, the drawing master who
began to attract her while Gabriel was away. Her suffering,
which is impressive because Miss Compton-Burnett underplays
it, does not prevent her from doing as she always has. At the

end of the book she is still head of a school where she dispenses justice and education with even-handed efficiency and consideration. The chorus of school mistresses communicates the author's judgment on the last pages. "'It had not struck me,' said Miss Luke, 'had it struck any of you—that Mrs. Napier is a tragic figure?' 'Yes, it had struck me,' said Miss Rossetti." And she, alone among them, knows of the murder Josephine Napier has committed. It is a great tribute to Miss Compton-Burnett's art that the reader agrees, for he has been made to see, with Miss Rossetti, "the many facets that go to make up the surface of the soul." "We must not find fault with what is natural," Josephine said before she had consciously contemplated anything but the beneficent exercise of power.

The four novels that succeeded *More Women than Men* are good, but not as good as it is. Each is concerned with grand and petty tyranny in the family and each is full of other fine things that arise naturally from the circumstances that are central in the novel. Artfully, Miss Compton-Burnett does not restrict the action so rigidly that there is no "irrelevancy" to enhance reality. Each of them is separately valuable.

*A House and Its Head* (1935), for example, is, in its not *too* controlled pattern, a novel that centers about Duncan Edgeworth. After the death of his wife, Duncan marries a very young woman and, when he discovers that the child she bears is not his, murders the child so that there will be a chance of a male heir from the next woman he marries. To present such bare bones without the flesh of texture will remind anyone who has read the novels how skillfully melodramatic events are underplayed in all Miss Compton-Burnett's work and how much more than the structure of plot the novels depend upon. Incestuous relationships, murders, and adulteries figure largely in all the novels just as they do in the tabloids. But they are never played up for sensational reasons. Rather, they are used as stimuli that make the characters reveal themselves as they would not under more ordinary circumstances, an aesthetic device Shakespeare and the Greek dramatists made full use of. Extra-ordinary events play an important part in the revelation of characters under stress, yet the reader of Miss Compton-

Burnett's novels does not remember these events any more specifically than the reader of *Hamlet* recalls the number of deaths in the play. It is the characters and the moral atmosphere one recalls rather than the sensational events that stimulate action and reaction. The sensational material is treated "as if one's next door neighbor leaned over the garden wall, and remarked, in the same breath and chatty tone, that he had mown the lawn in the morning and thrust his wife's head in the gas-oven after lunch," to quote Pamela Hansford Johnson's quotation from a review in the *Church Times* of *A House and Its Head*. Intentionally or not, this is a tribute to Miss Compton-Burnett's artistry, for is it not characteristic of the artist that he presents the sensational as if it were an ordinary occurrence that can help us to understand the nature of human beings?

So, in *Daughters and Sons* (1937), it is not so much the dramatic death of Sabine Ponsonby at a dinner party or the many marriages that one remembers. Rather it is the conflict between the family and Sabine, a matriarch so superhumanly rude that she is almost admirable, and Hetta, her daughter who tries to take over the family power when Sabine dies. One recalls, too, much of the dialogue which, while it is suitable to the characters in the situations in which they speak it, gives a running commentary on the action and establishes a "moral" atmosphere by which the whole may be judged. It reminds one of the relevant interruptions of the action of a Greek play by the chorus, except that what is said in no way interrupts the forward movement:

> "It would be good to have power."
> "No, we should use it. . . . No one can stand it."

> "Why is Aunt Hetta getting so much worse?"
> "She tried to live for others . . . and that is the end."

> "You really almost treat each others as strangers. It is the only way to keep family affection. One must never feel that one is in one's own house."

> "No one can look anyone else in the face. . . . So we are all equal."

A *Family and a Fortune* (1939) is about the way Dudley Gaviston's fortune brings more pleasure to others than to himself and about Aunt Hatty's attempts to use hypochondria as a way to power. In *Parents and Children* (1941), the central drama is the characters' attempt to get control of Fulbert's wife while he is on a trip to South America. In both novels, it is the conflicts within the family and the suggestions of the chorus of conversation about the universality of the struggle for power that are longest recalled:

> "Human beings ought always to be judged very tenderly, and . . . no one will be as tender as themselves."

> "Human failings, human vanity, human weakness! We don't hear the word applied to anything good. Even human nature seems a derogatory term. It is simply an excuse for everything."

> "Would it be better if Mother and Aunt Hatty did not address each other in terms of affection? . . . It is supposed to excuse everything else?"

> "Dear, dear, the miniature world of a family! All the emotions of mankind seem to find a place in it."

In context, these statements serve a dramatic function and arise out of the unusual happenings in the novels, but they also make us aware of the universal human plight that is Miss Compton-Burnett's central, artistically validated subject.

What can be called the first phase of Miss Compton-Burnett's development as an artist is climaxed in *Elders and Betters* (1944) and *Manservant and Maidservant* (1947). These are not better novels than *More Women than Men*, but perceptibly better novels than the four I have dealt with summarily above. They are fine dramatizations of what Miss Compton-Burnett has to say during her first phase about the ruthlessness of the power-seeker and the effect he has upon those he tyrannizes.

Anna Donne, the chief character of *Elders and Betters*, is more terrifying than any of the men and women who seek power in the other novels. Even in the opening pages of the book it is clear that there is no enlightenment in her self-interest.

She treats the servants like members of the family and the members of the family like servants; they are all furniture that must be arranged to suit her. Anna knows that "Nature is . . . red in tooth and claw," and that it "is not good to think that other people are out to serve our interests." She acts with frightening consistency upon these beliefs. When she perceives that she can profit from the one act of kindness she has shown, her visits to Aunt Sukey Donne while she is fatally ill from heart disease, she does not hesitate to destroy the last will that would keep her from an inheritance nor does she waver when Sukey's sister tries to persuade her that the money must have been intended for her rather than for Anna. Instead Anna drives the sister to suicide by playing upon her conviction that she was not good as either a mother or a wife. No one is able to oppose her successfully or uncover what she has done, and at the close of the story she is married to the son of the woman she drove to suicide and wears her rings as a token of family esteem. It is true, of course, that Anna, like all of Miss Compton-Burnett's characters, is following the law of her nature, but this does not mitigate the terror without pity that she arouses.

In the beginning of *Manservant and Maidservant,* Horace Lamb seems as horrifying as Anna. He tyrannizes through parsimony. An extra cutlet on the dinner table, a coal more than is needed for minimum comfort on the fire, and he is full of righteous indignation. His children are without love and without hope for a normal life. His wife intends to run away with his cousin so that both she and the children can escape from a situation that daily grows more impossible. But when Horace learns that his wife is to leave him and understands why, he changes. The children get new clothes, are urged to eat what they will, the house is kept warm, and he demonstrates his affection to such an extent that the children are uncomfortable under it. He even forgives a servant who plots without success to take his life. The fact that Miss Compton-Burnett makes his change plausible is the consequence of both fine art and a modification of her view of the unchangeableness of the nature each of us is given. Perhaps this was inevitable, for, after the presentation of Anna, and of Horace in the first part of *Man-*

*servant and Maidservant,* she could scarcely have gone farther in the exposure of the ruthless nature of absolute power or the lust for it that occurs in the miniature world of a family in which all the emotions of mankind find a place.

Ivy Compton-Burnett's second phase does not bring with it any obvious change in her view of the world. There is no sign of a benevolent deity who takes care of everyone and everything. Her people still fight for power as is their nature determined by Nature. The parents and the children still contend, with the children like the servants getting the worst of it—though not as consistently and not for as long. The late novels like the earlier contain a sufficient number of sensational events: two illegitimate children, a brother and sister who assume they are married to each other until they discover that the wife is really the illegitimate child of someone else, a father who is about to marry a girl forty years younger than himself until he discovers that the wife he presumed dead is alive. The characters continue to say what is usually not said, with wit and malice and wisdom. The difference is that Miss Compton-Burnett now concentrates her attention upon the good-and-bad characters (who always have been present in her books) and that she recognizes more than she has before the possibility of a change of mind and of action.

To a greater extent than in the earlier novels except *Parents and Children, Two Worlds and Their Ways* (1949) is child-centered. This leads to a gentling of view, to an emphasis upon the good that tends to preponderate in Miss Compton-Burnett's children and childlike adults. Clemence and Sefton Shelly are sent, from a home where they are reasonably adjusted to their mother's wish that they be superior, to private schools, other worlds where there is both exciting variety and, as they feel (projecting their mother's wishes upon the quite reasonable and amiable school masters and mistresses), an excessive demand that they demonstrate their superiority. Both cheat to show that they are as much better than their classmates as their mother would wish; both are found out and returned home disgraced. If the parents had been as demanding as those in the earlier novels, the result would have been tragedy. But the father, Sir Roderick, looks upon their stumble as something rather ordinary and the mother realizes that she has expected too much of them, made them cheat. She realizes that she does not differ too much from her children, for she had stolen from Sir Roderick's father to please her husband while he, in an interval between marriages, had had an affair and an illegitimate child. Because they recognize their own fallibility to a greater extent than any earlier parents in the novels, they recognize that "children are always reproached for doing what we do ourselves," and that parents and children alike are "human beings, liable to error." At the close of the novel, the outlook for the whole family is, without earlier parallel, at least bright gray. This chance of future brightness is plausible because it does not violate the conditions of Miss Compton-Burnett's world. We are still aware of the other side of the coin Miss Compton-Burnett has reversed. Indeed, we become aware that the brighter side of the coin appeared even in *Pastors and Masters,* for her children have always had resilience and intelligence and have rarely been defeated totally.

Though it contains two of her most successful portraits of pleasant old people, Sir Ransom and Selina, and is full of the good talk one finds in everything she writes, *Darkness and Day* (1951) is one of Miss Compton-Burnett's less successful novels. Perhaps this is because there is no real conflict between parents and children, masters and servants, husband and wife. The novel also lacks the usual trial by sensational events (though Edmund and Bridget are "tried" by the belief that they are brother and sister married). *The Present and the Past* (1953), on the other hand, is one of Miss Compton-Burnett's best novels. Like *Two Worlds and Their Ways,* it is child-centered and the children about whom it revolves are perhaps the most memorable to appear in all the novels (a dangerous judgment to make of a series of novels where plausibly good and uninnocent children abound). Henry, who sees things as they are with believable precocity, Megan, adept at rewriting the poems of others for her own purposes, and Toby, "who can still believe anything and be happy," are the children of Cassius Clare's marriage, his second, to Flavia. The oldest boys, Adrian and Guy, are from Cassius's earlier marriage to Catherine. When

Catherine moves nearby, Adrian and Guy suffer from divided loyalty to mother and stepmother while Cassius, Miss Compton-Burnett's most sympathetic muddler, thinks he is seen as a "common creature blundering between two high-minded women, and inflicting" himself on both. His tragedy is that he *is* a "common creature" and that he does not understand that the two women are more practical than high-minded. When he dies the reader is as genuinely sad as his children, Henry and Megan. Still, most of the reader's sympathy goes to Guy, who leaves the stepmother he has learned to prefer, to follow Adrian, whom Guy loves best of all; to Catherine, whom Adrian loves best, and to Henry and Megan, who now understand the nature of the death that they apprehended earlier when they witnessed the death of a sick hen and of a mole.

More than in any earlier novel the tone wavers movingly between pathos and humor that is only a little unkind. One smiles sadly with Toby throughout the book. "O dear people, we are gathered together. Dearly beloved brethern. Let us pray. Ashes and ashes, dust and dust. This our brother. Poor little mole! Until he rise again. Prayers of the congregation. Amen," Toby prays early in the novel. The mixture of feelings aroused by this prayer continues and applies to everyone involved. All the more so, I think, because we *feel* finally that no one is to blame. "We can only love according to ourselves. . . . We cannot alter our natures." In *The Present and the Past* we have something that transcends tragedy and comedy and is better, a gentle fidelity to "fact" that reminds one of Macaulay's and Huxley's views of life, that even suggests Waugh's stern Catholicism, yet is peculiarly and distinctly Miss Compton-Burnett's own.

*Mother and Son* (1955) and *A Father and His Fate* (1957) are not quite as good, though large things can be claimed for them even in brief summary. *Mother and Son* is the perfect fable of the man who loves all women because he knows no one of them will love him as much as his mother, who has kept him childlike to middle-age. (No villain appears. One never does in the later novels.) The mother loves according to her nature, the son invites perpetual childishness. *A Father*

*and His Fate* is about a reckless benevolent despot who intends
to marry Verena, his junior by forty-five years, until he
discovers that the wife he presumed dead is alive and anxious
to resume her place in his and the family's life. The chorus of
dialogue that is part of and apart from the action enhances (as
always) the value of the two novels:

> "So it is true that comedy and tragedy are mingled," said
> Adrian.
> "Really it is all tragedy," said his sister. "Comedy is a wicked
> way of looking at it, when it is not our own."

> "Yes, we all prey on each other. The jungle is never
> dead. . . ."

> "Can she be as much worse than she seems, as the rest of
> us are?"
> "Perhaps not. She does not edit herself."

> "I never know why self-sacrifice is noble," said Miss Burke.
> "Why is it better to sacrifice oneself than someone else?"
> "It is no better," said Hester, "and it is not really held to be."

> "But I should yield to temptation!"
> "People always do. . . . If they resist, it is something else."

> "We show the selves we are accustomed to show, and other
> people to expect."
> "I think I show my real self."
> "You show the one you have come to think is yours."

> "Why cannot you behave like a man?"
> "That is what I am doing, as she is behaving like a woman.
> As you say, there is little difference. We are both human
> beings."

> "Yes, it has made me see how seldom life is like that. It is
> everything else, and hard, happy, anything it may be, seldom
> strange."

> "Experience may go as deep in a quiet life as in any other."

> "Few of us would live at all, if we could foresee our whole
> future. . . . There are things beyond bearing in every life. We
> cannot escape them."

Nevertheless her last two novels—better than the two that preceded them if one can make distinctions with any accuracy among the works of a writer who has maintained always an exceptional level of excellence—do continue to show men as good-and-bad and life worth continuing despite inescapable ills. This is true of both *A Heritage and Its History* (1959) and of *A God and His Gifts* (1963), both somewhat diminished aesthetically by the repetition of thematic ideas phrased nearly as they have been before and by the too laxly structured section that precedes the magnificent conclusion of the latter—a conclusion that shows as close an approach to optimism as one can expect from a factualist of Ivy Compton-Burnett's integrity. Despite the adulteries coolly assimilated into the novel's lifelikeness and the persisting selfishnesses that enlighten her characters beneficently only sometimes, *A God and His Gifts* conveys in its last chapter an almost Shakespearean feeling, a feeling of life continuing to continue in its beautiful terror in the person of Henry, the end-product of a series of adulterous lives entered into or accepted by a group of unmalicious, very gifted, amoral factualists. Henry, the child who persists in his innocent cruel-kindness (or kind-cruelty), looks on life much as does Aunt Penelope, the wise old spinster who will not be perturbed. Having understood and faced the worst and the best of the characters who squarely face a world in which fiction and fact are horrifying and desirable, Aunt Penelope says, "I find you brave and kind and wise."

*The Mighty and Their Fall* (1961), the novel that preceded it, is as good as any novel she has written, better possibly than *A God and His Gifts*. The necessary prop of plot creaks with unexpected entrances, coincidences, twists in direction that stretch the limits of verisimilitude (as in Shakespeare, Sophocles, and Dickens). Widowed Ninian Middleton, surrounded by two children early in their twenties, one in adolescence, and two (Hengist, eleven, and Leah, ten) in their precocity, asks Teresa to marry him without telling her about his family. Wisely surveying the situation, she rejects him; wisely reconsidering her prospects of finding a man she likes more who is less surrounded, she writes a letter of qualified acceptance. Lavinia, the twenty-year-old daughter who seems mature because she is "an autocrat, an intellectual," and "a widowed father's companion," purloins the letter, blames its theft on her grandmother, Selina, surprisingly asserts herself (out of jealousy generated by the Electra complex that is nearly always suggested when daughter and father are together in a separated family?) by agreeing to marry her uncle by adoption. This she is able to do after Ninian marries, after the prodigal real uncle returns to die and leave his money to her, after her father tries to steal the will that leaves control of Uncle Ransom's money to her, so that he will have it. Well and sparely told, the creaks are almost soundless and the characters' witty wisdom would keep one with the novel even if the not-impossible plot thundered improbability.

As usual, but with the engaging variety of differentiation and penetration one finds always, the characters, their wording of their reactions, and the wisdom that comes from the reader's observation of their commingling, make the novel excellent. In their conversations, and it is conversation you want to overhear attentively, all amenities and inanities are omitted. No one neglects to say a harsh truth that may bring a brusque blessing; each character serves himself first, without ruthlessness or a pretense of saintliness. Unlofty, accurately humdrum human action prevails in talk and action. The reader finally agrees with Hugo, an amiable do-nothing who is willing, with only a slight twang of conscience, to marry his niece when he says

> "Why cannot we like people in lofty moods? . . . I suppose it
> is their being so unnatural to them. It produces discomfort."

All the characters Ivy Compton-Burnett conjugates in *The Mighty and Their Fall* find it difficult to speak without being wise wittily or without erasing a commonplace stupidity. Selina, for once a grandmatriarch with more wisdom than severity, stands out heroically in the constricted field of the family. She lives, like her expressions, fluctuating between grim "disillusionment and almost unconscious benevolence," and it is the good fortune of the family that her advice usually is taken, that the others end up nearly glad, finding the little that is more than they looked for, "much." All the others, except Egbert, have moments of revelation and revealing wisdom. The least likeable (as so often) is the central character, Ninian, who, far from being a hero, is gradually revealed as a respectable "man of family" who knows best how to pity himself, get for himself, and think only of himself. Next to Selina and the younger children, again a chorus frighteningly mature, the "bad" characters come off best: Lavinia, who is willing to marry incestuously to escape with Hugo from Ninian's second marriage; Hugo, who uses idleness to cultivate wise fatalism and wit; Ransom, the prodigal who returns with money made "in ways accepted in their time and place." The "sinners," like Lavinia, are not "better" for their "stumbles," but they "are wiser . . . [know] what [they] are." And this recognition of what one is and how he is conditioned socially and universally appears to be the closest to happiness that does not deserve contempt achievable by Ivy Compton-Burnett's characters. It comes naturally to the children when young, and returns after enough stumbles, comes to the servants (too little present in *The Mighty and Their Fall*, pleasantly vivid again in *A God and His Gifts*) through keyholes, and to us by turning pages that make lively what, experienced directly, would be pain alleviated occasionally by the good moments allowed by "Someone."

Perhaps that is why Ivy Compton-Burnett is so highly praised and so much less widely known than she deserves. Her universe, like Hardy's and Sophocles', promises neither nirvana nor security nor escape from mortality. Because it can't be undone, as one of her characters says, the past "is the one thing in a safe place." Miss Compton-Burnett's witty-wise truths come at us with such barragelike rapidity, destroy so thoroughly our cherished wishful-washy platitudes that the average mind reels and longs for the comforting tranquility of television. With near perfection in her peculiar way, her novels dramatize the conflict between what seems and what presently, in time's flow, will contradict its seeming. Her recurrent dim (not dismal) view is not unkind but uncovering and relentless. Like Yeats in his later poetry, Ivy Compton-Burnett appears to have looked so deeply into the Hell men have always made so capably that she can be gay even though she faces the somberness of "truth."

No, we cannot escape "truth" either in Miss Compton-Burnett's novels or in our own lives, though it can be borne, even smiled at, as the characters in the novels constantly show in their "quiet" lives where there are always signs that things strange and unpredictable happen. We all edit ourselves, prey on each other, prefer not to sacrifice ourselves, wickedly regard tragedy as comedy. Not wickedly, perhaps. Without mingling the sense of the comic with the sense of the tragic, our lives and the lives of the characters in Miss Compton-Burnett's novels would become unbearable. That she made us see and believe this with rarely flagging art, that she made her small world of several families reveal the large world of many, that she could be kind without overlooking the awful, that she could be gentle while seeing our manifold defects—these are Miss Compton-Burnett's great qualities. It will be a brave new world indeed that can afford to overlook her novels.

## Chapter Five

# Evelyn Waugh: Catholic Aristocrat

IN THE CLOSING PAGES of *Decline and Fall,* Professor Otto Silenus, the architect who thinks the problem of architecture is "the problem of all art—the elimination of the human element from the consideration of form," talks with Paul Pennyfeather:

"It's a good thing for you to be a clergyman. . . . People get ideas about a thing they call life. It sets them all wrong. I think it's poets that are responsible chiefly. Shall I tell you about life?"

"Yes, do," said Paul politely.

"Well, it's like the big wheel at Luna Park. Have you seen the big wheel?"

"No, I'm afraid not."

"You pay five francs and go into a room with tiers of seats all round, and in the centre the floor is made of a great disc of polished wood that revolves quickly. At first you sit and watch the others. They are all trying to sit in the wheel, and they keep getting flung off, and that makes them laugh, and you laugh too. It's great fun."

"I don't think that sounds very much like life," said Paul rather sadly.

"Oh, but it is though. You see the nearer you can get to the hub of the wheel the slower it is moving and the easier it is to stay on. . . . Of course at the very centre there's a point completely at rest, if one could only find it: I'm not sure I am not very near that point myself. . . . Lots of people just enjoy scrambling on and being whisked off and scrambling on again. How they all shriek and giggle! Then there are others . . . who sit as far out as they can and hold on for dear life and enjoy that. But the whole point about the wheel is that you needn't get on it at all, if you don't want to. People get hold of ideas about life, and that makes them think they've got to join in the game, even if they don't enjoy it. It doesn't suit everyone.

"People don't see that when they say 'life' they mean two different things. They can mean simply existence, with its physiological implications of growth and organic change. They can't escape that—even by death, but because that's inevitable they think the other idea of life is too—the scrambling and excitement and bumps and the effort to get to the middle, and when we do get to the middle, it's just as if we never started. . . .

"Now you're a person who was clearly meant to stay in the seats and sit still and if you get bored watch the others. Somehow you got on to the wheel, and you got thrown off again at once with a hard bump. It's all right . . . for me, at the centre, but you're static. Instead of this absurd division into sexes they ought to class people as static and dynamic. . . . I think we're probably two quite different species spirtually."

Paul Pennyfeather undoubtedly is, like most of Waugh's early characters, a static person who somehow got on the wheel and was thrown off with a hard bump. So, to a significant extent, is Evedyn Waugh, though he is also a person who hopes often that he has reached the very center where there's a point completely at rest. As far as one can judge from the novels, from his autobiography, and from Frederick J. Stopp's study, *Evelyn Waugh,* even his conversion to Catholicism in 1930 didn't help him stay still at the quiet center. Except for the time he served honorably in World War II, he hasn't stayed on the wheel much either. He sits and watches the antics of others, more and more often laughing a little bitterly. "To have been born into a world of beauty, to die amid ugliness, is the common fate of all us exiles," he wrote shortly before his death, recalling his early, stable, blessed, "aristocratic" years at Underhill, Hampstead.[1] Almost always in the early novels, very frequently in the later ones, static watching gave pleasure to both Evelyn Waugh and his readers, for he was a gifted artist so conscientious that he revised what he did every day so that, should he die suddenly, he would not leave behind him work he would be ashamed to have printed.

Part of the reason for his effectiveness as a social satirist is the static view of the world he assumed early in life. That his view of the world changed little from the publication of *Decline and Fall* (1928) to the publication of *Unconditional Surrender* (1961), his account of his early life shows.[2] At

[1] Quoted from *A Little Learning* (1964).
[2] Ibid., passim. See especially his asperities about Hampstead, Balliol, and the school he turned into beautiful absurdity in *Decline and Fall.*

twenty-five as at fifty-eight, he knew what he liked with singular exactness. Then he knew as later he knew, most surely, what he disliked, a valuable asset for a satirist. He never seems to have shared the illusions of those who were mature when World War I started or their loss of illusions after Versailles. Because he was not temperamentally disposed to cherish illusions, he did not experience either the spiritual flounderings or the disenchantment Aldous Huxley and Rose Macaulay did. Except that there's Heaven (the Middle Ages elevated to up there?), his view of people is like Ivy Compton-Burnett's but less charitable. He was eleven in 1914, seventeen in 1920. Frederick Stopp's account confirms his admitted self-portrait in the first chapter of *The Ordeal of Gilbert Pinfold* (1957). In childhood, he was "affectionate, high-spirited and busy." He was "dissipated and often despairing in youth." By the time he began to write his books—Stopp tells us he would rather have been a carpenter— he was "sturdy and prosperous." He appears to have always known enough of what he wanted to get it. Even his becoming a Catholic was not, any more than Gilbert Pinfold's, a conversion, for that word suggests "an event more sudden and emotional than his calm acceptance of the propositions of his faith."

His world-view was already aristocratic and disdainful. As a little boy, he "marshalled a 'pistol troop' for the defence of England against Germans and Jews." In his first book, *Rossetti* (1928), he accepts "both the aesthetic and moral visions of the pre-Raphaelite conception of medievalism," and relishes "the stimulus it gives to one's restiveness in an era of complete stultification." His novels, early and late, exhibit artfully the prejudices one would expect from these early attitudes. For Kafka, Kierkegaard and such he shows the contempt of an upper-caste for the low-brow; he uniformly deprecates modern painting and architecture, "progressive novelists," and the left-wing poets of the thirties. Negroes, such as Chokey in *Decline and Fall* and Seth in *Black Mischief* (1932), he makes absurd because of their inadequate aping of an efficiency and a culture Waugh dislikes anyhow, anywhere. With the exception of Father Rothschild, who is made usually intelligent and good, no Jew in the novels is estimated highly or treated fairly. Neither is any Frenchman, German, or American. Democracy is "equality through slavery," communism rather worse. If things go as they have been going, and Stopp says Waugh thought they would, society will become what it becomes in Waugh's only story about the future, "Love Among the Ruins" (1953). The law will be that no man can "be held responsible for the consequences of his own acts," everyone will be "strictly schooled to a life of boredom," their usual greeting will be "state be with you." Even if the future is no worse than the present, Waugh believes "that man is, by nature, an exile," that "the inequalities of wealth and position are inevitable," that British prosperity need not be inimical to anyone else, "but if, on occasions, it is," he will hope that Britain will prosper, "not her rivals."

My emphasis upon Waugh's reactionary ideas should not make one overlook the views he shared with intelligent liberals. As he tells us in his self-portrait as Pinfold, his "idiosyncratic toryism . . . was quite unrepresented in the political parties of his time (except during the brief Churchillian renascence) and was regarded by his neighbours as being almost as sinister as socialism." His idiosyncratic toryism enabled him to see many aspects of modern life quite as liberals do. His portrayal of war as "order, counter-order, disorder," where the stragglers frequently "seem to be in front of the firing line," resembles Hemingway's and Norman Mailer's, although he stresses, as they would not, the courage of the officers who are gentlemen and the cowardice of the men at arms who are not. He speaks against the "Boy Scout honour" of English imperialists, of the similarity between prisons and English public schools, of the jumbled name-calling that accompanies modern war and peace, against news-paper owners like Lord Coppers who prefer the common lie to common humanity, against customs officers who want to "stamp out literature," against warmongers who protest too much their pacific intentions, against army life that is like the "drab compass of marital disillusion," against Hollywood's reluctance to even use the word death, against the "beauty parlour as the school of democracy." With Hemingway and Faulkner and his peers in contemporary British fiction, he believed in honor, in courage, and in love that transcends egocentric bickering and reciprocal flattery (though he most often praised these by deriding their opposites). He was against Nina's conception of physical love as "a thing one could grow to be fond of after a time, like smoking a pipe," was for the love of a particular person that can take you out of yourself and towards the love of God. There are many aspects of his idiosyncratic conservatism that readers of and writers for *The New Republic* and *The New Statesman* would agree with. Indeed it would be difficult for any honest liberal to disagree with his ideal of an English aristocracy: "a combination of heredity and talent rising to the top," that can contribute "statesmanship, intelligence, low cunning," qualities Roosevelt and Churchill shared.

I hope much of Waugh's interpretation of the world is not valid. But one can't be sure. One is not certain that Mr. Prendergast, created in 1928, was not right in his inability to understand "why God made the world at all." One is not sure that Guy Crouchbank's gentlemen, with their dedication to duty and courage, with their amused and stoical endurance of SNAFU, are not to be preferred to Cockney Trimmer and "idealist" Colonel Marchpole and "Bourgeois" Sarum-Smith. In other words, although it appears reactionary, Waugh's worldview is neither ridiculous nor impossible. Readers of all sorts of persuasions can suspend disbelief and enjoy his incurably artful body of work.

The early characters Waugh created for us to laugh at, as they jump on and are bumped off his Luna Park wheel, are as improbable a group of plausible characters as one can find in modern fiction. No one except Candide and Gulliver was ever as naïve as Paul Pennyfeather in *Decline and Fall* (1928). As he is moved from Oxford to Llanabba Castle School, from there to the terrifyingly inhuman functional architecture of King's Thursday to become engaged to Margot Beste-Chetwynde, from King's Thursday to prison, from prison back to Oxford to study theology, he never reacts intelligently to nor is perturbed by an experience. His imperturbable naïveté makes plausible an unbelievable series of events acted by characters of irreproachable unreality. Only when one reflects afterwards does one realize that the absurd exaggerations he tumbles through with incredible rapidity represent accurately the awfulness of a world totally divorced from God, that *Decline and Fall* is a farcical morality "play."

Llanabba Castle is the English public school raised to absurdity. Dr. Fagan, the headmaster who thinks his teachers must "temper discretion with deceit," has assembled Captain Grimes, a not-gentleman who knows God's in his heaven as long as one "does exactly what one wants to and when one wants to," Mr. Prendergast, a lapsed clergyman who can find no better job until he becomes a "Modern Clergyman" who "draws the full salary of a beneficed clergyman and need not commit himself to any religious belief," and Paul Pennyfeather, who has been sent down from Oxford because his classmates exposed him indecently and he was too passive to blame anyone but himself. About all they have in common is an entire distaste for teaching and a complete incompetence in the subjects they profess.[3] Except for Lady Circumference's son, who dies from a shot in the foot inflicted by Prendergast when he starts a race with a gun he doesn't know is loaded, the students like it well enough, especially since the most difficult task they are set is to write an essay for which a prize will be given to the one who writes the most words regardless of content. The school is made still more lively by the butler, Solomon Philbrick, who is thought to be either a novelist, a ship-builder, or a burglar in disguise—who *is* an entrancing liar and perhaps, one wonders afterwards, a representative of those who know that honesty is the worst policy.

At King's Thursday, formerly the seat of the Earls of Pastmaster, Margot Beste-Chetwynde, Professor Silenus, Peter Beste-Chetwynde, Sir Humphrey Maltravers, and some others as appropriately named as if they were out of Restoration comedy, Dickens, or P. G. Wodehouse, bump each other, and particularly, Paul Pennyfeather, about on the wheel. Professor Silenus, obsessed by man's lack of the grace of machinery,

---

[3] Compare Ivy Compton-Burnett's *Pastors and Masters*. No inference that Waugh was influenced is intended.

redesigns King's Thursday into a functional monstrosity appropriate to its inhabitants. Peter, fourteen, tipples constantly and reads Havelock Ellis whenever he becomes bored with *The Wind in the Willows.* Margot proficiently introduces Paul to the mechanics of sex, gets his witless help in running the foreign houses of prostitution on which her fortune rests, then lets him go to prison as a white slaver. There she keeps him well supplied with caviar and sherry until he escapes by being declared dead from an operation on his appendix. This act of benefaction is Margot's, after she has married Sir Humphrey, shortly to become Lord Metroland.

My account necessarily omits much—the ludicrous reformed prison, where a Laborite mispractices progressive penology, Paul's resurrection as an improperly qualified student of theology. Except for one serious scene where Arthur Potts and Paul inappropriately talk sense, it is a finely integrated farcical morality where one finds, when laughter stops, a thorough indictment of the modern world Waugh detests. No liberal can ever be solemn about his prejudices after he has read Waugh's dramatically appropriate airing of *his* prejudices against sports, public schools, penny-pinchers, ill-founded fortunes, preposterous modern architecture, Labour and Liberal politicians, penal reform, casual sex, casual religion. That Waugh became a Catholic after writing *Decline and Fall* hardly surprises us: he left himself no secular activity or ideology to turn to.

But *Decline and Fall* is not as good a novel as *Vile Bodies* (1930), written while he was still on the threshold of Catholicism. Under the laughter of his first novel one barely detects the seriousness. It almost seems he is for what he hates, it provokes such delighted laughter. Yet its unsurpassableness is surpassed in *Vile Bodies* where the cause for laughter is as frequent but blends more skillfully with sympathetic castigation of the entire modern world. No one who has read *Vile Bodies* can be startled by Pinfold-Waugh's self-characterization in *The Ordeal of Gilbert Pinfold:*

> His strongest tastes were negative. He abhorred plastics, Picasso, sunbathing and jazz—everything in fact that had happened in his own lifetime.

The chief character in *Vile Bodies*, Adam, although he too is naïve and passive, is sophisticated compared to Paul Pennyfeather. Adam is one of the "Bright Young People" who get mild pleasure out of fornication and adultery, going some place in a dirigible, beating a track record in auto racing, party-going —though this last usually becomes "blind-making" or "sad-making" if not "spirit-crushing." He is a novelist perpetually out of funds who figures that if he wrote a book a month he'd become solvent; for a time he is the second Mr. Chatterbox (after the bored suicide of the first) for Lord Monomark, the owner of the *Daily Excess*, where he spends his ingenuity inventing shocking doings of imaginary people the public thinks real. But mostly his function is to be one who has things done to him, who looks on while the absurd wheel spins. Jobs, money, partying, adultery, ultimately war, are thrust upon him, but mostly he is one on the sidelines who watches.

What he has to watch is hilarious enough to keep one less designedly tired than Adam in constant laughter. He watches Mrs. Ape, who looks like a "procureuse" and is, like Aimee McPherson, with complete lack of disinterest saving souls by having her angels (Chastity, Christian Endeavor, Divine Discontent, etc.) sings "There ain't no flies on the Lamb of God" before they leave England to "ginger up the religious life of Oberammergau." With similar ennui he observes "last week's Prime Minister," the Right Honourable Walter Outrage, who never quite has an affair with the ever ready Baroness Yoshiwara; Lord Metroland, who in "his years in the Commons . . . always liked a good scrap, and often thought a little wistfully of those orgies of competitive dissimulation in which he had risen to eminence"; Margot (still imperturbably amoral), who gives a party for Mrs. Ape and feels sorry enough for Chastity to offer her a place in one of her foreign houses of prostitution; Agatha Runcible, who, while dying from an auto accident, "Moved her bandaged limbs under the bedclothes in negro rhythm"; Mr. Isaacs, the film producer who makes a film about Wesley he says will be "the most important All-Talkie super-religious film" ever to be done by British actors on British capital. Though Adam frequents, a little implausibly,

Shepheards, where one can go "parched with modernity . . . and still draw up, cool and uncontaminated, great, healing draughts from the well of Edwardian certainty," he is more resignedly at home when he attends the riotous party at No. 10 Downing Street, which, as it reaches the papers, helps this week's prime minister to fall. Probably the main reason the reader is delighted by all of this is that Adam finds all monstrosities run-of-the-mill and keeps his mind and face dead-pan through it all.

Reflecting afterwards, the effect is a good deal more like remembering *Candide* or *Gulliver's Travels* than recalling something by Ronald Firbank or P. G. Wodehouse, both of whom Waugh *does* resemble superficially. Firbank, whom Waugh admired, helped him to his use of tersely absurd dialogue that makes the story run, but Waugh used flippancy mordantly as Firbank didn't. Partying, politics, philandering, marriage, love, peace, morality, war, are all a hideous joke one has laughed at because to be annihilated laughing is perhaps as good a way to go as any. As the epigraph from Lewis Carroll suggests, there is no place for real tears in this country where "it takes all the running you can do, to keep in the same place." What occurs in *Vile Bodies* may be, as Father Rothschild suggests, "in some way historical" since people never "want to lose their faith in religion or anything else." Nevertheless the over-all impression is of "a lot of parties," of "all that succession and repetition of massed humanity. . . . Those vile bodies," inevitably hurried towards another war, where we "shall all be walking into the jaws of destruction again, protesting our pacific intentions." It is appropriate that the last scene is on the battlefield of a war Waugh made occur a little too soon. It is fitting also that we find there the drunken major, that he gives Adam the £35,000 he never gave him while there was peace, that the final look is at the drunken major to whom bedraggled Chastity is starting to make love.

Still worth rereading and still serious light amusement, *Black Mischief* (1932) and *Scoop* (1933) seem less rewarding to me. (Frederick J. Stopp's apologetics for them nearly convince me that I am wrong.) Both of them take us into Africa, about which Waugh has written travel books with "disgusto," where he did not find more than feeble premonitions of humanity in either the Emperor of Abyssinia or his subjects. Most of the malicious fun in these novels is at the expense of Seth, the Negro emperor who should never have been contaminated by Oxford, the diplomats who are even less aware of Negro humanity than Waugh, and the Red and White blacks who fight a ridiculous war which the meek naturalist, William Boots, reports with absurd literalness. One laughs at the excesses of Seth in *Black Mischief*—the abolition on paper of the death penalty, marriage, infant mortality, Totemism, Inhuman Butchery, Mortgages, Emigration, and the native languages (in favor of that silly Esperanto, of course). But the early laughter diminishes as we read of Seth, "his eyes wild with the inherited terror of the jungle, desperate with the acquired loneliness of civilization," and as we learn of Basil Seal relishing the flavor of his sweetheart in a soup prepared by cannibals. (Admittedly he didn't know till afterwards and it is not impossible that this, like some earlier and later deaths Waugh reports with deadpan casualness, is intended to symbolize modern man's preying upon himself.) *Scoop*, with its splendidly ingenuous reporter, William Boots, and its inexculpable satire on journalism, is fine going until it dulls down into repetition of the mixed-uppedness of black folks one found more vivid in *Black Mischief*. And, thinking back, one does not recall much relevant sense behind these intermittently amusing devastations of press, primitives, and diplomatists who tend their gardens while revolutions occur just over the wall. Forster, Joyce Cary, and William Plomer have done with successful seriousness what Waugh does here with comic bad taste.

*A Handful of Dust* (1934) is Waugh's first "serious" novel, With minor exceptions, the characters are realistic in the traditional sense of the word, round rather than flat as the characters in the farcical moralities were. Except for the scene where Tony Last listens politely to his vicar read a sermon written twenty years before for soldiers in the tropics, and the sad-making comedy of his weekend at Brighton to give his wife grounds for divorce, there is little that is funny and few witticisms. The plot is the banal one of the good stodgy man who at first intends to give his unfaithful wife a divorce, sees her awfulness, refuses, and goes away. But it is an excellent novel.

Its excellence is due largely to Waugh's characterization of Tony Last. Apart from his dullness, which is never portrayed dully, Tony resembles Waugh himself. He believes in the old Edwardian certainties: marriage that is love forever, the child the center of the household, the household that is neither beautifully medieval nor very modern, the church one attends regularly even if one nods, decency. Even when delirious in the South American jungle, where he has gone to seek a city (like Waugh when he sought the Roman Catholic Church after his first marriage broke up and other disillusions?), he remains admirable: "I know I am not clever but that is no reason why we should forget courtesy."

The other characters are rounded too, if less pleasantly. His wife, Brenda, who thinks him pompous and "too madly feudal," is as complete a portrait of a wife who loves only herself as we have in modern fiction—Lady Brett with no impulses towards tenderness. Her lover, John Beaver, mother-ridden and penny-pinching, is her male counterpart, his authenticity made complete when he deserts her. Mr. Todd, the man who keeps Tony with him by force when his search for a city leaves him lost in the jungle, is a plausible psychopath, equally in love with power and with the sentimentalities of Dickens. Tony Last's son, whose pathetic death contrasts strongly with the casual deaths in the early novels, is as convincing a child as his father is a man. These characters, in their complicated interrelationships, make *A Handful of Dust* tragic and support the positive side of Waugh's world view as effectively as the farcical moralities do his negative convictions. It is something like what Shakespeare might have written if he had paired Othello and Goneril.

During the years that followed the publication of *A Handful of Dust,* and preceded World War II, Waugh travelled a good deal, wrote about it with angry vividness, married again, and settled down in Piers Court, Gloucestershire, where intrusions were not welcome, wrote a biography of Edmund Campion, the

Jesuit martyr of Elizabethan times, and published the fictional by-products of his travels in Abyssinia, where he favored Mussolini's fascists. When World War II broke out he was commissioned company commander in the Royal Marines. Later he served as a commando in the Middle East; still later he went to Yugoslavia as a member of the British military mission to Marshall Tito. Clearly he had little time to perfect a novel, though he did write *Put Out More Flags* (1942) and a number of shorter pieces of fiction.

Except for a few excellent short stories—"Cruise," as devastating a satire of feminine silliness as Ring Lardner's "I Can't Breathe," "Excursion in Reality," an angry funny story about what the films might do if they turned *Hamlet* into modern speech and dress, and "Mr. Loveday's Little Outing," a story that annihilates humanitarian insane asylums—and some portions of *Put Out More Flags*, his work of these years is not particularly memorable. It seems quite sensible that he should find more "food for thought in the follies of Basil Seal and Ambrose Silk than in the sagacity of the higher command," that he should show the amoral aristocrats of his early novels becoming serious when the "Great Bore War" becomes hot, as he did effectively in *Men at Arms* (1954), *Officers and Gentlemen* (1955), and *Unconditional Surrender* (1961). But *Put Out More Flags* is not as successful as *Black Mischief* or *Scoop*. It only comes to a boil when Basil Seal amuses himself with his billeting racket with the Connolly children and when it tells of the insanities of war office work and spying. It is implausibly cruel when it satirizes the thinly disguised intellectuals who were left-wing, implausibly kind when it shows us Basil Seal and Peter Pastmaster starting towards heroism.

*Brideshead Revisited* (1945) is a different matter. Certainly it is his richest novel, possibly his best, for there is no place else in his work where such complexities of felt life are so unobtrusively controlled. The reasons for this are not too difficult to find. In the Brideshead Estate, a thoroughly unmodern place, Waugh felt spiritually at home; with the Marchmains, Catholics for generations, Waugh felt more than at home—he felt as if he were part of a family of aristocratic Catholics such as he would like to have belonged to. With them an interest in wine and architecture did not have to be acquired (as it did with Waugh); the Marchmains had lived their interest for centuries. They were, moreover, eccentrics of deep faith and feeling, wise in much they did, witty in most of what they said. As in no other book of his, there was room for the aesthetic convictions he expressed in his book on Rossetti, for the admiration for Catholics more saintly than he ever pretended to be that he expressed in his fine book on Campion, for his convictions about the virtues of the aristocracy to which he did not quite belong. Even more important aesthetically, to present this richness he made a first-person narrator very like himself in Charles Ryder, whose prejudices, convictions, and tastes are almost identical with Waugh's own. Ryder also can look back at Oxford and at the days when he was an agnostic who cared nothing for the Roman Catholicism to which he is finally "converted."

As he looks back without anger, Charles Ryder recovers the past with Proustian thoroughness. He recalls, for example, the time when his father kept a young Englishman unamusedly perplexed by treating him as though he were an American and unfamiliar with the English language, the time when his father, enjoying it with cruel immensity, pretended not to understand that his son needed money badly. He remembers Rex Mottram, "a tiny bit of a man pretending he was the whole," his mitigatedly crass opportunism and his worry that when he became a Catholic he could send a man to Hell by putting a pound in the right box and be compelled to accept the "fact" that the Pope once made a horse a Cardinal. He recalls the affectation and charm of Anthony Blanche, particularly as displayed in a long monologue about the Marchmains that is at once amusing, annoying, and a necessary means of advancing the reader's curiosity about them. As the narrative shuttles back and forth skillfully in time, Ryder retrieves much more that is grave and gay and essential to the narrative: his managing, faithless wife (a more temperate treatment of a woman like Brenda in *A Handful of Dust*), a drunken Oxford party that ends in jail, travel in South America as an architectural painter,

Mr. Samgrass, a more preposterous and more deadly phony than Philbrick or Captain Grimes. All that Ryder retrieves is fitted casually and relevantly into the major recollections that form the core of the story: his relations with the Marchmains and how he changed from agnostic to Catholic.

Ryder's long journey to faith starts when he meets and falls in love (not homosexually) with the Marquis of Marchmain's second son, Lord Sebastian. The reader does too, in spite of or because of the teddy bear he carries, his compulsions about clothes and conduct, his excessive drinking, his sweetness and charm with everyone. Ryder (and the reader) continues to love him even when he becomes a thief, a vagabond, and an alcoholic. Sebastian is one of Waugh's most considerable achievements, a saint manqué, an Edmund Campion fallen upon times too evil to demand saintliness, a worthy (dissimilar but like) predecessor of Graham Greene's whiskey-priest.

Through Sebastian, Ryder comes to know the rest of the Marchmains: the older brother, Brideshead, and the younger sister, Cordelia, both "fervent Catholics"; half-heathen Julia, with whom he falls in love and who is his second station in his passage through love of man to love of God; the mother and father, she an almost-saint whom people often despise because they hate her conception of God as a well-intentioned matriarch who frequently does the wrong thing, he an excommunicated Catholic who lives in Italy with his mistress, a dancer who looks like a respectable bourgeoise. In his relationship with the Marchmains, Ryder uncovers nearly all the possible varieties of Catholics and grows to understand them both as human beings and as members of a faith. He honors the serious, slightly stodgy Brideshead for his conviction that God must enter the most minute crevices of our lives; the gay, plain Cordelia, who is unsolemnly devout; Julia, who loves him and gives him up because she cannot set up "a rival good to God";[4] the mother who teaches him that even riches can be sanctified and makes him appreciate "the Alice in Wonderland side" of religion; the father who, at his death, realizes how God has caught him "with an unseen hook and an invisible line which is long enough to

4 Compare Graham Greene's *The End of the Affair.*

let him wander to the ends of the world and still bring him back with a twitch upon the thread." With great art, Waugh makes convincing the restoration of all the Marchmains to Catholicism and makes one believe aesthetically that "all our loves are merely hints and symbols; vagabond language scrawled on gateposts and paving-stones" to lead one finally to the love of God.

*Brideshead Revisited* was followed by two returns to the manner of the first novels, *Scott-King's Modern Europe* (1946) and *The Loved One* (1948). Though the saga of Scott-King's journey into Neutralia, where he gives a dim speech on the dim Bellorius he and a few Neutralians alone know, takes us into a police state a good deal more amusing than any actual one, there's nothing particularly new in matter or manner to linger on. There is in *The Loved One*.

*The Loved One* is a macabre tale that centers about Dennis Barlow, attendant at the Happier Hunting Ground, where animals are given full rites before luxurious interment. He falls in love with Aimée Thanatogenos, cosmetician at the Whispering Glades, where people are buried a little more elegantly, and woos her with poems from the *Oxford Book of English Verse*. Torn between two suitors, Dennis and Joyboy, an artistic embalmer, Aimée commits suicide, and Dennis helps Joyboy, who feels it a duty to dispose of a death that occurred in his workroom, cremate her at the Happier Hunting Ground. This macabre morality concentrates its satire upon the modern "cult" of death as unnatural. It is also seriously amusing about the American way of insarcophagusement, about bad modern writing (for Waugh, most of it), commercial radio ("the raucous stream of misinformation gave place to a gentler voice advocating a brand of toilet paper"), about sentimentality for "Dog that is born of bitch" and "cometh up, and is cut down like a flower," about Whispering Glades Memorial Park Works of Art. These last, of course, include the corpses, and Aimée and Waugh, for once agreeing, think them "an epitome of all that is finest in the American Way of Life." It is Waugh's most expert novel, a brilliantly condensed letter of hate to America and the modern world America has infected with its unrealism, yet it is amusing enough for William Buckley to laugh at. The key passage is a parody Dennis applies to another suicide:

> They told me, Francis Hinsley, they told me you were hung
> With red protruding eye-balls and black protruding tongue
> I wept as I remembered how often you and I
> Had laughed about Los Angeles and now 'tis here you'll lie;
> Here pickled in formaldehyde and painted like a whore,
> Shrimp-pink incorruptible, not lost nor gone before.

The entirety has to be read to see with what skill Waugh ties all the satirical threads together, how well he blends anger and humor.

*Helena* (1950), which Frederick J. Stopp considers a major work, seems to me almost as bad as its reviewers said it was. No doubt it is an act of piety and an ingenious historical reconstruction intended to show dramatically the importance to Christianity of the finding of the cross. It is also Waugh's only novel to combine overseriousness and unintentional humor. *Men at Arms* (1954), *Officers and Gentlemen* (1955), and *Unconditional Surrender* (1961) make an impressive trilogy about World War II, though the last volume, despite its base in the first two, should be, I believe, treated separately.

Interrupted by his work on Ronald Knox and *The Ordeal of Gilbert Pinfold*, it doesn't seem to me that Waugh quite succeeded in tying *Unconditional Surrender* to the first two novels so that it completed a trilogy that unifies diversity, as does Cary's Gulley Jimson series. This does not mean that *Unconditional Surrender* is not immensely good. It is Waugh's best and final say (there has been no word of any posthumous work and he sounded in his *Paris Review 30* interview as though he had no more to say). The experience, throughout the trilogy, of war on the battlefield and on the home front during 1940 and 1941 is seen through the eyes of Guy Crouchbank, a Catholic and an idiosyncratic conservative like Charles Ryder and Waugh himself. The account includes serial bombing, stupid bureaucracy, a retreat no more disorderly than an advance, personal heroism and cowardice, boredom, stupidity about clearance for security, over-all SNAFU somehow sometimes leading to sacrifice and glory. It differs from all other war novels in its emphasis upon an aristocracy of officers who have nearly "everything that one needs for survival," in its emphasis upon not-gentlemen who are usually good when they follow dutifully, generally bad when they are on their own. It is a tribute to Waugh's art, particularly to the skill with which he compels identification with Guy Crouchbank, that the reader believes as he reads in the superior virtue of heroes like Guy's father, Waugh's most vivid creation whose only activity is brave, inconspicuous sacrifice at home, and like Ritchie-Hook, "enfant terrible of the First World War . . . often decorated . . . twice courtmartialed . . . twice acquitted in recognition of the brilliant success of his independent actions."

The officers who are gentlemen and men at arms are presented without obvious heroics, with humor as well as seriousness. Ritchie-Hook, Guy, Ivor Claire, Apthorpe, and Tommy Blackhouse are anything but demigods. Tommy Blackhouse sums up the attitude of most of them: "It's going to be a long war. The great thing is to spend it among friends." Apthorpe gets drunk too often and is helped to his death from drink by Guy himself. Guy is as seriously hurt when he tackles a drunken officer who is using a wastebasket as a football, as he is when he retreats with honor in Crete. And those from other classes are presented as a believable mixture of good and bad, for the most part. Jumbo Trotter, a barber and a middle-aged masher, comes off well as a run-of-the-mill soldier who tries to do his duty and have a good time in spite of it. Corporal Major Lodovic, an intelligently malicious proletarian, keeps a journal about the others that hits close to the truth and he performs more honorably than the officious and cowardly Major Hound, who is not a gentleman, or than Crouchbank's friend, Claire, who sees life *sub specie aeternitatis* with melancholy humor. What somewhat diminishes the authenticity of the picture for one who does not share Waugh's prejudices and convictions is the occasional angry interpolation, such as "in the next war, when we are completely democratic, I expect it will be quite honorable for officers to leave their men behind," or the picture of

Ivor Claire, "putting his horse faultlessly over the jumps, concentrated as a man in prayer. Ivor Claire, Guy thought, was the finest flower of them all. He was quintessential England, the man Hitler had not taken into account." But this, in view of Claire's anomalous behavior at the close of *Officers and Gentlemen,* is an irony, probably unintended. Perhaps, despite or because of its limitation of characters and its inclusion of prejudiced fatuity, these two novels are the best dramatizations of modern war's essence yet published.

*The Ordeal of Gilbert Pinfold* (1957), Waugh's first novel "written from direct experience," may come to be his most remarkable book. Gilbert Pinfold is Waugh seen by Waugh from an aesthetic distance, for in 1954, Waugh "had the pleasant experience" of going off his head for "a week or two" because of a muddle over some sleeping stuff injudiciously mixed with too much to drink. As a case history, a friend of mine who went through the same thing assures me, it is vividly authentic, but Waugh's account of his auditory delusions is a good deal more than that. The voices that accuse him of imaginable and unimaginable attitudes and actions are clearly representations of what he sometimes thought and felt about himself. Pinfold-Waugh is a likeable, intensely imaginative, divided man, far less sure of himself than the writer of the moral farces, less sure of himself than the writer of the serious novels from *A Handful of Dust* onwards. He is a good deal more than the "combination of eccentric don and testy colonel" he acted "before his children at Lychpole and his cronies in London." It seems possible that this temporary psychotic condition gave a better understanding of himself than he had ever had before and that this is why *Unconditional Surrender,* which followed the biography of Monsignor Knox, is better than the first two novels of the trilogy, for here he misunderstands himself and his significant limited powers less (as the cryptic interview in *Paris Review 30,* confirms).

Waugh's self-evaluation in *The Ordeal* is an underevaluation:

> He regarded his books as objects which he had made, things quite external to himself to be used and judged by others. He thought them well made, better than many reputed works of

genius, but he was not vain of his accomplishment, still less of his reputation. He had no wish to obliterate anything he had written, but he would dearly have loved to revise it, envying painters, who are allowed to return to the same theme time and time again, clarifying and enriching until they had done all they can with it. A novelist is condemned to produce a succession of novelties, new names for characters, new incidents for his plots, new scenery; but, Mr. Pinfold maintained, most men harbor the germs of one or two books only . . . all else is professional trickery.

Waugh is right to the extent that all of his books tend to fall into two basic patterns: The *Candide*-like satire of *Decline and Fall* and *The Loved One,* and the "novel" about an aristocrat unattuned to his time, regretting if not despising the most typical products of modernity. He is right also to imply that a good many of his farcical moralities are "professional trickery," though the least of them are deft and worth reading. He is wrong about the one or two books. Indeed one can say that he has exercised something of the prerogative of the painters he envies. Is not *Vile Bodies* a better *Decline and Fall* (though he has said he dislikes the first), *The Loved One* a better *Scott-King's Modern Europe?* Is not *Brideshead Revisited* a better *Handful of Dust* and is not *Unconditional Surrender* as good as or better than *Brideshead?* Though I cannot agree with all the ingenious intricacy of Frederick Stopp's interpretation in his *Evelyn Waugh,* both his book and my own reading of Waugh suggest that this is so.

*Unconditional Surrender* is a beautiful flawed novel. To get rid of the duty of severity quickly, it doesn't tie in too well in mood or in plot with *Men at Arms* and *Officers and Gentlemen.* It contains dramatically irrelevant incidents and comments and interpretations about Yugoslavia, Tito, and the partisans; about homosexuals, communists, intellectuals (these three nearly alike in activity and character when Waugh lets the unreasonable part of himself take control); and bravuras I can't credit about *his* kind of Catholicism and the kind of aristocrat he never was. But I hasten over these rapidly to come to the good that overweighs the bad.

After the halting synopsis and prologue, needed connections

even if you've read the two first parts of the "trilogy," *Unconditional Surrender* becomes a rarely interrupted moral parable (a good novel, too) about the redemption of Guy Crouchbank, who goes as far a step towards blessedness as a character who represents Waugh and improves on Charles Ryder could. For two years disgusted by the alliance with Russia, and out of touch, Guy's restiveness returns when there's a chance for redemption as a commando. This he does not achieve because he is caught up in the Automated War's red tape, though he does jump as a parachutist, get disqualified by age and malicious protocol, and save part of a group of old Jews who are all too believably mistreated or ignored because of the mistakes and conflicts that mismeet when the British, the Americans, and the Russians contend for control of Tito and the partisans in Yugoslavia. What Guy tries to do but does not achieve enables Waugh to plausibly fill out his dramatization of war in peace and in mixed-up battle with  accurate adroitness (one presumes and believes). It also, on a group scale, dramatizes, through the saving of the Jews, the personal redemption and the Catholic and catholic redemption Guy himself arrived at more significantly and in another way.

Skillfully interwoven with the part of the plot that has to do with war is the stay-at-home's actions that circle around Virginia, Ian and Kirstie Kilbannock, the unsuccessful effort to get Virginia's illegitimate child aborted, Guy's father's death. In the Prologue is reproduced the last letter Guy's father wrote him, containing the repeated passage that, acted on by Guy, gives the novel its stature and universality:

> The Mystical Body doesn't strike attitudes and stand on its dignity. It accepts suffering and injustice. It is ready to forgive at the first hint of compunction. . . . Quantitative judgments don't apply. If only one soul [is] saved that is full compensation for any amount of loss of face.

Guy saves that one soul, prodded perhaps by God's manifestation in the magnificently significant funeral of the father who wrote the letter. (No world will let that section of the novel die if it is worth living in.) Possibly he saves two souls, his son's and Virginia's; for he remarries Virginia, knowing that she is to bear Trimmer's child she could find no one to abort. About Virginia we do not know at all securely that she has changed from the awful gasper for pleasure who can also be "nice" when what pleases you pleases her, though we're led to hope that she'll reach Waugh's Heaven (which must be lovely indeed contrasted to the horrible modern earth he presents to us), after a long stay in purgatory. We know the son is saved though we are only told. And the saving of this one or two souls by Guy in the midst of such infamous life, confirms, like the saving of the Jews, not only Guy's sufficient compunction but the saving remnant of individuals of integrity that Waugh hopes, despite his cry of despair at automated earth, will survive.

However this may be (and away from the novel's intermitted magnificence I become sceptical again), whether he is read from the Catholic point of view of Frederick Stopp and Christopher Hollis or from the point of view of Stephen Spender and myself, clearly Waugh is an original novelist of importance. The bitter comic spirit that pervades the early fiction reminds one of a similar spirit in Rose Macaulay and Aldous Huxley, the style in a limited way, of a happy amalgam of Hemingway, Firbank, and Wodehouse. There are times when his angry caricatures recall those of Voltaire, when the gusto of his anger reminds one of Fielding in *Jonathan Wilde*. But all these resemblances are superficial, as superficial as the criticism that links him with Graham Greene and Mauriac because of their commonly shared Catholicism. The sardonic squire who wonders, as Pinfold, why everyone except himself finds it "so easy to be nice," is conjoined to a sensitive, idiosyncratic conservative who is a Catholic not unjustly angry at the phoniness and sordure of the modern world. A discomforting writer, yes; also a purveyor of delight who can force the "stiff upper lip of the soul," to use David Daiches's phrase, to maintain its dignity by smiling. A limited writer, yes, but one who suggests in a distinctive manner "truths" as important as those we find in "many reputed works of genius."

## Chapter Six

# Mid-View: The 1930s

THE FIRST WORLD WAR, Stephen Spender wrote, "had knocked the ball-room floor from under . . . English life. People resembled dancers suspended in mid-air yet miraculously able to pretend that they were still dancing." The writers who started towards artistic maturity in the twenties did have a ball-room floor under them, however much they felt they must dance suspended. There is gaiety in the fiction of the twenties—sometimes despairing in Rose Macaulay, bitter in Huxley and Waugh, grim in Ivy Compton-Burnett, resigned in Maugham, glittering in Coward and Arlen, frivolous in Ronald Firbank. There is hope in the writers who matured before the twenties. Galsworthy and Wells still hoped for reform; Galsworthy thought that to be a gentleman was important; Bennett thought realistic documentation would help one understand enough to help. Virginia Woolf hoped for the salvation of individual sensibility, Lawrence for the man completely animal and completely human, Joyce and Yeats for the preserving of their individuality and for a reversal in the cyclical course of history that would someday make the good life possible for men like themselves. Eliot thought Christian salvation possible.

For the writers who matured in the thirties, salvation of any kind was difficult to conceive, since, for good or for ill, it was now necessary to think in terms of mankind as a mass on many continents. Neither gaiety nor salvation seemed likely for the separated person when huge holes appeared in the walls and the floor of the ball-room and one looked through or down on the misery of poverty or out to the fright of international discord.

To any sensitive person who matured in the thirties, mere dates have a symbolic significance. 1921 was the first year that showed, in minimum, what was to come: a million unemployed, the dole, the Great Coal Strike. 1926: the General Strike; two and a half million strikers, many upper- and middle-class people strikebreaking and fearing revolution, Evelyn Waugh among them and Cary, as his last trilogy shows, fearing. 1929: the crash on Wall Street (though the effect was not too obvious in England until the suspension of the gold standard in 1931 and the concurrence of the first National Hunger March, carrying a petition signed by a million). 1930: the *Daily Worker* began, shortly to be followed by the *Week,* communist-dominated and, according to Robert Graves and Allan Hodges,[1] one of the few places where one could get accurate information during the thirties. 1933: the failure of the World Economic Conference, Walter Greenwood's *Love on the Dole* published as a novel, shortly to become a play with a long run. 1934: Mosley's Black Shirts organized; the Disaffection Act's passage that prompted the organization of the National Council for Civil Liberties with E. M. Forster as president, Rose Macaulay active. 1938: the National Unemployed Worker's Movement dramatized by having two hundred stop traffic by lying down in the middle of Oxford Street, by the invasion of the Ritz with appeals for tea, by a black coffin carried to No. 10 Downing Street (inside was the message, "Unemployed—No appeasement"). All this, although from 1935 on domestic misery was alleviated, finally dissipated by the increased production required to prepare for a war Baldwin and Chamberlain said couldn't happen.

Undoubtedly foreign affairs affected the sensitive more than what occurred at home. The long build-up to the war, that Churchill, the communists, and most of the intellectuals feared would come, began in 1931 with Japan's unimpeded occupation of Manchuria. In 1932 reparations were abolished, war debts cancelled. France proposed a League of Nations army, Russia proposed *total* disarmament. 1933 saw Japan withdraw from the League and Hitler came to power in Germany. (By clever exploitation of private affairs more alluring than the depression and the world crisis, the *Daily Herald* and the *Daily Express* became the first British newspapers to gain a circulation of over

[1] Most of my information comes from their book *The Long Week-End,* and from *Britain between the Wars* by Charles Loch Mowat.

two million.) Italy invaded Ethiopia, and Mussolini, who had said in 1930, "Words are a fine thing; but rifles, machine guns, warships, aeroplanes, and cannon are still finer things," was supported, reluctantly or ignorantly in the war that finally showed the League's impotence, by the *Daily Mail*, the *Observer*, and the *Morning Post* (the other papers opposed him). In 1934 the Disarmament Conference failed and Hitler reintroduced conscription. The *Daily Worker* and Churchill predicted the consequences of German rearmament, Baldwin reassured, and Mussolini said, "War is to man as maternity is to woman. I do not believe in perpetual peace." In 1935, with Rose Macaulay and Aldous Huxley among the leaders, the Peace Pledge Union was formed. One hundred and thirty thousand belonged by 1937. In 1936, Hitler reoccupied the Rhineland with troops that carried no ammunition because they expected no resistance and, with Mussolini, began to test out modern armaments in the Spanish Civil War that Franco's invasion began. In 1937, Neville Chamberlain succeeded Baldwin as prime minister, and the Chinese-Japanese war started. Hitler, whose name now appeared constantly in the headlines, annexed the Sudetenland after the amicable agreement at Munich in 1938. In October of the same year, the "reliable" Lloyd's of London offered odds of thirty-two to one against war within a year. In January 1939, Barcelona fell; in February, Great Britain recognized Franco; in March, Madrid fell; on March 15, Czechoslovakia was occupied; on March 22, Lithuania ceded Memel to Germany; on April 5, Italy invaded Albania. Within a month, the autonomy of Poland, Greece, and Rumania was guaranteed by Great Britain and an antiaggression pact was signed with Turkey, conscription was introduced in England, and the Anglo-German naval agreement was denounced by Hitler. In August, the Nazi-Soviet Pact; September 1, the invasion of Poland; September 2, mobilization; September 3, war.

Happier things that have and may fructify occurred during the decade. Steps were taken toward helping the unemployed, a start was made toward national planning; sulfa drugs and nylon appeared. A good many went to international peace conferences, ungovernmental of course, as they do still. More tried to urge their governments into a stand against fascism, as they do still for coexistence. Some found consolation in the Left Book Club (started in 1936), the new Penguins (begun the same year), or found consolation in agreeing with the Webbs that the Soviet Union was a new civilization, because they misunderstood it, half-understood it, or mis-saw it. The actual masses were diverted by the funeral of George the Fifth, the accession of Edward the Eighth, the coronation of George the Sixth, impropriety in high places, and the Loch Ness Monster.

For the thinking and feeling man, these were minor diversions and dubious hopes. Spain was a death, Munich a mourning, the Soviet trials a disillusionment, the Nazi-Soviet Pact a disenchantment. Probably no other decade is more difficult for those who did not live through it to understand; no other decade is more troubling for the creative artist to create. Except in the poetry that saw through much, though it overlooked much, too, in the work of the novelists who had matured in the twenties, the thirties, which they nearly foresaw in their maturing years, were a dim, hopeful time for man and those who wrote about man. It was not (though so it seemed on September 1, 1939) "a low, inglorious decade," but those who lived and wrote during it resembled too closely "children / afraid of the night / who had never been happy or good"—or feared they did, or recognized the many who did not, perhaps would not, could not.

## Chapter Seven

# Graham Greene: Stoical Catholic[1]

I<small>N HIS ESSAY ABOUT</small> Dickens in *The Lost Childhood*
(1951), Graham Greene remarks that he is "inclined to believe"
that "the creative writer perceives his world once and for all
in childhood and adolescence, and his whole career is an effort
to illustrate his private world in terms of the great public world
we all share." Whether this is generally true or not, Greene has
made out a convincing case for its truth about himself. When, at
the age of ten, he read H. Rider Haggard's *King Solomon's Mines,*
he was most impressed by the figure of Gagool, the old witch,
for someone very like her waited for him in dreams "every night
in the passage by the linen cupboard, near the nursery door"
and she still continues to appear, "when the mind is sick or
tired . . . now . . . dressed in the theological garments of despair,"
the garments Waugh had feared too, that affected in a different
way the other novelists who represented the uneasy armistice
that preceded World War II. Quartermain and Sir Henry Curtis
seemed too heroic to Greene at ten: "These men were like
Platonic ideas: they were not life as one had already begun to
know it."

The years between ten and fourteen, when "the future for
better or worse really struck" with the reading of Marjorie
Bowen's *The Viper of Milan,* accentuated the feeling of despair
that frequently masked itself as boredom. In *Journey without
Maps* (1936) Greene recalls seeing a dog that had been killed
in an accident, lying in the bottom of his pram, where it had
been placed by his nurse to get it out of the way. This, the
first thing he remembers, "was just a fact," and was later joined
by a recollection of a man who rushed out of a cottage with a
knife in his hand to kill himself, and the memory of wishing to
experience "the pleasure of cruelty" with a girl who lived close
by when he was fourteen. It was also during these years

probably (Greene is not very exact in his chronology) that he tried three different ways of suicide, ran away from Berkhamsted school (where his father was headmaster) because of boredom that had reached "an intolerable depth" and started the six-month psychoanalysis that taught him correct orientation and wrung him dry, "fixed in boredom." The consequence of this fixation in boredom did not leave him often until hope resurged in his late fifties.

At the age of seventeen he began his several-times-repeated experiments with Russian roulette, pulling the trigger of a revolver with one of its six chambers loaded. It is likely that his later dangerous ventures into Liberia, Mexico, Indochina, Cuba, Haiti, Vietnam, and a leper colony in Africa served much the same purpose as the Russian roulette he abandoned, that these journeys were night journeys like Marlow's in *The Heart of Darkness,* Céline's in *Journey to the End of Night,* and Orwell's among the down-out-out in Paris and London. We have Greene's word for the fact that, after almost dying on his dangerous trek through Liberia, he "discovered in himself a passionate interest in living," though he had always "assumed before, as a matter of course, that death was desirable." This experience, like the experiences with attempted suicide and Russian roulette, "was like a conversion" which at least left "a little sediment at the bottom of the brain" that enabled him to strengthen himself "with the intellectual idea that once in Zigi's town" he had "been completely convinced of the beauty and desirability of the mere act of living."

Why despair and boredom were and are so prominent a part of Greene's character, he nowhere reveals unless it is by the implication in all his work that they are the inevitable consequence of "some terrible aboriginal calamity" in which "the human race is implicated."[2] But his revelations about himself do make it possible to understand why he early preferred *The Viper of Milan* to the books of Anthony Hope, Haggard, and Westerman (although there is a residual trace

---

[1] The suggestion for this title I owe to Ronald Bryden's brilliant "Graham Greene, Alas," published in the *Spectator,* September 28, 1962.

[2] Cardinal Newman in his *Apologia pro Vita Sua.*

of these last in his first three novels and in his "entertainments").
For Greene, *The Viper of Milan* colored and explained

> the terrible living world of the stone stairs and the never quiet
> dormitory. . . . It was no good in that real world to dream
> that one would ever be a Sir Henry Curtis, but Della Scala
> who at last turned from an honesty that never paid and be-
> trayed his friends and died dishonored and a failure even at
> treachery—it was easier for a child to escape behind his mask.
> As for Visconti, with his beauty, his patience and his genius
> for evil, I had watched him pass by many a time in his black
> Sunday suit smelling of mothballs. . . . Goodness has only
> once found a perfect incarnation in a human body and never
> will again, but evil can always find a home there. Human
> nature is not black and white but black and grey. I read all
> that in *The Viper of Milan* and I looked around and saw that
> it was so.

Marjorie Bowen gave him the pattern he believes he has
exemplified "in terms of the great public world we all share":
"perfect evil walking the world where perfect good can never
walk again, and only the pendulum ensures that after all in
the end justice is done."

With the not small qualification that he rarely approximates
perfect evil in the characters he creates, this is the pattern of
Graham Greene's world. Hell lies about his children in their
infancy and one starts to believe in heaven only because one
imagines that all societies, the creation of gray and black
characters, are "in a true sense discarded from" God's presence,
and, "implicated in some terrible aboriginal calamity." The
game Monopoly says, "the object is to collect rent," and its
players "may land in gaol," symbolizing capitalist society,
which, Greene points out, papal encyclicals have condemned
"quite as strongly as Communism." England is a place where
men "live in an ugly indifference"; America is where the disparity
between the comfortable and the impoverished shows up most
shockingly against the background of "the drugstore and the
Coca-Cola, the hamburger, the graceless sinless empty chromium
world." Mexico and Russia, *all* welfare states, are the worst
because they offer inadequate palliatives: "Even if . . . there
were no God, surely life was happier with the enormous super-

natural promise than with the petty social fulfillment, the tiny pension and the machine made furniture." Even primitive societies are better than any of these, for in squalid Liberia one could have moments "of extraordinary happiness, the sense that one was nearer than one had ever been to the racial source, to satisfying the desire for an instinctive way of life, the sense of release, as when in the course of psychoanalysis one uncovers by one's own effort a root, a primal memory." In primitive societies one finds too, among the natives in the interior, "gentleness, kindness, . . . honesty which one would not have found, or at least dared to assume was there, in Europe." On his return from each of his journeys among the less "civilized," to the "seedy level" of civilization, he feels, as he did after his trip to Liberia, that "this journey, if it had done nothing else, had reinforced a sense of disappointment with what man had made out of the primitive, what he had made out of childhood." This realization is dramatized effectively in Querry's realization in *A Burnt-Out Case* (1960), that primitives still *are,* that God *is,* if not for him.

In his latest phase, Greene is almost optimistic about some of those who have undergone civilization. Brown, in *The Comedians* (1966), at least hopes for a future less awful than today while he observes the faith and acts of the Smiths, who are absurdly heroic, of Jones, who, under stress, becomes the hero he only pretended to be until crisis makes him brave, of Dr. Magiot, who believes the state may wither away in a far future. Brown, of course, is not Greene, but his feelings about the human condition, like those of the "I's" in *May We Borrow Your Husband?* (1967), seem appropriate to the Greene whom Greene creates in *In Search of a Character* (1961) and implies in the sympathetic characterizations in his fiction of the sixties.[3]

Even though Greene may reject "faith in the future" as too

---

[3] In *Travels with My Aunt* (1969), the gaiety seems to be forced, many critics feel. I find it pleasant, as I do the aunt's "harmless" amorality that counterpoints the horrifying "morality" of Ida in *Brighton Rock* (1938). Greene is near both cheerfulness and carelessness in the latter part of the novel where he consciously or unconsciously parodies himself. By turns farcical, amusing, "tragic"—his latest work is the only approach he has made to a comic novel and is a charming book in spite of the failure to prepare adequately for the somberness of the main character in the last part of the book.

strong a phrase for his feeling about man's fate, he appears to feel affection for comedians who mean well and admiration for heroic absurdities like the Smiths and the priests at the leproserie. The comedians do little harm, the heroes may keep the world from getting worse. Brown, early in *The Comedians,* feels we are all "driven by an authoritative practical joker towards the extreme point of comedy." After watching the absurd but heartening heroism of those who fail to overthrow Papa Doc, he agrees with some observations that are, at the least, a contrast to those any character makes in *The Power and the Glory,* Greene's other serious novel about a dictatorship:

> The Church condemns violence, but it condemns indifference more harshly.
> Catholics and Communists have committed great crimes, but at least they have not stood aside, like an established society, and been indifferent.

By having Brown concur with these statements, the first by a priest, the second by an atypical communist, Greene does not demonstrate, even dramatically, a liking for communism or capitalism or Catholicism. The close conjunction of these remarks and their appositeness to *The Comedians* do show his realization that the good continues to appear in unlikely forms and places. Perhaps the best those who do not stand aside can expect is that those who act with good intentions hold up the regression that has appeared to be dominant since the days when Greene says "the Victorians kept skeletons in cupboards," that God, something of a comedian himself, knows the good end, and acts more for what we can reasonably desire than our nescience realizes.

Still, even as it diminishes into comedy in the later books, Greene's is a pessimistic reading of life and the world in which it is lived, much closer to that of Pascal than to that of St. Thomas Aquinas. A Roman Catholic since 1926, and one assumes as good a one as he can be, Greene when he writes is more the product of his lost childhood than a Catholic "with an intellectual if not an emotional belief in Catholic dogma." In the November 1948 issue of *Partisan Review,* Graham Greene wrote, "Literature has nothing to do with edification." And he continued, "I am not arguing that literature is amoral, but that it presents a personal moral, and the personal morality of an individual is seldom identical with the morality of the group to which he belongs." Never a liberal who "thought men could govern themselves if they were left alone to it, that wealth did not corrupt and that statesmen loved their country"; once briefly a communist; never a capitalist with "the power of elimination" that enables one to forget "the people behind the shares"; always inclined to prefer the ruled to the rulers; frequently and surprisingly, considering his view of life, a popular success, never quite consistent in his representation of his views —Graham Greene is an artist committed to the faithful representation of his personal vision, a vision he realizes with usual fidelity.

Before his first published novel, *The Man Within* (1929), Graham Greene published a volume of poems, *Babbling April* (1925), and wrote two novels and part of a third that have never been printed. The poems confirm what he has said about himself in "The Lost Childhood" and elsewhere. Sensations do not delight him: he is "ignorant of the way to speak to God,/ Whether Father, Majesty, or simply You There"; his ideal of happiness is to be like "the insentient stone"; he thinks of love as a "brief ecstasy and a lengthy pain." Significantly, in "The Gamble," about the playing of Russian roulette, he wonders:

> Will it be mist and death
> At the bend of this sunset road,
> Or life reinforced
> By the propinquity of death?

Of the unpublished novels, John Atkins tells us in his comprehensive *Graham Greene,* one was about a black child born to white parents, one was a detective story about a murder committed by a child of ten ("Hell lies about us in our infancy"), and one was about the Carlist activities of Spanish exiles living in London. If we can judge Greene's judgment by his good taste in not permitting *The Name of Action* (1930) and *Rumour at Nightfall* (1931) to be republished, their only interest would be in what they reveal about his own obsession, not in their artistic merit.

The first three novels Greene published show, as Kenneth Allott and Miriam Farris say in their admirable study, *The Art of Graham Greene,* "the divided mind." Andrews in *The Man Within* (1929) is "embarrassingly made up of two persons, the sentimental, bullying, desiring child and another more stern critic," the "man within . . . that's angry with me." Oliver Chant, the protagonist of *The Name of Action,* is unable to decide whether he is for or against dictator Damassener, who is trying to coerce the people of Trier into puritanical moral conduct. But Chant becomes glad, as one presumes Greene does, that life there is uncertain "in place of the regular succession of meals, theatres, parties. . . ." The two protagonists in *Rumour at Nightfall* appear to be two sides of one personality rather than separate individuals.[4] Crane, a coward who fears and hopes to believe in God, is opposed to the rather indifferent Chase throughout most of the action, but in the end Chase becomes a whole person because of the guilt he suffers after betraying Crane to his death. "I suffer, therefore I am," he thinks. This continues to be a preoccupation of Greene's as the slightly "diminished" comment of Querry shows in *A Burnt-Out Case* (1961): "I feel discomfort, therefore I am alive."

Except in *The Man Within,* which is still a readable and significant novel, Greene succeeds poorly in dramatizing the divided self. There are good things in both *The Name of Action* and *Rumour at Nightfall.* The characterization of Damassener, who sometimes thinks he is "the only man existing who can see . . . things as they must appear to a God who is not smirched by living in the world," is admirable caricature, but those who conspire against him and the protagonist Chant are types. Despite Greene's failure to make plausible two aspects of a character acting as separate persons and the implausible melodrama of the action, *Rumour at Nightfall* is the better of the two, particularly in the minor characterizations. Riego, who worries more about the souls of his men than the success of

---

[4] Rather like the many voices Conrad uses. The Conrad influence on Greene is put convincingly by Ronald Bryden in "Graham Greene, Alas," and by Greene himself in *In Search of a Character* (1961).

their actions, and the incidental descriptions predict Greene's mature manner:

> A manageress in velvet with a mass of hair and a smile. A drawing room with cheap mirrors and a red plush sofa. And finally a rather squalid bedroom with lace curtains, not quite clean sheets, a dressing table littered with hair combings . . . and a naked, ill-shaped prudish woman, who is determined to give as little as possible for your money.

But neither novel has either the technical or the substantial interest of *Stamboul Train* (American title, *Orient Express*) which followed in 1932 or of *The Man Within* that preceded.

*The Man Within* has the intensity of a nightmare occasionally interrupted by pleasant dreams. From the first page, when Andrews is discovered in full flight from his friend Carlyon, whom he has betrayed, to the conclusion when he feels he has conquered the lower self that led him to betray his smuggling comrades and behave with intermitted cowardice, the reader identifies with the struggle that goes on within him, and is carried ahead by nightmare plausibility. If Greene had not, by the intensity of his own identification with Andrews, made the reader live within him, a good deal might not seem probable: the extent of Andrews's hatred for his father, a good leader of the smugglers with whom the son is compared invidiously; the rapt love he feels for Elizabeth because, like a mother, she shelters him from Carlyon (his still warm cup of tea that she drinks to make Carlyon believe he has left becomes a chalice, symbolic of the sacred love he does not believe he deserves); the very profane love of Lucy that he wins by testifying in court against the smugglers (typically, after they have slept together, Lucy says, "Have you enjoyed yourself?" and Andrews replies, "I've wallowed"); the facing of danger at the end that leaves Andrews with Elizabeth's suicide to expiate by the false confession that he killed her, which makes up for the cowardice of leaving Elizabeth alone to face the smugglers. Finally the man without becomes the critic within. But Greene's art, here as in many of the novels and "entertainments" that followed, is equal to his task of making you see, feel, and live within the bad dream of life *The Man Within* presents. Even after you have put down the book, you wonder which is dream, which reality, and you are left, as in Greene's other books, with a residual enlightenment about the horror of existence for those who live with minds alternately haunted by heaven and hell.

*Stamboul Train,* which followed the lesser successors to *The Man Within,* is the first of what Greene calls his entertainments. In these novels, as Allott and Farris point out, there is a "comparative lack of development in the characters . . . , wilfull use of interesting background for its own sake," and a linking up of "the various sections of his narrative by coincidences and improbabilities." These entertainments, as a rule, move so rapidly in short, sharp, cinematographic flashes that the reader has no more wish to weigh probabilities than he does when he watches a good Hitchcock film (as *Stamboul Train* became). So the reader does not consider the unlikelihood of the many interestingly unusual characters who are thrown together on one train and experience so many sensational events. He does not question the probability of the relationships among Dr. Czinner, the socialist leader, Myatt, the insecure Jewish businessman, Carol Musker, the homely dancer travelling to a foreign engagement, Miss Warren, the aggressive Lesbian reporter, and the popular "cheerful" novelist Savory. Nor is he upset by the sudden melodramatic events that bring death to Czinner and turn Carol into Miss Warren's next convert to Lesbianism. It is an entertainment, perhaps, only because the unlikely characters and happenings seem so plausibly removed from our everyday realities and one reads entertainments, even Greene's, rapidly. But the aftertaste suggests a world similar to that of *The Man Within* and the other novels: a world in which betrayal, lust without love, and violence without motive are more likely to occur than fidelity, true love, and kindly gentle action. This is true in the films that have been made of Greene's entertainments, of quite a few of the "novels."

As we approach the novels that preceded *The Power and the Glory* (1940; American title, *The Labyrinthine Ways*) it is necessary to remind ourselves that the real world in which Greene lived was full of lust, betrayal, violence, and exploitation, that during the years in which he wrote *It's a Battlefield* (1934), *England Made Me* (1935), *A Gun for Sale* (1936; American title, *This Gun for Hire*), *Brighton Rock* (1938), and *Confidential Agent* (1939), everybody's world was a fallen world. The years that saw the Great Depression, Manchuria, Ethiopia, and the Spanish Civil War, can easily be seen as a "low, inglorious decade," possibly a little worse than the decades that have followed. Graham Greene cannot be accused of misrepresenting the thirties in his most pessimistic novels. Indeed, since his novels are as critical of capitalists as of communists, of the men who uphold the law as of those who are lawless, it is possible that the novels from *It's a Battlefield* to *Confidential Agent* give a more accurate picture of the decade than the "Marxist" novels of Dos Passos and Steinbeck.

It is puzzling, however, that these novels became popular, both in England and in the United States. There are no heroes, capitalist or communist; happiness occurs only in incidental snatches; there is no hope for a better world on earth, only a slight hope of heaven. The characters who stand out most memorably are Conrad Drover, who tries ineptly to reverse his brother's sentence of death, sleeps with his brother's wife, and dies unheroically; the Assistant Commissioner, who says "God help the men responsible for the way that life is organized; I am only a paid servant, doing what I am told"; Anthony Farrant, a ne'er-do-well who uses charm like a revolver; his sister, whose love of him is nearly incestuous; Krogh, the dictator of an industrial empire who does not believe in God but in the lines on his hand and in the manipulation of men as integers in the game of finance; Raven, who has never been loved and prefers killing for pay to the dangers of loving; Pinkie, who is always ready for more deaths because hell lay about him in his infancy; Ida, a convincing and horrifying parody of a liberal whose "big breasts, which had never suckled a child . . . , felt a merciless compassion." All of these and minor others comprise a fallen world more terrifying than Dante's *Inferno* because it contains our living and is the world we read about in the daily newspapers.

*It's a Battlefield* (1934) is a more fully realized novel than

any Greene published earlier.  Like *Stamboul Train* it is cinematographic in technique, giving a broad social picture, rarely
going very deeply into any of the characters, relying on
suggestion for emotional depth.  It is, however, more carefully
centered than *Stamboul Train*.  All of the action circles about
the attempt to reverse the sentence of death passed on Jim
Drover, a communist, who killed a policeman for striking his
wife while the police were putting down a communist demonstration.  Involved in the effort are Jim's brother, Conrad, who
is not a communist but believes injustice has been done; Milly,
Jim's wife, who sleeps with Conrad out of loneliness and pity;
Surrogate, a Fabian turned communist who would like to have
Jim die a communist martyr; the Assistant Commissioner, who
knows all justice is imperfect and rarely dares to think of
anything but doing his job, and a number of others who
represent differing and representative attitudes towards communism and social justice.  The point the action as a whole
emphasizes is that each of those involved in the battlefield
centering about Jim Drover tends towards the condition of
"the private soldier fighting in a fog, like the men at Inkerman,
in a fury of self-preservation," that in such a mixture of ignorant
motivations justice happens only accidentally.  Greene's point
is brought out most effectively when, after the muddle is nearly
over, the prison chaplain resigns because he "can't stand human
justice any longer.  Its arbitrariness.  Its incomprehensibility."
When the Assistant Commissioner replies that divine justice is
"much the same," the chaplain replies, "Perhaps.  But one can't
hand in a resignation to God. . . . And I have no complaint
against His mercy."

Judged by conventional standards of realism, the novel is
not an entire success.  Though all of the characters have an
exterior plausibility, and depth is suggested, the fury of self-
preservation the characters are made to exemplify is overdone.
Surely, one feels, there would have been some "noble" characters
involved in the muddle, whether they were able to help Jim
Drover effectively or not.  Surely human justice, which must
dimly reflect God's, cannot be quite that arbitrary.  Nevertheless, if one views the novel as a projection of Greene's peculiar

—and powerful—nightmare vision of the worst that often happens, the novel is good. Greene's skill is so great that one believes thoroughly while he reads and continues to wonder afterwards if Greene's exaggeration may not be closer to the truth than the cosier realisms we prefer. Sacco and Vanzetti are only one of a long succession of inexplicable miscarriages of human justice that have become symbolic in post-1918 life.

*England Made Me* (1935) is at once more plausible and less important. The portrait of Krogh, based upon the figure of the Swedish match king, Kreuger, is impressively probable, and so is the portrait of Minty, the ticket-of-leave man who clings pathetically to the respectability of a Harrow tie while he buys and sells scandal and rumors of misfortune. What keeps the novel from impressiveness is the supine conduct of the two chief characters, Anthony and Kate Farrant. One believes in and remembers their unnatural attachment to each other, but it is difficult to feel any identification with two characters so dedicated to letting what must be, be. Their only gesture against the domination of Krogh seems half-hearted and theatrical and one scarcely cares when Anthony is killed by Krogh's chief henchman and Kate decides to leave Krogh for a new way of life somewhere between the disreputable and the reputable. Though, like most of what Greene writes, it is readable, it does not leave one wondering or worrying about either man's or God's injustice.

In *The Confidential Agent* (1939), D, the economic materialist with whom Greene identifies, is afraid "of other people's pain, their lives, their individual despairs. He was damned like a creative writer to sympathy." It is Greene's damnation to sympathy that makes his nightmare picture of the world bearable and believeable. Though one dares not always find plausible what his characters do or the background against which they act, Greene's identification with extreme characters in extreme situations is so adequate that one lives the books until their nightmare becomes one's own. He does not portray "perfect evil walking the world," unless the perfect evil is the direction of modern society rather than the men who make it. Neither the communists nor the Assistant Commissioner in *It's a Battlefield*, nor Krogh nor the Farrants in *England Made Me* are portrayed without sympathy. Except for Sir Marcus in *A Gun for Sale,* Hall in *England Made Me,* and Ida in *Brighton Rock,* Greene identifies sympathetically with all his characters, Catholic or opponents of Catholicism, murderers, or those set to catch murderers. This identification and his conception of the mercy of God that may save Pinkie, Scobie, the whiskey priest, and all the rest of his sinners, may make him a poor apologist for Catholic orthodoxy as it is conventionally viewed, but it does make him a good artist, angry with circumstances that corrupt, gentle with the corrupted—as perhaps God is, too.

Though it is flawed by a happy ending that can only satisfy the most wilfully sentimental reader, *A Gun for Sale,* which would have been a good novel with the last chapter omitted, and *The Confidential Agent,* which would have been a good novel with the omission of the last page, illustrate Greene's art as vividly as the books he labels novels rather than entertainments. Raven, the paid killer who nearly starts a war with the innocence of a man who is just doing what his managers say he should do, has everything against him. Hare-lipped and too poor to do anything about it, fatherless from the age of six when his father was hanged, motherless when his mother cuts her throat on the kitchen table, he seems predestined for efficient killing. He is plausible as one who is comforted by the kind feeling of Anne, who does not notice his hare-lip and listens to his confessions like a psychiatrist or priest. When she betrays him, our sympathy is with Raven, who has by then killed Sir Marcus, the evil capitalist, and his henchman. Indeed we have something of the same feeling for him that we have for Macbeth, though it is tinged with the feeling we have for pathetic Falder in Galsworthy's *Justice.* If Greene's theology were different, he might have concluded with "the President of the Immortals had finished his sport with Raven."

In *The Confidential Agent,* D is a creative artist who has accepted economic materialism with such dedication that he is obsessed by the need to get coal for the Loyalist government of Spain during the Civil War. (It is worth noting that D is a character comparable to the fellow travellers pilloried by Waugh in his trilogy.) Though the novel is full of the improbabilities

Greene allows in an entertainment (and makes plausible while one reads), the characterization of D is quite as moving as that of Raven. His side, Loyalist though not called so, is shown to be as flawed as Jordan's in *For Whom the Bell Tolls,* but one sympathizes, as I believe Greene did, with his feeling that the poor right or wrong is as justifiable a slogan as my country right or wrong. Unobtrusively, Greene makes his religious point, as he did with Raven when Raven feels he might not have had to kill if he had a priestlike listener, when D thinks, "If you believed in God," you could leave punishment to Him. One agrees also with D, who hadn't "that particular faith" and believed that "unless people received their deserts, the world . . . was chaos." One is happy with him when he learns that the coal that did not go to the Loyalists at least did not go to the rebels who almost thwart him. Indeed it is with the rebels and the businessmen who will sell to anyone for a profit that one is really angry in *A Gun for Sale.* If they do not make the circumstances that make D and Raven, they are partially responsible for the continued existence of injustice, as they continue to be as late as *May We Borrow Your Husband?* (1967).

*Brighton Rock* (1938) Greene first labelled an entertainment, later called a novel. Though there are incidents that require an unusual willingness to suspend disbelief, it deserves the name of novel because of its over-all probability and seriousness. I do not mean that it is a realistic novel, though it is based upon an actual series of murders that occurred in Brighton. None of Greene's novels are "realistic." But it is a vividly plausible nightmare that suggests, by exaggeration, truths about men and the moral and social universe God may have made.

The center is Pinkie, a lapsed Catholic who retains a knowledge of good and evil different from the secular conception of right and wrong. He believes in hell and lives in it, dimly sees the possibility of a heaven that is not his destination. Like Raven, he has never known love, unless it was his parent's weekly exercise in bed, which he witnessed and which made him think of sexual desire as a sickness. His wish for recognition, for him a substitute for love, has made him a killer, an inept, merciless, and credible leader of a gang. He is not sentimentalized (in him hate runs stronger than blood) but he is presented as salvageable human material in his awkward and diffident approach to love for Rose. Rose resembles an animal whose hole for hiding contains "murder, copulations, extreme poverty, fidelity, and the love and fear of God." Pinkie accepts also Satan, the coincidence of good and evil, that God may save him "between the stirrup and the ground." Both he and Rose seem more worthy of salvation than their pursuer who believes in the secular punishment of wrong by right, than the big-breasted Ida, with her merciless compassion for Rose and her sense of "fair play" as an eye for an eye that actually means death for Pinkie. One does not like to believe that such people exist, but they do in the terrifyingly convincing nightmare world of the book that does, after all, resemble life more than our daydreams do. One hopes strenuously, while and after he reads, that the priest Rose visits after Pinkie's death is right when he tells her, "You can't conceive, my child, nor can I or anyone—the . . . appalling . . . strangeness of the mercy of God."

Greene's more recent novels—from *The Power and the Glory* (1940) to *The Comedians* (1966)—are his best. One continues to find the familiar obsessions with the awfulness of life, with the strangeness of the mercy of God, so odd "it sometimes seems like punishment." Now, however, it is with the mercy of God and the need to believe in it and with the way awfulness is made by hubristic idealists that Greene is mainly preoccupied. Because of the plausibility of his view of God and the world, the novels are less realistic nightmares, more realistic novels in which nightmares appear. Because he has matured both as thinker and artist, Greene's control of his material is better, too. Though he continues to use, when it is necessary, the vivid cinematographic technique he used first in *Stamboul Train,* the quick flashes that suggest a multiverse are subordinated to the steady progression of a conflict in which only a few characters are involved.

To see how much he has progressed as an artist one has only to compare *The Lawless Roads* (1939; American title, *Another Mexico*) with *The Power and the Glory.* In *The Lawless Roads* righteous indignation at the treatment of Catholics in Mexico often obscures his vision, both his insight and his outsight; in *The Power and the Glory* he dramatizes fully and fairly the insights that are nearly buried in *The Lawless Roads:* that the peasants are perhaps "the population of heaven," that "these aged, painful, and ignorant faces . . . are human goodness"; that even the communists are compelled to their view of the world, for "no one can live without a philosophy"; that what is typical in Mexico is perhaps typical of the entire human race: "violence in favor of an ideal and then the ideal lost and the violence just going on."

Where the whiskey priest goes, pursued by God and the police, he finds human goodness. He finds it most among the peasants who risk danger by coming to him and by sheltering him, in the mestizo Judas who ashamedly betrays him, in Coral Fellows, who lost her religion at ten. He finds it even in the Lieutenant, his and God's opponent, who despite his mystical "certainty in the existence of a dying, cooling world" where people should have the "right to be happy in any way they chose," befriends him as long as he does not know he is a priest. Certainly Greene does not sentimentalize the goodness of any of these: the peasants haggle over the price of a baptism, the mestizo betrays him, the Lieutenant orders his execution. But without Greene's picture of limited human goodness, both the priest's fearful efforts to serve people and God's efforts to save the priest would seem utterly futile.

It is what happens within the priest that holds us. He is so thoroughly oppressed by the awfulness of the world, "the way things happen," and the evil he sees in himself—his early mistaking of ambition for a sense of vocation, his dreams of luxury, his sleeping with Maria and his love of his child above other children when he should "love every soul as if it were one's own child," his cowardice and his drunkenness—that his persistence in his priestly function resembles saintliness. Indeed, as we watch him learn in his corruption what he had not known in his innocence, we agree that "when you visualized a man or woman carefully, you could always begin to feel pity," that hate, even of his opponent, the Lieutenant, "was just a failure of imagination." As he argues Catholicism with the Lieutenant while he is nearly overcome with fear of death, he seems specially favored by God, certainly not despised. Assuredly all but the blindly prejudiced must agree with Greene's judgment of the man upon whom he based his characterization (from *The Lawless Roads*): "Who can judge what terror and hardship and isolation may have excused him in the eyes of God?"

In the entertainment that followed—*The Ministry of Fear* (1943)—Greene develops further his preoccupation with the excesses of secular power unchecked by belief in a supernatural power. Like all of Greene's entertainments it relies a great deal on coincidences and does not attempt depth of characterization, but it does illuminate the problem of idealism run amok in idealists (like Dr. Forrester and Poole) who don't see blood like you and I do. . . . It's all statistics to them."

The central character, Arthur Rowe, unwittingly receives some films the Nazis and their "idealist" allies need. As a consequence he becomes involved in melodrama that includes two bombings, confinement with amnesia in a sanatorium, and pursuit by and of the secret agents who form a Ministry of Fear in England. The action, of scenario swiftness, is handled admirably, but what remains after the aesthetic pleasure, is a brooding worry over a world in which man acts so unworthily with such idealism. " 'Let not man prevail,' " Rowe reads in a Roman missal, "and the truth of the appeal chimed like music. . . . It wasn't only evil men who did these things. Courage smashes a Cathedral, endurance lets a city starve, pity kills. . . . We are trapped and betrayed by our virtues." (How like Hawthorne, and Greene's more ambiguous irony in *A Burnt-Out Case*, where the lapsed Catholic acts out a close approximation to saintliness he cannot credit to either himself or God.) This irony is dramatized vividly by the entire novel, for almost everyone means well and expects to accomplish too much— even Rowe, who had killed his suffering wife out of pity. Although it is clear that the Nazis and the idealists who "can bear . . . other people's pain endlessly" if it seems justified by their ends, are worse than those who cannot outlive pain "like sex," it is clear also that we are all involved in a Ministry of

Fear larger than any the Nazis ever made, "a Ministry as large as life to which all who loved belonged. If one loved one feared." And there is the further implication that it is only God's mercy that permits escape.

The three later entertainments—*The Third Man* (1949), *Loser Takes All* (1955) and *Our Man in Havana* (1959)—are entertainments only. Fast pace and plot ingenuity are their virtues. *The Third Man* is the most typical of the three because it does suggest one of Greene's preoccupations: "In these days . . . nobody thinks in terms of human beings." Greene himself properly characterizes *Loser Takes All* as a "frivolity," and though *Our Man in Havana* is unique in the gaiety of its satire of secret agents and their superiors, it is barely consequential.

*The Heart of the Matter* (1948) is, in a different way, as good as *The Power and the Glory*. Appropriately its epigraph is from Péguy: "No one knows as much about Christianity as the sinner unless it is the saint." Even more than in *The Power and the Glory*, the conflict is within the protagonist. Scobie, the sinner, is also an upright man, so unimpugnably honest that the civil servants under him dislike him and the Commissioner above him looks upon him as his logical successor. Like Greene himself when he made his journey without maps and when he served in West Africa during World War II, Scobie is kind to the African natives, to his subordinates, to everyone, even the smuggler Yusef (of the "wide, pastry, untrustworthy, sincere face," a fine characterization of a man who is sincerely sentimental and unavoidably unscrupulous). Like Greene again, Scobie is a Catholic convert married to a woman who was born Catholic. I do not mean to imply that Scobie is a self-portrait; I only suggest that there may be an autobiographical reason why Greene identifies with him.

Scobie's gentleness is interpreted as the consequence of the sin of pity, which resembles the damnation of the creative artist, sympathy. He does not, as he feels he should, love his wife Louise, for she wants him to get ahead, to move some place where cultivated company is possible, and cannot comprehend how he loves Africa because there nobody talks foolishly about a heaven on earth (as did the Lieutenant and the "idealists" of *The Ministry of Fear)*, because there you "could love human beings nearly as God loved them, knowing the worst." This is a major reason, one suspects, why Greene himself journeyed to Liberia, to Mexico, to French Indochina, to the Congo. Greene—like an inverted Thoreau, like Orwell, like Hemingway—seems to want to go where the going is worst so he can confront the human situation at its most basic and rediscover whether the world is really of God or of the Devil.

Scobie loves Louise most in her times of ugliness, "when pity and responsibility" reach the "intensity of a passion in him." Because of the "pity that smouldered like decay at his heart," Scobie becomes involved in an impossible series of situations. He borrows from Yusef so that Louise can get away to something like happiness in South Africa; he falls in love, during her absence, with Helen Rolt, for with her he feels to excess "the loyalty we all feel to unhappiness, the sense that that is where we really belong." Deeply involved in the complications to which pity leads him, he can only wonder, "If one knew . . . the facts, would one have to feel pity even for the planets? if one reached what they called the heart of the matter." He wonders, he cannot accept. He cannot accept the Church's dogma that "one should look after one's own soul at whatever cost to another," since he feels one cannot truly love God "at the expense of one of his creatures." Consequently he succumbs to despair, "the price one pays for setting oneself an impossible aim": kindness to everybody that hurts no one. Despair is, he thinks, "the unforgivable sin, but it is a sin the corrupt or evil man never practises. . . . Only the man of good will carries in his heart this capacity for damnation." His despair leads him to suicide which he tries to make appear a natural death so that his wife and Helen Rolt will not suffer. This is not because he does not recognize the probability of his own eternal damnation, whether he makes an act of contrition before dying or not. His wife, a more devout and/or orthodox Catholic, is appalled, but the priest to whom she talks says, "don't imagine you—or I—know a thing about God's mercy. . . . The Church knows all the rules. But it doesn't know what goes on in a single human heart."

In my account of this novel and the others, I have stressed the structure at the expense of the texture, which is everywhere realized admirably. One gets to know the people, the weather, the insides of houses and the suggestive outsides of the minor characters, the total atmosphere of the place where Scobie's tragedy occurs. Without the texture, one would not care about or believe the meaning Greene unobtrusively conveys. In this, as in all of his better novels, the meaning becomes universal because it is particularized vividly. But here as in the better novels it is the meaning, artistically translated into an ambiguity as obscure as the will of God, that remains with us forcibly. One is left wondering about the close alliance of sin and virtue, perplexed, whether one is Catholic or agnostic, about the working and judgment of whatever transcends the world we see and die in. *The Heart of the Matter* may not represent *the* truth, but it does enrich our stumblings towards it and makes us realize the importance of the quest.

Most critics consider either *The Heart of the Matter* or *The Power and the Glory* Greene's best novels, *The End of the Affair* (1951) and *The Quiet American* (1955) inferior. Though there are parts of both of these that hurt effectiveness—the planting of Sarah's baptism as a Catholic in *The End of the Affair* to make plausible her wish to be buried a Catholic, the inept moment in *The Quiet American* when Pyle thinks of the shine of his shoes rather than of the bloodshed his ignorant idealism has caused—I consider *The End of the Affair* among Greene's best novels and *The Quiet American* very little below his best level. Perhaps this is because I prefer flawed intensity to diffused "perfection." Without detracting from the excellence of the other novels, I believe that Greene's most recent novels are the most intense he has written, both because they are more deeply felt and because this deep feeling is represented by a greater concentration on fewer characters, with the cinematographic flashing over a broad surface reduced to a minimum.

In *The End of the Affair* the reader may identify closely with the good-and-bad man and writer, Maurice Bendrix. He is, he says at the beginning, writing a record of hate "far more than of love." He hates particularly Sarah Miles, who became his mistress while he was trying to get material from her about her husband Henry Miles, a prominent civil servant whom Bendrix despises as a representative of unimaginative bureaucracy. Whatever he says in favor of either of them, he writes on the first page, can be trusted. "I am writing against the bias because it is my professional pride to prefer the near-truth, even to the expression of my near-hate." As his record continues to struggle towards the near-truth, it becomes clear that his hate of both Henry and Sarah is caused by jealousy, for Sarah, after being his mistress for five years, suddenly and unaccountably breaks with him after an intense meeting that is followed by his close escape from death by a buzz bomb. As he thinks, she either returns to her husband or goes on to another lover (she has had lovers before). His hatred of her is the consequence of great love intensely shared. The description of this love affair is the first in Greene to be presented as passion that brings happiness while it lasts. Out of the desire to hurt both Sarah and her husband, Bendrix hires a private detective who uncovers evidence of her apparent double infidelity and brings to him, finally, Sarah's journal that covers the time of the affair and afterwards.

Reading it, "over and over again," he has to skip "when a passage hurts him too much." So does the reader, for the journal shows that Sarah gave up Bendrix because she made a promise to God that she would leave Bendrix if He restored him to life after his *actual* death from the buzz bomb he thought only stunned him. The diary is mainly about the conflict between her "ordinary corrupt human love" and her desire to love God, who has saved Bendrix and deprived her of him with that "odd sort of mercy" that "sometimes looks like punishment." The intensity of her struggle to give up a human love that has enabled her to understand how God can be loved and hated, is superlatively executed. Sarah finds it as difficult to believe God can love her immortal soul as it is to give up Bendrix. No excerpts can do the journal justice, but he who reads it entire is convinced that Sarah means the words that come repeatedly to Bendrix's mind after reading it: "But You are good to me. When I ask You for pain, You give me peace. Give it him too. Give him my peace—he needs it more."

Her ultimate forgetfulness of herself in her love of God, who can work miracles for others, turns her into a saint. The very ill son of the detective who followed her is made well by a book she lends him, as if it were a sacred relic; the rationalist to whom she goes to cure herself of her growing love of God, although he is literally defaced, is cured when she kisses his defacement. In the end, after her death, caused by the conflict of her desire not to hurt either God or Bendrix, he is still unconverted, but the reader feels sure Bendrix cannot escape Him, though the last words of the book are "O God, You've done enough, You've robbed me of enough, I'm too tired and old to learn to love, leave me alone for ever." Querry feels the same in *A Burnt-Out Case;* so does Morin (who "believes," in one of Greene's better short stories in *A Sense of Reality,* 1963).

What has caused many modern readers to refuse to acknowledge the book's excellence, as it has, I suppose, kept most viewers from accepting Greene's plays, such as *The Potting Shed* (1958), is the occurrence of the miracles and the conversion of the adultress Sarah into a saint. Why this difficulty should occur when we accept the miraculous change of Saul to Saint Paul and know the early life of Saint Augustine, puzzles me. As Greene comments in *The Lawless Roads,* "We are too apt to minimize the magic elements in Christianity—the man raised from the dead, the devils cast out. . . ." Evidently most modern readers cannot agree with Hardy, the agnostic, who would go to the manger on Christmas Eve, hoping the miraculous were so, or with that devout agnostic, Gilbert Murray, who felt the same. I must agree with William Faulkner, who was not a Catholic, yet called *The End of the Affair* "one of the best, most true and moving novels" of our time.

The way Greene shocks one into taking a position that it is disreputable to take in a sophisticated gathering is again illustrated in *The Quiet American.* Greene's tale of Pyle, the innocent American, "impregnably armoured by his good intentions and his ignorance," a man who must blame even the violence he causes on the communists, has not been very sympathetically received. It is evident that the narrator, Fowler, though he shares only some of Greene's views, as Greene has pointed out in a letter printed in the *New York Times,* does believe American foreign policy in Indochina and elsewhere is dominated by an innocence that is "like a dumb leper who has lost his bell, wandering the world, meaning no harm," dominated too by diplomatic correspondents who get "hold of an idea" and then alter "every situation to fit the idea." Greene's dramatic pillorying of such innocence is not, of course, confined to what he observed of Americans when he spent some months in Indochina. The Englishmen who belonged to the Ministry of Fear and the Mexicans who pursued the whiskey priest are found guilty (insofar as a novel can hand down verdicts) of similarly well-intentioned idealism. I cannot understand how intelligent American readers can believe that only other countries would benefit from the acknowledgment of a "few bad motives" that might make them "understand a little more about human beings." Our recent interventions in the Middle East, for example, would have seemed more palatable if the State Department had admitted that our intervention (like that of the "communists") was not a crusade but, as the *Wall Street Journal* said, an attempt to protect our oil interests.

Aesthetically, *The Quiet American* is very good indeed. The I, Fowler, is a convincing portrait of a man who refuses engagement only to become involved when he sees the harm Pyle's naïveté is doing. (A somewhat comparable theme is perhaps better dramatized in *The Comedians*.) Another plausible part of Fowler's motivation is his jealousy of Pyle, who has taken from him his native mistress, Phuong, and who envies him his faith in God though he distrusts faith. The characterization of the others—the soldiers reluctantly managed by politicians who will ultimately settle for a state of affairs similar to what prevailed before the fighting started, the Vietnamese, the other Americans, the communists, everyone but Phuong, who seems a stereotype once one finishes reading—is vividly gray. The action of Pyle in trying to form a Third Force that is neither communist nor imperialist is thoroughly plausible, the jungle warfare managed with a skill comparable to John Hersey's in *Into the Valley*. It is, furthermore, like all of Greene's middle novels, religious as well as political in theme. The significance of the whole action is the awfulness of what occurs when man alone tries to prevail and the last sentence implicitly decries even Fowler's intervention in Indochinese affairs which helped cause Pyle's death: "Everything had gone right with me since he had died, but how I wished there existed someone to whom I could say that I was sorry."

This sentence, the latter part of it, states again the fundamental preoccupation of Greene in all his better novels of the forties and fifties. With an art and an insight that approach with incremental repetition the consummate, Greene dramatizes man's hope of God and the danger of his frequent hubristic self-reliance. These novels are never cozy. They emphasize the loneliness of human beings that has caused even the pretentiously rational to invent God or something very like Him —"a being capable of understanding" ourselves or others. Perhaps Greene overdoes his case against contemporary man and what, without God, he has made and may make of this world, but who can disagree with Fowler's casual comment after seeing an American film: "It was what they call a film for boys, but the sight of Oedipus emerging with his bleeding eyeballs from the palace at Thebes would surely give a better training for life today."

A *Burnt-Out Case* (1960) could never be mistaken for a film for boys. Querry, *the* Querry of architecture, like Scobie of *The Heart of the Matter* and Brown of *The Comedians,* is an intellectual, "a character with Catholic ideas" he has rejected reluctantly. His retreat to a leproserie on the Congo, away from fame and "civilized society," where Marie Morel killed herself when he stopped letting her love him, is also a pilgrimage, partly conscious, towards learning to suffer rather than to feel only discomfort. In the first part of the novel, he is "cured" of fame, love, religion; he is as burnt-out spiritually as the lepers he lives with are burnt out physically, and faintly hopes that seeing suffering and its assuagement by the priests who care for him and them may enable him to feel more than "the reflection of another's pain."

This hope, dramatically implied but never explicit, leads him into a physical, intellectual, and spiritual pilgrimage, from indifference to a kind of "absurd" yea-saying when he becomes "the innocent adulterer" by saving the wife of one of the few husbands he does not cuckold, and is killed by the mistaken, wronging husband. (Much could be made, but I won't, of the conscious or unconscious naming of Querry—a querier of God's grace?—, of the leproserie's Superior—the Church?—, and of Father Thomas's parallel journey from pride through scepticism to faith. And *Marie* Morel dies for Querry; he comes to love *Marie* Rycker aphysically.) Along the way out of a retirement in which "human beings are not [his] country," through something like St. John of the Cross's dark night of the soul, by increasing participation in living, he begins to experience suffering, God's gift to those who cannot feel, and probably earns God's grace as he dies, saying "Absurd . . . or else." (The close reminds one of the agnostic Catholic conclusion of *The Heart of the Matter.*) This good novel is nearly as intense as the best of those that precede it, particularly in its believably melodramatic climax. But like some of his later short stories and *The Comedians* (1966), it is unusually full of intellectual paradox, especially in the somewhat leisurely first two-thirds, compared to its predecessors. The characterizations of Dr. Colin, who "doesn't care" to believe in a God who "cannot feel disappointment or pain," of Father Thomas, of the Superior, of the cynical Parkinson, who makes of Querry a feature-story saint, provide tension and give intellectual variety to a novel that is aesthetically satisfying. Their dialogues and multilogues, good talk about the human condition as life in and around the leproserie reveals it, are as dramatically complex as any that one finds in Conrad, though they lean undogmatically towards *a* Catholic view.

The stories of *A Sense of Reality* (1963), particularly "A Visit to Morin," are told in the more leisurely pace of the first two-thirds of *A Burnt-Out Case* and prepare us for the mixture of horrifying, exciting action and quizzical talk about man's fate that has, in varying proportions, marked Greene's work since *The Man Within*, that coalesces best in *The Comedians*. Perhaps, since Greene appears to have relaxed into a usually benign observer of man's absurdity in *May We Borrow Your Husband?* (1967) and in *Travels with My Aunt* (1969), *The Comedians* is intended to be his closest approximation to a definitive statement of his convictions, by way of the dramatic counterpointing of dialogue and action.

Haiti, realistically portrayed, as Greene admits in his prefatory letter, dominated by the pathological Papa Doc and his Tontons Macoute, is a fitting background for Greene's comedians and not a background for a child's story. Jones, Smith, and Brown— underlinedly representatives of common contemporary varieties of everyman—are supposed to be the comedians, the not-heroes. Brown is the observer-narrator, pigmented for transcience. Against the judgment of his "comic" intelligence, he is drawn into action by Smith, by Jones, and by Martha, his mistress and the wife of one of the few remaining ambassadors. Finally he escapes to Santo Domingo, no more unhappy than usual, in his final comic, unheroic, wise act. Brown is like Ishmael, if Ishmael or any product of the long "enviable Victorian peace," could be expected to look at the white whale of Haiti with a sense of humor that makes life seem to him "a comedy, not the tragedy for which [he] had been prepared," in which we "were all . . . driven by an authoritative practical joker towards the extreme point of comedy."

Captain Ahab, or his similar, does not appear. He stays in his cabin, afraid, while Captain Concasseur and the Tontons Macoute assure his unenjoyed luxury. Or can one say that Jones and Smith, at least in a Don Quixote way, are out to cleanse the world as Ahab was and as Papa Doc no longer is? Smith, a naïve American idealist kindly portrayed, would like to help build a Haitian counterpart of Brazilia, but he sees through Papa Doc's concept of social welfare before he is conned into believing it Utopian and achievable. Jones, who is out to get a fortune without sweat or much danger, is forced by circumstances to become the hero of a revolt that shows, at the least, that the Haitians are not inert, only unable.

Indeed, though Brown's conviction that one can no longer think in "Big Terms" like "Mankind, Justice, the Pursuit of Happiness" in Haiti, which is "a small slice of everyday taken at random," seems proven by the action, a lot of temporarily inert goodness shows up. Martha, Brown's mistress, has "that vague thing . . . 'goodness.'" She is faithful to Brown, good to her ambassador husband. The prostitute, Tin Tin; the madame, Mère Catherine; Henri Philipot, the son of the murdered secretary of social welfare; Brown's castrated servant, Joseph; Doctor

Magiot, who believes in communism somewhat as many Christians "believed" during the time of Nero—these represent a hopeful portion of goodness in their highly varied ways. Given the chance, one feels they might have become—those left alive may become—what Brown calls the Smiths, "heroic." Brown, the teller of the tale, in his Berkeleyan self-centeredness, is really the least admirable of the characters in spite of his percipience about those from whom he keeps as detached as possible. Protagonist, author's eye, nevertheless he is what one should not be, for "the Church condemns violence, but it condemns indifference even more harshly," and Brown slips safely away to Santo Domingo though he agrees with the priest who says this.

Like all the novelists I write of, Greene survives because usually he writes so well: sentence to sentence, character to character, scene to scene, action to action; movement and tension nearly always as he goes from each to each. His seamy people and places, where the going rarely is good, presented by acts and images that are seedy and overdone and memorable, conflict to resolutions that satisfy aesthetically. Andrews, Pinkie, the spoiled priest ("Behind all of us in various ways lies a spoilt priest," Querry says), Sarah—how good that Greene is an artist who makes us believe in them and what they do. But believing Greene as one reads provides more than temporary aesthetic respite, far from negligible though that is. Reading Greene's work carries over into our lives a sense that indifference is frequent, forgiveable, and wrong. As the testing of his last book of stories shows, with a comic sense that is not funny:

> "Perhaps the sexual life is the great test. If we can survive it with charity to those we love and with affection to those we have betrayed, we needn't worry so much about the good and bad in us. . . ."

Not inappropriately it is Brown's mistress in *The Comedians* who says this. And, as *May We Borrow Your Husband?* shows, it is a variedly universal test that may be a station of the cross Greene would like to add to Catholic doctrine. Surely those who pass it will not love indifference and may, like Greene's seedy, admirable characters, pass other harsher tests.

## Chapter Eight

# Joyce Carey: Christian Unclassified

MUCH AS HE MIGHT HAVE disagreed with him in other ways, Joyce Cary would have agreed with Graham Greene's conviction that childhood and adolescence are fundamental in determining "the private world" the writer expresses "in terms of the great public world we all share." It is arguable that the many differences between these two writers have their source in their disparate childhoods. Greene's unhappy childhood made him conclude that this is a world where perfect evil walks, "where perfect good can never walk again, and only the pendulum ensures that after all in the end justice is done"; Cary's happy childhood led him to believe that there was no "grief that has no cure." While Greene remembers the wish for death that hung over his childhood, Cary, in *A House of Children*, recalls a happy drift through sensations and a succession of pleasant excitements about swimming, hunting, boating, rugger, writing poems, putting on *The Tempest*. In this admittedly autobiographical novel, he and the older brother he made up to represent the adolescent side of his then-self "were not the pathetic deceived infants of the story-books, entering step by step the prison shades of grown-up disillusionment." They "were confident of happiness" because they "had had it before." When they shrieked it was in "joyful terror." Throughout this convincingly happy novel of childhood, Evelyn and Harry Corner represent Cary's early life, grow "drunk with expectation" which increases "all the time." They feel "dizzy with the weight of experience." For them words "like beauty, death, love, took living form and sang . . . like angels."

As Cary grew up and his feelings and thoughts about life became more like Greene's, he did not lose the gusto Greene seems to have lacked. "I don't know when my childhood ended or if it is all ended now," Cary wrote in 1941. Pamela Hansford

Johnson remembers her first meeting with him—a good deal later—when he appeared "alert as a blackbird hopping through a hedge." After they had eaten together, "Coming suddenly on a greengrocer's barrow he gave a sudden hop—one step forward, two steps back: 'Look at that! Just look at those lemons and beetroots! Look at them!' And he saw such colour that it stopped him short, he was filled with delight, not a bit urgent that I should be filled with it too because he was so dead certain that all saw as he did, twice as large and nine times as lovely." Even during his long last illness he forced the London *Sunday Times* into a typical Caryan paradox to describe his way of facing death as "stoical gaiety." And like his best known character, Gulley Jimson, the closeness of death did not make him stop. He finished *Art and Reality* (1958) during the last few months of his life and almost finished *The Captive and the Free* (1959) during his last year, while paralysis spread and killed him.

But it should not be assumed that Cary led an easy life or came to easy, comfortable conclusions about it. Though he was born at a lucky time—in 1888, seven years later than Rose Macaulay, four years earlier than Aldous Huxley, fifteen years before Evelyn Waugh, sixteen before Graham Greene—and was fortunate enough to have an independent income that permitted him to do what he willed, he did not escape trouble either as a child or as an adult. His mother died when he was eight. In apparent contradiction to what he fictionalizes in *A House of Children*, he has written of how, as the son of a dispossessed English landlord in Ireland, "from earliest childhood . . . the fundamental injustice of things, the cruelty of blind fate, was as natural as the air we breathed." (Though he adds characteristically, "and, as I think now, probably as important to our health. We lived more intensely, and we set a far higher value on what we had of secure happiness.") As his shifting from a Paris art school to the Art School of the University of Edinburgh to Oxford indicates, he had a hard time finding himself, for he felt "the rootlessness and restlessness of a boy uprooted from the long domestic tradition of a family domain." He was wounded and decorated in the Balkan war to which he went in 1912 because he "wanted the experience of war" and, like most of his contemporaries, thought "there would be no more" of them. In 1913, after a brief period in Sir Horace Plunkett's Cooperative Society in Ireland, he discovered himself no cooperator. Later in 1913 he began his service as a "road-builder, a general Pooh Bah of State" in Nigeria, a position that held him until 1920 except for his second experience with war as a soldier in the Cameroons Campaign of 1915–1916 in which he was wounded again. In 1920 he was invalided out of the Nigerian service and from then until 1932, when *Aissa Saved* was published, he fumbled about as a writer who wrote much but was never satisfied with what he did. (Though again characteristically he was consoled by his happy family and by his capacity to believe that there were no griefs without a cure.)

Intellectually, one gathers, he was unsettled too. He abandoned his Church of England faith before he was twenty and, long after he had *made* his own religion, he told the *Paris Review* interviewers that he didn't suppose any church would accept him. He was incapable temperamentally of the profound disenchantment of Aldous Huxley and Evelyn Waugh, but anyone who has read his novels knows that he was disillusioned by the war, the General Strike of 1926, and the atmosphere of pointless hedonism that seemed to afflict the twenties. Indeed, it is likely that he, like Gore and Stoker in *An American Visitor* (1933), often felt that "the world is a hopeless mess," though certainly he did more than "get up in the morning and shave and carry on" with a job that may as well be done properly. We know from Andrew Wright's *Joyce Cary: A Preface to His Novels* that Cary felt the reason he could not finish most of the many novels he attempted in the twenties was that he believed he had to have a philosophy that suited him before he could be successfully an artist, and that this he achieved only just before he began *Aissa Saved* in 1929.

How this happened we do not know yet. But some time in 1929, as he tells us in his preface to the Carfax edition of *Aissa Saved,* his view of the world began to become clearer. He arrived at his own tentative answer to "the fundamental question for everybody . . . what they live by; what is their faith. Why don't they cut their throats; why is the fakir happy on his nails; why does the millionaire shoot himself at the dude ranch." He "waked up to the fact that all evil is not the result of an evil will; that the innocent may suffer misery." He realized "the fundamental injustice of the world," a recurrent phrase throughout the rest of his work, and having found his own answers, tried to put them into *Aissa Saved.* So, "like any one who has broken, with difficulty, out of a confused foggy disintegrated state of feeling and thought into moderately clear going, I wanted to tell everyone how to find the road. I did not realize that everyone has his own fog and therefore, needs a special map; that most of those who wanted a way out had found it for themselves, and that the rest would rather stay where they were; that is, different people needed different kinds of faith: 'true' for them." This passage was in the first and unpublished version which, as his own critic, Cary rejected.[1] Before he was satisfied enough to publish *Aissa Saved,* he tried to cut out "the religious philosophizing" and rewrote "the book several times in forms of increasing simplicity."

From the time of the publication of *Aissa Saved* (1932) on, Joyce Cary's novels, with ups and downs, reflect his growing maturity both as an artist and as a thinker. The growing pains are evident in the novels that precede *Mr. Johnson* (1939). Thereafter, with lapses in *The Moonlight* (1946) and *A Fearful Joy* (1949), the pains are successfully concealed. As early as *Aissa Saved* he believed, I feel confident, in "an immanent world spirit." As late as *The Captive and the Free* (1959), his "profoundly religious spirit" continued to be of "that intensely individual and protestant kind that cannot find fulfillment in any corporate body," to quote Lord David Cecil's preface to it. What he learned more and more as his artistic control and philosophic certainty increased, was that each of his characters had his own fog and needed his own special map. Consequently he was able with great sureness to become the characters who were warring parts of himself, to become what V. S. Pritchett has called "the chameleon among contemporary novelists," what

[1] According to Andrew Wright, from whose *Joyce Cary* I take the rejected passage.

Walter Allen has called " 'the one Proteus' of the English novel today."

Judged by severe standards of excellence, Joyce Cary's first four novels are not particularly good. They all have too many characters, too much incident imperfectly controlled, too many themes imperfectly illustrated. But they remain interesting reading even for those who do not care to observe the development of one of the finest novelists of our times.[2]

The first three are without parallel for the comprehensive picture they give of Nigeria in transition: juju and African witches in process of being replaced by Christianity, tribal despotism on the verge of succumbing to benevolent colonial despotism. In portraying this change, which Cary thought symbolic of the change that is always occurring everywhere in less obvious ways, he is objective and vivid. Though these novels, when they appeared first, were often understood to be, alternatively, against missionaries or against juju, against colonialism or against tribalism, actually the balance is held remarkably even. Aissa, the primitive who dominates sections of *Aissa Saved* (1932), is only more unusual, not better, than Mr. and Mrs. Carr, the missionaries, and Bradgate, the district officer who does what Cary himself was told to do in Nigeria: "Act always so that the local native government, however primitive, can carry on without you." Marie Hasluck of *An American Visitor* (1933) has been called a caricature of an emancipated American woman journalist who writes out the "resuscitated fancies of Rousseau," but she is not implausible to anyone who has read the hopefully progressive journals of England and the United States. Nor is she portrayed as inferior or superior to Obai, the native convert who kills his master, or to Gore, the "inelastic" district officer who cannot adjust to the transition going on in his section of Nigeria. Similarly in *The African Witch* (1936), all of the main characters are treated with impartial vividness, whether they are traditionalists like

---

[2] A comprehensive and perceptive study of the first four novels that contains supplemental material from his letters and political writings is M. M. Mahood's *Joyce Cary's Africa* (1965).

Rackham, half-liberated natives like Aladai (who resembles Hamlet and Forster's Aziz and is different from either), or a strong believer in juju like Elizabeth. Though he has not yet learned how to integrate theme, character, and action, Cary has learned how to give life sympathetically to anyone who is free enough to have "strength in the faith, the only true faith, of the autonomous individual soul," to quote from his posthumous novel, *The Captive and the Free* (1959). As a consequence these early African novels are not mere colonial novels any more than *A Passage to India*, William Plomer's *Turbott Wolfe*, or Alan Paton's *Cry the Beloved Country* are. Cary's too many characters in too much action *are* plausible and significant enough to increase our understanding of man in the modern world anywhere and of the moral universe Cary sees everywhere.

Though any reviewer who did not see its promise was unperceptive, *Aissa Saved* is, apart from *Castle Corner* (1938), the least successful of these four early novels. Its principal action is the attempt of Ojo, Aissa, and the Carrs to convert the Mohammedan and pagan-dominated village of Kolu. Its principal interest is in the portrayal of Aissa and Ojo, who take Christianity, with the exception of its admonishment to be charitable, with disconcerting literalness. Ojo's illiterate translation of the Passion is magnificent.

> Then Jesus gave himself to the wicked judge . . . and they nailed his hands and feet to a wooden cross so that he died slow—slow. . . . He screamed for a whole day, friends—the pain was worse than fire—but in that way he made God sorry. . . . Now Jesus sits up there (he pointed to the sky), and if you ask him he will speak to God for you. He will ask God to forgive you and send you the rain.

Aissa's death at the end of the book, when she has a vision of heaven while she is being devoured by ants, is not imcomparable to the death of Christ that Ojo described:

> Jesus had taken her, he was carrying her away in his arms, she was going to heaven at last to Abba and Gajere. Immediately the sky was rolled up like a door curtain and she saw before her the great hall of God with pillars of mud painted white and red. God, in a white riga and a new indigo turban,

his hands heavy with thick silver rings, stood in the middle and beside him the spirit like a goat with white horns. Abba [Aissa's child] was sitting on its back and looking frightened and almost ready to cry. One of the angels was holding him and putting his cap straight. . . .

Aissa fearing that he would cry and disgrace himself . . . waved and beckoned to attract his attention. At once as if feeling that she was there he looked down at her and smiled gravely.

Aissa held out her arms to him and shouted, "Oh, you rascal." She could not help laughing at him. She was helpless with laughter.

There are no characters as movingly human as Ojo and Aissa in *An American Visitor* (1933), but, as a whole, it comes off better than *Aissa Saved.* One reason for this is that the novel has a closer approximation to an aesthetic center in the character of Marie Hasluck, the American visitor. Though Cary strays into the minds of nearly everyone at one time or another and though there are long intervals when the action is seen from other points of view, the novel centers about the transformation of Marie from a naïve Rousseauean to an intelligent accepter of the "fundamental injustice of the world" and the permanence of change.

At the start, because she is determined to find an earthly paradise among the Birri, Marie can write, "To pass from what we call civilization into this obscure district of Nigeria is like going out of a lunatic asylum where the keepers are crazier than the patients into a spring-morning of the Golden Age." Since Monkey Brewsher, the district officer, is opposed both to his Nigerian superiors and to missionaries such as the Dobsons who think "love . . . stronger than guns," and since he wants to work out a native creed from juju and "pump in the right kind of ethics," Marie is attracted to him, marries him, and works with him to bring all the Birri, who laugh even at the "word for nation," together under one great chief who will preserve them as they are and keep them from violence. As Marie observes increasingly the impossibility of her ideas, she wants to cry "for the silly young woman who had seen in a little community of naked savages the pattern of an earthly paradise," though she continues to admire Brewsher's faith even after he is killed in a native uprising by the most promising of his converts, Obai. And, after this uprising has been quelled by the civilizers and the Birri have been made safe for exploitation, Marie, looking back at her "education" in Nigeria, is given the final word:

> I didn't see that if Birri was safe, Monkey wouldn't be Monkey, and if the world was meant to be a safe place there wouldn't be any man like Monkey, and if no one was to die or suffer there wouldn't be any love, and if no one was to get killed there wouldn't be any life worth living.

This is very much like what Cary himself said in 1955 to the *Paris Review* interviewers:

> Roughly, for me, the principle fact of life is the free mind. For good and evil, man is a free creative spirit. This produces the very queer world we live in, a world in continuous change and insecurity.

Against this queer world in continuous creation and insecurity, all of Cary's characters are seen and contend. Indeed, one surmises that the obviously transitional character of Nigeria gave him the clue, as it did Marie Hasluck, to the "intensely dynamic world in creation" that all his novels explore with differing effectiveness. What he at first observed in the apparently primitive world of Africa he was later to find in his house of children (did Africa make him see his childhood in Ireland better or did his childhood in Ireland prepare him to understand Africa better?), in his Charlie, who is very like Aladai, Aissa, and Mr. Johnson, in his Sara, Wilcher, and Gulley, in the equally creative and equally disturbed characters of his political trilogy and of *The Captive and the Free*. There is an almost steady progression in his novels from the relatively simple character facing confusion to the very complex character facing it. Marie Hasluck is more complex than Aissa, Aladai than Marie, and so on throughout the novels.

Aladai, in *An African Witch* (1936), is the most complicated and sophisticated of Cary's native Nigerians. Well-educated at Oxford, heir presumptive to the Emirate in a part of Nigeria divided among pagans, half-Christians, Mohammedans, and white colonials, he becomes involved in inextricable difficulties as soon as he comes home from the university. When we first see him he is shocking the colonials by crossing the polo field with Judy Cotte, fiancée of Rackham, the district officer who thinks "there's nobody can be a bigger danger to himself and everyone else than the half-educated nigger." Before the novel closes Aladai discovers the impossibility of behaving as a "civilized" human being, for the half-educated white residents rebuff him either immediately or finally and he feels compelled to fall back upon the clever leadership of his sister, Elizabeth, who has never had her philosophy of life upset by contact with a culture other than her own. He dies a sacrificial death to show the white man and the natives that there is inherent virtue in Nigerians. He does not succeed in showing them this, but he does succeed in showing the reader, as Elizabeth does in another way, that there is a "fragment of spirit" in all Africans "which knew freedom and had pride, was enslaved inside them, blind and helpless, and forced to eat humiliation every day."

To this "fragment of spirit" which, one should remember, Cary saw when colonial civilization had barely begun to rise to the level sometimes achieved in Ghana and Nigeria,[3] Cary returns again in *Mr. Johnson*, 1939 (after *Castle Corner*, 1938, in which Andrew Wright counts ninety-three characters, in which I found none who arrested me for more than the briefest moments). In this novel artistic and philosophic maturity cohere. The very queer world of Africa is much the same as in the earlier novels—with poverty, ignorance, native despotism, and fumbling colonialism combining to make Fada more a confusion than a society—but this novel does not date as the others do. The major reason for the success of the book is the character of Mr. Johnson, the aesthetic center of the book with whom Cary empathizes more fully than he has with any earlier character. Mr. Johnson is a realistically conceived character, a symbol of the emergent African, of the emergent continent, and of the artist-rebel who, like "every living soul

---

[3] The current (1969) difficulties in both states show the persistence of both tribalism and disguised colonialism.

creates his own world and must do so." Small wonder that Cary did not write another novel about Africa, for in *Mr. Johnson* he both said what he had been trying to say about Africa and Africans and reached the central insight the remainder of his novels illustrate dramatically: Each man "uses his mind and his imagination to create a world satisfactory to himself. . . . He has to create, from childhood, because isolated. You see, he's free, and therefore he's isolated—the two things go together."[4]

Mr. Johnson is very isolated indeed. When he first appears he falls (through his freedom) into instantaneous love with Bamu, who is conservative as only a tribally conditioned native can be, and he determines to make his union with her a civilized marriage that will conform to his ideas, which are based upon a few novels, store catalogues, and what he has observed of missionaries at the school that miseducated him—"a compound of romantic sentiment and embroidered underclothes." His determination to create his own world is not confined to his marriage with Bamu, a failure he does not allow himself to recognize. He creates himself into becoming the good friend and advisor of Rudbeck, the district officer, into becoming the hero of the native population, an expert thief and informer, a cajoller of natives and Rudbeck into finishing the road that is to bring change, if not civilization, to Fada. Only with the roadbuilding does he succeed, for none of the district officers and none of the natives *are* able to see him with his own eyes. But he is never daunted, for he is a poet who can sing his way out of disaster. Like Cary he sees everything "twice as large and nine times as lovely." In the moods of gaiety that preponderate, "the more he swaggers the more he is charmed by all these nice people in this nice world; the nice trees, the nice sky, the nice sun. The very curve of his hat is a gesture of universal appreciation. He is full of gratitude to the whole world." Work is for him, when he sees sense in it, "a kind of festivity." When he is high with poetry and sings the poems that cannot be quoted out of context, he is welcome everywhere.

[4] As he told Sir David Cecil in a recorded interview published in *Adam*, November-December 1950.

His short, happy life—for he is executed when he is eighteen—is not all happy, of course. Deep depression, brothering deep joy, is often upon him because, like Padsy in *Castle Corner,* he created "an ideal world for himself," but unluckily "did not build facts into the structure." Yet gaiety is uppermost. Before his execution he dictates a letter to Bulteel, Rudbeck's superior who understood him not at all, which says, "I bless you and Judge Rudbeck for my happy life in de worl." No one who reads the novel can doubt either the sincerity or the accuracy of his judgment.

His death is inevitable, and it is at an earlier age than usual because he is a victim (he would never call himself that) of sudden transitions in the peculiar African situation that exaggerates and epitomizes the human situation. He likes "everybody who gives him the least excuse to do so," such as Rudbeck, who treats him with the "ordinary politeness which would be given to a butler or a footman." No one really understands *him.* Not his wife, not the colonial officers, not the natives. He is doomed to create his own happiness and his own death, a primitive existentialist who represents the total situation Cary sees. His tragicomedy is the prototype of what Cary presents in all his sad and gay novels that unsentimentally affirm the grandeur of being a human being in whom God tries his endless, incomprehensible, and glorious experiments.

Except in *A House of Children* (1941) in which Cary presents the nearly unmitigated happiness that may be the foundation of his happy-sad acceptance of this very queer world, all the novels that follow *Mr. Johnson* are tragicomedies. *Charley Is My Darling* (1940) is the saddest of all of them, though happiness often prevails. Like all Cary characters, Charley is in a jam. ("For me all characters are in a jam, all of us are in a jam, a special and incurable difficulty from which there is no escape. It contains all our lives and affects every aspect of our existence—we are born to freedom in a world condemned to be free, for its own good, for its own maintenance and for its own destruction," Cary later wrote.) Charley's jam is peculiarly difficult. Cary himself summarizes the novel in the preface to the definitive Carfax edition:

> Charley is a small boy, an evacuee, sent to the West Country from a London slum. He is found to have a dirty head and has to be shaved. This gives him a bad start with the other evacuees, who, jostling for position among themselves, unite to jeer at him. But being a child with imagination and nerve, he recovers his position and self-respect, and finally becomes a leader of gangs by various bold enterprises which at last land him in the courts.

Cary's summary is the bare bones of a very complicated novel that might be a transformation of Mr. Johnson to a slum evacuee, a novel about juvenile delinquency, a transformation of Gulley Jimson to childhood in the slums. Told in the historical present, like *Mr. Johnson,* in a dialect superlatively fitted to Charley and carefully centered about him, it is as good a novel as its immediate predecessor. One identifies with Charley as he submits to the shaving of his head and becomes "Lousey" to his associates, with his fearful joy when he becomes a gang leader, discovers a cave, paints a Jimson-like picture, makes love to Liz (a masterfully crude idyll), is host at a banquet at Burl House, where he and his gang have come to steal and destroy, lives for a while with Liz as his wife while the police hunt them, is finally separated from Liz by the police—all his created world crushed. What Charley experiences, Cary tells us in his preface, is what Cary might have experienced had he been born in similar surroundings. The crimes of the children, he says, could alternatively be called succumbing to temptation or to inspiration—moral experiments to find out what is good and what bad. The wrecking of Burl House (compare with hundreds of contemporary incidents) comes from "a rage against beauty and dignity by those who have neither but feel the want . . . above all from the secret hunger of a starved imagination, not only for aesthetic but moral comprehension."

There is another important meaning in the book, as Cary points out in his preface. Charley is entrapped like Hitler in "the ordinary dynamics of gangster politics" (which now rule half the world), the leader's need to invent new and exciting enterprises for his band. Neither in the preface nor in the novel is this implication stressed very strongly, but the book is given a philosophic dimension in such completely believable conversations as the following:

> "It's cruel," Harry says [about bull-baiting].
> "Cruel," Charley stares at him in contemptuous amusement. "Oos this chap?"
> "Don't mind im," Bill says. "E's a cissie—e's a Christian."
> "I ain't," Harry shouts.
>
> . . . . . . . . . . . . . .
>
> "Why are they so cruel?" [Liz asks after they have been discussing the beatings they've experienced]. "It ain't no fun hurting people."
> "They wip Jews to death in Germany," Charley says. "Jus go on beating till they pass out."
> "It's so wicked—arn't they afeard to do such turble things?"
> "You don't believe in hell, Lizzie, do you?"
> "I don know."
>
> . . . . . . . . . . . . . .
>
> "Burning fire for ever and ever. Thass cruel if you like."
> "But what you going to do with cruel people like they?" Lizzie gives a deep sigh.
> "I don't know, Lizzie. Shoot em. But they might shoot you first."
> "Perhaps there isn't no god neither," Charley suggests.

This conversation suggests quite as vividly and naturally as Ivy Compton-Burnett's similar choruses that Cary is "essentially a philosophical novelist," as Walter Allen says. "For Cary," he continues, "the central fact about man was his imagination, which was nothing if not creative, and involved every man in the effort 'to create a universe which suits his feelings.' Since each man's shaping fantasy was unique it clashed inevitably with those of his fellows and with the established order of society, and the result was tragic or comic, depending on how you looked at it." The truth of Allen's generalization can be seen in any of the novels, no matter how faulted. It is pre-eminently, dramatically, and unobtrusively true of the two trilogies that are his best work.

The first of these trilogies—*Herself Surprised* (1941), *To Be a Pilgrim* (1942), and *The Horse's Mouth* (1944)—is as experimental in form as any modern novel that avoids the portentously esoteric. The first two can be read as merely readable realistic fiction, *The Horse's Mouth* as high farce or as expressionistic fiction that resembles in mode and manner Gulley Jimson's own painting. The three of them together extend Conrad's method of circling "the truth" by the use of multiple narrators into a form that Derek Stanford has called (in *Books and Bookmen* for May 1957) "contemporary fiction according to the theory of relativity; a theory which, as Cary employs it, takes us much closer to the 'truth of personality' than any doctrine of realism." (Closer, I think, than Durrell's comparable experiment in the *Alexandria Quartet.*) In *Herself Surprised* you get Sara Monday as she sees herself as well as what she understands to be Tom Wilcher and Gulley Jimson. In *To Be a Pilgrim* you have Tom Wilcher's perception of himself and his world that extends back to the late nineteenth century and includes a group of men and women who represent different and important facets of the world that led to 1938, the year in which he writes his autobiographical memoir. In *The Horse's Mouth,* which is appropriately placed last, you get through Gulley Jimson's first-person narrative his view not only of Sara, Wilcher, and some Bohemian and lower-class others; you get also a statement of and an acting out of the Blakean philosophy Cary and Jimson accept. (In an unpublished essay on Blake quoted by Andrew Wright, Cary says that Blake "introduced me into a highly complex universe where what is called material is entirely dissolved into imaginative constructions and states of feeling, where matter, mind, and emotion, become simply different aspects of one reality.")

The quotations from Blake that go in and out of Gulley's mind throughout *The Horse's Mouth* are an unintrusive *coda,* like the conversation in earlier books, that gives a key to the significance of the entire trilogy. I have to be abstract about this significance, as Cary fortunately is not. Sara is the earth mother, concentrated on subsistence and persistence, generous and wayward, kind and uncomprehending, a more complex and completed Molly Bloom. Wilcher is the dreamer and reflector, torn between the pull of tradition and the thrust of change, compelled to be a pilgrim though only within himself. Jimson is the active, impulsive, feeling force that must realize itself in artistic creation, that uses the earth mother, that cares little for reflection or for those who reflect. To be still more abstract and Blakean, Sara is matter, Wilcher mind, Gulley emotion. Cary's scheme is quite as complex as Joyce's in *Ulysses* or Yeats's in *A Vision,* but he is also a novelist who is difficult in sense rather than in its communication, who has "a power of empathetic impersonation so far unequalled" in our age, as Pamela Hansford Johnson has said. "So that in the end," Lord David Cecil said in his recorded interview with Cary, "your book if it's going to mean anything really significant will be an illustration of the general law of life as you see it as well as a picture of that particular age—that particular man." Wisely for a novelist, Cary replied, "You start from the other end in fact . . . stick to the character wherever it leads."

It was admirable strategy for Cary to start his first trilogy with the first-person narrative of Sara Monday, *Herself Surprised.* Her narrative takes us from her early life as a servant through her marriage to Matt Monday, her alliances with Gulley Jimson and with Tom Wilcher, to her imprisonment as a thief that gives her the chance to write about her life. Though she is a free spirit within the limits of necessity, like all of Cary's favored characters, events happen to her; she does not make them happen but accepts what occurs with a joy that has little fear in it. Although she sees herself as "that fat, common trollop of a girl with a snub nose and the shining cheeks," and thinks she must have done wrong because she is imprisoned, she moves with marvelous amoral aplomb always. Though she gestures conventionally to please others, especially when she is with Matt Monday, conventionality is always for her a facade demanded by others. When Mr. Hickson, Gulley's "patron," tries to make love to her, she thinks, "after all, it was no great crime in Mr. Hickson, to be a man and like me as a woman. Or if it was so, then providence must answer for our shapes." When she poses half-naked for Gulley, she cannot tell whether she is doing "a religious thing or a bad one," anymore than she can be sure in church whether she is laced and dressed and scented "to an inch of my life, for the honor of God, or the lusts of the flesh." Almost anything can send her into ecstasy: a new Paris hat, a good kitchen (nowhere in literature, except sometimes in Thomas Wolfe—he and Cary would have liked each other—are the delights of the kitchen so beautifully celebrated as here), Matt's or Gulley's or Wilcher's delight in her, "three larks at a time trilling and tweeching as if the sun had got into their brains and made them glorious," clouds melting into the sky "like suds." She is herself and the earth mother who accepts everything that happens because it is in the nature of things.

But, though she accepts Matt Monday, Wilcher, and Mr. Byles because they need her and to be needed is pleasing, it is Gulley Jimson only that she accepts wholeheartedly. "Gulley was the most of man I ever knew. For he carried his own burden, which was a heavy one; and even if he was cruel, it was only when driven mad." At their best times, Sara says "it seemed to us both that the world was not big enough for our joys." And it is what she quotes from Gulley that represents best the attitude towards life she lived: "We ought to live in God as familiarly as in a lodging, diningroom, drawing-room, bedroom and kitchen. . . . Don't worry. . . . You're Mrs. Em and I'm Gulley Jimson and that fly on the wall has its own life too—as big as it likes to make it, and it's all one to God as the leaves to the tree." Sara's attitude towards Gulley points forward skillfully to the concluding novel of the trilogy that contains the heart of Cary's matter: "Oh no," she says of Gulley when he is under attack, "he's very sane—the other people are mad—to live as they do without happiness or God." Nor is this attitude pointed too tendentiously, for Sara, as she is presented in *Herself Surprised*, is immensely interesting and plausible for herself alone as well as for what she points forward to.

Tom Wilcher in *To Be a Pilgrim* is the man between, appropriately enclosed in the middle volume of the trilogy. He is not an accepter like Sara or a rebel like Gulley. He is free, like the two of them, but in his soul rather than in his actions. Of himself he says, "I have always been a lover rather than a doer; I have lived in dreams rather than acts; and like all lovers, I have lived in terror of change to what I love." Despite his terror of change and his feeling that the family place, Tolbrook, is "a holy place" rather than a relic, he is not merely a traditionalist. He is within himself a pilgrim, somehow forever deflected from action by meditation. He is a conscience that violates itself, a stingy man, an exhibitionist, a man almost senile who is wise and generous about the many and disparate people he loves and the times he knows must change and wishes would not. His account of his life is more intricately involved than Sara's or Gulley's, a slow rewarding second movement that necessarily follows the first and leads to the third.

Tom Wilcher's progress, as he tells it in old age, adds the dimension of time to the trilogy. Sara takes the changing times in her stride, barely noticing; Gulley seems to live outside both time and change, in the eternity of creating something permanent. Wilcher, as his telling goes back and forth from Victorian to Edwardian to Georgian to Hitler time in an old man's ramble that makes sense, impresses upon us both change and the permanence in it. Through his eyes we see the time when Gladstone was a hero to his father, an impediment to progress for himself and his brother Edward, who became a successful "radical" politician; the early-century time when his brother William was a stolid soldier who married Amy simple-mindedly, expecting to be happy and succeeding, while Edward became eminent despite his life with his mistress Julie that was always about to become a public scandal; the time of war, Boer and First World, when Tom was a hospital nurse and when one of his nephews was killed in action; the unquiet twenties when change was for its own sake and a palliative to the immense injustice of things; the thirties when, dying, he lovingly disapproves of his relatives Robert and Ann, who have an unhappy "modern" marriage, are very "practical" about material progress and very worried about Hitler. His never-satisfied pilgrim's quest is to fit the old and the new together, to love the good in the old and recognize the inevitability of the new—even if it concentrates more on an improvement in mattresses than on an improvement in manners and morals. But, though Wilcher is intensely aware of time and change and rebels against those "who hate the past, not because it is old, but because it might give . . . something unexpected, and disturb . . . complacent littleness," he is, like Sara and Gulley, the creator of his own universe. Generally too intellectual and knowing it, he is capable of ecstasy in his love of Sara, in Blakean moments when, looking at a lime tree, he feels God's presence "within that burning tree," and feels his "very consciousness . . . dissolved in sensation." Intensely aware of time and in rebellion against many of the changes he must accept, still he transcends time and his own intellectuality to live in others with whom he empathizes rather than sink into excluding self-centeredness. For him Sara is the ideal, "one of those people to whom faith is so natural that they don't know how they have it." And, despite his almost perpetual meditations about God's way as bad and good times reveal it, what he admires most is the people unlike himself, "like those simple Indian nuns, who, unable to comprehend anything of theology or even to read, nevertheless are so often closer to God than the most learned professors. They are free. . . ." The man between who never knows freedom as fully as Sara or Gulley or his sister Lucy, who does God's work "out of deviltry," he is a pilgrim in his meditative quest of freedom and would have admired Gulley had he known him better.

Gulley lives freedom with an energy that is eternal delight. From the time he gave up respectability to become an artist, he has been his own law though he is not without awareness of the laws that he disregards. He is a Blakean anarchist who makes allowances for other people doing what they like as well as himself. With cheerful laughter and unscrupulous cunning, he goes his own way, stealing, cheating, accepting the blocks to his own way happily, never complaining when necessity knocks him down. He knows there must be millionaires who want to own art they cannot understand, critics who try to make themselves more important than those they criticize, women like Sara who can "commit adultery at one end and weep for her sins at the other, and enjoy both operations at once," accepters like Plantie who have had a hard time and like to be told that in God's sight they are dirt, philosophizers like Wilcher as he

misunderstands him, "murmuring to themselves and uttering
faint sighs in a spectrous world of abstractions, gibbering and
melting into each other like a lot of political systems and
religious creeds," ugly boys like Nosy "who aspire to martyrdom
or fame," dictators like Hitler who have ideas and want to see
them omnipotent, *the* law: "A man who cuts a throat because
of imagination is hanged by a judge who is appointed to keep
imagination in order."

But all of these are obstructions he must love (like Sara and
Nosy), use (like the collectors), disregard (like the philosophizers, weepers, and dictators), or overcome, like the law and
the raw material out of which he creates art, like old age to
which he refuses to give in. He lives freedom in his life and
art. He is always serious, never solemn, as able to laugh at
himself as at anybody else. He does not pretend to judge the
epic paintings of the fall and the creation he must paint. Looking
at his painting of the fall, he cannot decide whether he sees
something the critics would wordily call great "or a piece of
barefaced pornography that ought to be dealt with by the
police." With the multiple irony that characterizes most of his
sayings, he talks about his son Tom, who "went to a good school
and it cured him of art before he was fifteen. And see where
he is now. A gentleman and a scholar. Who doesn't know an
illustration from a picture." In context, what he says means
that he is against art, against schools, against the proper
gentleman and scholar, against the many who have no feeling
for art, yet *for* all of them too, for art must be for *his* own
sake, and schools, gentlemen and scholars and dim viewers are
part of the unavoidable surroundings of any artist or rebel at
any time. With irony multiplied, he speaks of the Beeders'
freedom and friendliness: "Liberty hall. Everything shared
because there is too much. . . . Richesse oblige. . . . They get
past being shocked before they are out of school, just as they
get over religion and other unexpected feelings. . . . God bless
the millionaires who can forgive everything unless it bothers
them too much."

Gulley's energy is eternal delight, an expression of what
everyone might become and rarely does, what Sara often uncon-

sciously is, what Wilcher would like to have. The starting paragraph sets the tone that is never violated:

> I was walking by the Thames. Half-past morning on an autumn day. Sun in a mist. Like an orange in a fried fish shop. All bright below. Low tide, dusty water and a crooked bar of straw, chicken boxes, dirt and oil from mud to mud. Like a viper swimming in skim milk. The old serpent, symbol of nature and love.

> Five windows light the caverned man: through one he breathes the air
> Through one hears music of the spheres; through one can look
> And see small portions of the eternal world.

Gulley is always seeing small or great portions of the eternal world firmly fleshed and transfigured by imagination. Like Blake, whom he resembles and quotes with insistent pertinence, he can love without the help of anything on earth. He loves Adam's leg in the painting of the fall because it says: "I walk for you, I run for you, I kneel for you. But I have my self-respect." He loves, because they are, "old black rooks flapping down the sky and old black taxicabs flapping down the street." Thought he likes Plantie, the weeping spinozist, he doesn't like Spinoza, for Gulley doesn't have any self-respect and is an optimist: "I get a lot of fun out of fun, as well as the miseries." He can't hate an individual man: "To forgive is wisdom, to forget is genius." He doesn't care about fame, "a grass that grows in any dirt, when no one's looking." He cannot pity himself or others: "Pity is a whore. It gets inside you and sucks your blood." He has no time for the God of creeds (nor do any of Cary's major characters): "Vengeance is mine, saith the Lord. Safer to leave it to him. He won't do anything about it. It's not his game. He's too busy getting on with the next thing." For Gulley the fall is a fine thing: "Science destroying the law of the old Panjandrum. The fall into manhood, into responsibility, into sin. Into freedom. Into wisdom. Into the light and the fire. Every man his own candle." He has Emerson's temerity about sometimes being like God. Painting Sara's top arm, he blows "an angel's trumpet." Painting he transforms a canvas "into a spiritual fact, an eternal beauty. I am God." Dying of a stroke he incurred (appropriately) while working on his painting of the creation, he tells Nosy, his one faithful hero-worshipper, "Get rid of that sense of justice, Nosy, or you'll feel sorry for yourself and then you'll soon be dead. . . . Go love without the help of anything on earth." On his death bed, when the nun says, "It's dangerous for you to talk, you're very seriously ill," he replies:

> "Not so seriously as you're well. How don't you enjoy life, mother. I should laugh all around my neck at this minute if my shirt wasn't a bit on the tight side."
> "It would be better for you to pray."
> "Same thing, mother."

Gulley Jimson's pilgrimage, dramatized by a multitude of seriously amusing incidents is, like Aissa's, Mr. Johnson's, Sara's, Wilcher's, a journey to joy that recognizes the misery included in the immense injustice in the universe. Soberly, improbably, believably, Cary's account of this pilgrimage in *The Horse's Mouth* caps the realism of *Herself Surprised* and *To Be a Pilgrim*. It says with almost hilarious seriousness what life can nearly be, could nearly be, if we were all as sane as Gulley, not mad like the people who do not believe in or try for happiness. With the exaggeration of expressionism, it tells how a violent, innocent urge for freedom can transcend the conditions of necessity to which it must also submit. It shows what is incipient in the partially captivated lives of Sara and Wilcher while it admiringly and implicitly criticizes their more realistic ordinariness. *The Horse's Mouth* is, I believe, Cary's best novel, the appropriate climax to his other good and middling and bad novels as well as to the trilogy that it concludes. But this is not to say that it should have concluded his work as a novelist. Very good, perhaps more soberly commendable, novels were to follow. The great gusto, the insight into joy's possibility, diminish; Cary's wisdom and command of his art fortunately remained undiminished, almost.

As Andrew Wright and others have observed, Cary is more notable for his creation of characters than for his command of plot. This does not mean that there is not enough action in all the novels. Each of the many short chapters in the novels from *Aissa Saved* to *The Captive and the Free* contains an incident. Once Cary conceived a character in a situation, his imagination rioted with possible happenings. Though he controlled these happenings after his apprentice period better than some critics will allow—for example, he cut out his favorite chapter from *The Horse's Mouth* on structural grounds—there can be no doubt that he always allowed the happenings he so quickly created to tumble over each other. When he was intimately enough inside the controlling characters, as in *Mr. Johnson, Charley Is My Darling,* and the first trilogy, the rush of incidents does not too much matter since we, like him, are intensely curious about *anything* they may do. Indeed, it is as silly to complain about the way the incidents tumble over each other in the better novels as it is to complain of a similar plethora of incidents in Fielding or Dickens. It is enough to note that he is not a master of structure like James or Forster. Then add: he has virtues they have not that redeem him.

These virtues are evident even in the two poorest of his later novels, *The Moonlight* (1946) and *A Fearful Joy* (1949). Both of them are lively, sometimes wise, almost all the time very readable. *The Moonlight,* a favorite with Cary himself and intended to be an answer to Tolstoy's *Kreuzer Sonata,* is a good fictional argument against the suppression of the sexual impulse (though not as good as several of Lawrence's novels and stories with the same theme) and an interesting chronicle of the way two Victorian women's lives interlock in love and hate. Rose Venn, who has "terrible power" because she is too unselfish, and Ella Venn, who instinctively rebels against both the Victorian distrust of passion and the Victorian admiration of "unselfish" power, are admirably characterized with the appropriate amount of sympathy and deprecation dramatically implied. But the other characters, of whom there are too many involved in too many incidents, blur into the background instead of standing out. This fault in artistic handling that always plagued Cary when he was determined to cover too much time, is still more apparent in *A Fearful Joy.* What Tabitha, a middle-class Sara Monday, and Bonser, a debased Gulley, do

is interesting on a first reading and so is the hurried survey of
the intellectual and social currents from the 1880s to the 1940s.
On rereading, it appears that Cary too courageously tried to
get every kind of character and movement into one novel. The
consequence is that Tabitha, the author's eye rather than a
real self like Sara, and what happens to her and in history, are
not memorable but unrememberable. The few sections that
stick in the mind—such as Ella's plotting to get her daughter
Amanda and Harry together in *The Moonlight,* and Tabitha's
grand days as a grocer's mistress and accepted hostess to the
liberated—do not justify the quantity of pages, incidents, and
characters spent, except as one recalls them as pleasant reading
amidst too much that nearly becomes dull. Perhaps they were
an inevitable marking time until Cary became engrossed in his
last four novels.

The Nimmo trilogy—*Prisoner of Grace* (1952), *Except the
Lord* (1953), and *Not Honour More* (1955)—lacks the verve and
gusto of the earlier trilogy, but it has virtues that almost or
quite raise it to as high a level. The very fact that it can be
called the Nimmo trilogy points to one of its virtues. Though
he is seen from the point of view of Nina, his wife, and Jim
Latter, his enemy who becomes Nina's second husband, as well
as from his own point of view, Chester Nimmo is the center
of all three novels. The early trilogy might be called the Sara-
Wilcher-Gulley novels because of the almost equal emphasis
upon three totally different representatives of humanity. There
is another differing virtue in the Nimmo trilogy. It deals with
more complex individuals involved in more complicated situations, for Nina is Cary's one portrait of a highly aware woman
and Chester is perhaps the most fully realized representation
of a politician in modern literature.

As the reader pieces the story together from Cary's intricate
presentation of three points of view, it goes something like
this. Chester Nimmo, the poor son of a lay preacher who
thought the second coming was at hand, becomes first a union
leader, then an adroit Liberal who rises to power with Lloyd
George, becomes a member of the cabinet, falls from power at
about the same time Lloyd George does, and tries without

success to rise to power again by manipulating the various forces at work in the General Strike of 1926. His rise and fall as a politician are intimately involved with his personal life. The impetus for his becoming a union leader comes from his personal experience with extreme poverty in the 1870s, from sharing the evangelical fervor of his father (though not his father's acquiescence to what seems to be the manifestation of God's will), and from his contact with Marxist and non-Marxist radicals. His rise to political power is partially, perhaps importantly, due to his marriage to Nina, whom he marries when she is pregnant with Jim Latter's child. His fall is in part the consequence of external circumstances, in part the consequence of a worsening of his relationship with Nina.

These are the bare bones of a plot that has depth, coherence, and vividness. Nina and Jim Latter, though their positions in the novels are secondary to Chester's, are of interest in themselves, and so are a multitude of minor characters who fill out the background but do not clutter it. Nina, though she calls herself "a very ordinary kind of woman who simply wants to be happy without giving too much trouble," is actually extraordinary emotionally and intellectually. Emotionally her desire to be happy includes her desire to love Jim Latter in a way that reminds us of the way Constance Chatterley loves Mellors. Her three children, one conceived before her marriage to Chester, one while she is married to him, one after she has married Latter, are all Latter's. Yet she feels the emotional necessity to comfort Chester by going to bed with him even after she has divorced him and married Latter. Intellectually she comes closer than anyone else in the trilogy (and without any violation of her character) to understanding politics, Chester Nimmo, and Jim Latter. Latter is simpler but not simple. Preeminently a soldier who feels he could not love Nina so much if he did not prefer honor, he is also ardently in favor of letting the African Negroes develop their own civilization, is against any kind of pacifism, is very much opposed to the organized workers in the General Strike and to the communists he thinks are behind it, is for a kind of honorable fascism, for adultery while Nina is married to Chester, against it when she is married to him, is simple-minded (perhaps) in his acceptance of conservative clichés but not simple-emotioned nor unadmirable, though he tries to kill Nimmo and does "execute" Nina. The minor characters, except for Pring, a Liberal's caricature of a Marxist, are both vivid and relevant. Nimmo's father, a believable and likeable religious bigot; Georgina, the sister who rebels against her father though she dies of tuberculosis rather than leave him uncared for; Aunt Latter, an off-beat aristocrat; Fred Coyte, the worthless, pathetic son of a too-domineering mother—these and others make the texture within which Nimmo is seen, rich, to say nothing of the physical background which is seen extensively with Cary's distinguished intensity.

But the political, philosophical, human mystery that holds the trilogy together and provides its psychological suspense is the character Nimmo and his actions as they are variously interpreted by himself, Latter, and Nina. Is he the dangerous humbug Latter usually sees him as, the fundamentally religious man (who has inevitably sinned) he sees himself to be, the combination of hypocrite and great man Nina sees him to be? As Granville Hicks has said, Cary never tells you; it is up to you as reader to draw your conclusions. Certainly he is, like almost every politician or man of note, something of what he himself, Nina, and Latter believe him to be. Nina, I think, comes closest to seeing him whole; Latter is farthest from seeing the truth about him (naturally). Nina says "that Chester's imagination suggested to him every day hundreds of truths and it was always easy for him to find among them one that 'suited' him." She says also that he was "a religious man"; even "if he had stopped taking much interest in God, he still believed in 'freedom' and 'brotherhood' and the 'rights of the individual.'" She says that "he really did believe that if you pretend people are good (as he had praised my 'goodness' to make me better) they will become good." She says also, though there are times when she denies this judgment, that there "is less 'hypocrisy' and 'machiavellianism' among politicians" than there is among ordinary people.

What Nina says of Nimmo and even what Latter sometimes says of him or reports him as saying, all of the complex and beautifully integrated sayings and doings of the trilogy, make us believe that Chester believed in his father's favorite Psalm: "Except the Lord build the house, their labour is but lost that build it; except the Lord keep the city, the watchman waketh but in vain." Whatever his falls from integrity—those he admitted, those he did not, those of which he was not aware—Chester Nimmo was more a good than a bad politician, even a great though humanly limited man, the sort of man Cary explicitly in his political pamphlets, implicitly in his novels and poems, hoped would recur and have more importance than he feels such a man does in our times, against which he writes:

> The world itself is young, we are but little removed from the time when writing was a wonder, when any written speech was magic. Words printed in books—Rousseau, Proudhon, Owen, Marx, what power they can wield. But it is the power of sorcerers—the spell they cast is abracadabra. And the fruit of their sorcery is egotism and madness, war and death.
>
> So evil is the brood of the slogans that the most splendid and noble cries, Liberty, Equality, Fraternity, bred nothing but new and more cunning, more hypocritical despots, better organized murder, popular nationalism drunk with the conceit of hooligans, militarism as the tool of demagogues, hatred not to be assuaged by the blood of millions and a century of tears.
>
> Trace now the record of another, a modest and unconsidered force, an influence little more noticed by the learned and the propagandists, the word-wielders, than the play of the English weather—the daily, weekly ministrations of fifty thousand servants of the Lord.

The words are Nimmo's and appropriate to his character, but they are Cary's also, as his last novel, *The Captive and the Free,* makes clear. It is about the learned and the propagandists and the word-wielders and the servants of the Lord, those who are captive and those who are free because they are not soft idiots murmuring "me" but liberated servants of Cary's unconventional God who permits immense injustice in order to allow freedom of choice.

In *The Captive and the Free,* Cary is more explicit about what he is for and what he is against than in any of the other novels. Since he knew he was dying when he was writing this novel and revising his Cambridge lectures, *Art and Reality*

(1958), it is not unnatural that he became in these two books less the chameleon of modern fiction, more the seer who would persuade us to rejoice while we recognize fundamental injustice. That there was much he held against the changes in modern times which he held to be inevitable, every reader who has penetrated the consummate disguise of his art must have recognized long before. The African novels are against the necessary fumbling of colonialism in an age of transition. The two contrasting pictures of childhood in *A House of Children* and *Charley Is My Darling* are implicit condemnations of what adults have made of children. His first trilogy is a condemnation of a society that cannot accept a naturally religious woman who also does what is natural, a dreamer and seeker who finds his truth only by exploring himself intensively, an artist who can neither conform nor give up. Not that Cary ever complains about what he condemns. In some form or other what is has always been and will forever be. Man can never escape "the dilemma of the free individual soul, separated by the very nature of his individuality from the real of which he is nevertheless a part." "The world is inescapably shot through with luck, because it is also shot through with freedom." An even more explicit statement than the above (from *Art and Reality*), is quoted by Andrew Wright from an unpublished play in which an African faith-healer, a combination of Preedy and Syson in *The Captive and the Free,* says:

> The truth is "That life is hard and dangerous; that he who seeks his own happiness, does not find it; that he who is weak, must suffer; that he who demands love, will be disappointed; that he who is greedy, will not be fed; that he who seeks peace, will find strife; that truth is only for the brave; that joy is only to him who does not fear to be alone; that life is only for the one who is not afraid to die."

Not his best novel, because he was unable to complete it himself and because he more obviously takes sides than in his better books, *The Captive and the Free* is a fitting last testament to the world he loved and found fault with. Preedy, the faith-healer who has seduced a girl of fourteen, the girl he seduced, and Syson, the modernist clergyman who opposes Preedy violently and is led to faith by him, are the free, those who can love without the help of anything on earth (like all of Cary's sympathetic characters). They are set against this "modern world of pressure groups and propaganda," against its representatives, such as Hooper, who will publicize faith-healing if it diminishes his feeling of nothingness by bringing him success, against Clarry, who shrugs off the problem of evil, against Syson's bishop, whose "qualified optimism . . . had got him a bishopric and might take him even further if he could keep in with the press." All of the free characters lose, as far as the world outside themselves is concerned. Preedy, at the end of the novel, is about to become, with Alice Rodker, whom he seduced, "the story of the year": "the poor little girl seduced and ruined by a person who . . . has such power over her still that he recalls her to his side and beats her up as a reward." Syson goes to prison for libel but he finds there an individual truth that replaces his institutional one and that makes him free and happy, just as Alice and Preedy will remain as free and as happy as the universe allows despite becoming "the story of the year." It is, like most of Cary's books, a tragicomedy that is neither dispiriting nor incompatible with an intense joy in living.

Appropriately so, for Cary is, in a sense that goes beyond all pigeonholing, a writer comparable to Shakespeare. He identifies with his major characters, with their feeling for the fearful joy of existence so purely that, while one reads, one lives them rather than judges them. But, when one thinks back, one sees that all of them, from Aissa to Syson, are products of the tragic vision, as Richard B. Sewall has recently defined it: "It sees man as questioner, naked, unaccommodated, alone, facing mysterious, demonic forces in his own nature and outside. . . . It is not for those who cannot live with unsolved questions or unresolved doubts." Cary's tragic vision—nearly always in his better novels, sometimes in all of them—happily presents the fearful joy of the sensitive and maladjusted who are never defeated totally by conditions within or without themselves. Overcome by flaws within and circumstances without, Cary's characters continuously affirm the joyful dignity of the human individual who must say yes to what he knows will overwhelm him.

## Chapter Nine

# L. P. Hartley: Diffident Christian

IN A SYMPOSIUM ABOUT the "new novelists" in *The London Magazine* (1958), L. P. Hartley was ranked among "the best" of them by three of the four contributors. Since Hartley was in his mid-sixties it is slightly strange that the well-informed contributors thought of him as a contemporary. Although he is esteemed in England and, to a lesser degree, in America, there is no mention of even his name in seven books having sections on contemporary British fiction that have appeared within the last ten years. In five other recent books and pamphlets of about the same time, he is dismissed with a flattering paragraph or page. The one exception among these is Walter Allen's British Council pamphlet, *The Novel Today,* in which there are two perceptive pages devoted to Hartley.[1] None of Hartley's novels has sold as well as several of those of Kingsley Amis and Elizabeth Bowen, whom he surpasses or equals in stature. There has been only one extended treatment of his work, Peter Bien's *L. P. Hartley* (1963), which exaggerates the effect of psychoanalysis upon him and deals with his novels too much as though they were case histories, though Hartley, characteristically, speaks well of a book that overplays an influence he believes he acquired by osmosis.

From what I have seen and heard it appears that there is only desultory knowledge of his work even among such informed contributors as those in *The London Magazine* symposium. Anthony Quinton calls *The Boat* (1949) "the nearest thing to a great novel that I can discern in the postwar years," apparently disregarding the trilogy *Eustace and Hilda* (1947) and Hartley's other fine novels. Lettice Cooper agrees about Hartley's stature but selects as examples *The Go-Between* (1953) and the first volume of *Eustace and Hilda* (*The Shrimp and the Anemone,* 1944; American title, *The West Window,* 1945), about which she talks as though it were a separated novel. Maurice Cranston is the only one of the three who speaks of Hartley as a writer "over forty," and therefore, though he agrees about his excellence as a novelist, he specifies no books. Such desultory comment may be English offhandedness or legitimate difference in taste, but I wonder why no one mentioned *My Fellow Devils* (1951) or considered his trilogy as an entity. Perhaps, even in these days of quickly swelling and subsiding reputations, Hartley is, as Cranston says, "the sort of writer who has to win his recognition slowly"; perhaps the fact that he published no novel between *Simonetta Perkins* (1925) and the first volume of the *Eustace and Hilda* trilogy (1944) accounts for his neglect. Certainly Hartley's quiet, unpretentious fiction, which to an unusual degree only *implies* our age of anxiety, deserves consideration as serious as that which should be given any written in our century.

Admittedly it would be easy to underestimate Hartley if one happened to pick up the wrong novel or even the wrong two or three novels. Despite the fact that he has never written meretriciously and has always felt it to be the novelist's responsibility to show in his work a feeling "as strong as, or stronger than, the feeling he has for his own life," like every novelist he has sometimes failed in part. All of his novels are worth reading but it scarcely seems mandatory that the reader who has time for only the best should read most of his short stories (five volumes, including *Night Fears*, 1924, his first, and *Two for the River*, 1961, his best), or his novels *Simonetta Perkins* (1925), *A Perfect Woman* (1955), and *The Hireling* (1957). Although one of his major preoccupations—the difficult fight of the individual to distinguish between God's orders and what society, increasingly oppressive and increasingly inclined to level down, demands—appears in both his first novel and in *Facial Justice* (1960), *Simonetta Perkins* is spoiled a little by too sedulous apeing of Henry James, just as *A Perfect Woman* is hurt by a plot that commands the characters' actions too clearly,

---

[1] Allen treats Hartley more extensively in *The Modern Novel in Britain and the United States* (1964), which is titled *Tradition and Dream* in England. Anthony Burgess's page on Hartley in *The Novel Now* (1967) is perceptive. So is James Hall's essay in *The Tragic Comedians* (1963).

and *The Hireling* is marred by its melodramatic ending. Better than these three but not as good as his best are *My Fellow Devils* and *Facial Justice*. His best novels are the *Eustace and Hilda* trilogy, *The Boat*, and *The Go-Between*, three of the most significant works published in our century. Though it is better than *A Perfect Woman* or *The Hireling*, Hartley's recent duology —*The Brickfield* (1964) and *The Betrayal* (1966)—does not seem to me to be as good as the three I consider Hartley's best. *The Brickfield*, an experiment in handling a tale within a conversation, is an illuminating variation on the theme of *The Go-Between*. *The Betrayal*, which shows the consequence of overtrusting and misunderstanding the conversation of *The Brickfield*, reveals many interesting things about Richard, the not-hero but is structured loosely.[2]

Hartley's three most distinguished works do not make their claim to permanence in an obvious way. (Except in *The Brickfield*, one does not find startling stylistic innovations in his work.) Though he has learned the lesson of Henry James about a central point of view defined clearly, he allows himself liberties that suggest the "old fashionedness" of E. M. Forster and the nineteenth-century English novelists. His style does not call attention to itself as frequently as that of, say, Virginia Woolf, because it is submerged in substance. Though he has read widely and has lectured often about the novelists of the past and present and has absorbed more about depth psychology than many psychiatrists, he never gives a pyrotechnical display of what he knows, as Aldous Huxley upon occasion does. His apparent scope is not a great deal wider than that of Jane Austen or Ivy Compton-Burnett. Like them, his method is to suggest the great world by intensively representing the smaller world most individuals habituate. With Hartley, substance is the main thing and even this he approaches cautiously, circuitously, more like a birdwatcher than a hunter. As Walter Allen says in his pamphlet *The Novel Today*, "On the face of it, his world is a small one, and apparently demure; yet it reflects in the uncanniest way the violence and the moral con-

---

[2] *Poor Clare* (1968) is a better novel than its two predecessors. The disposing of Poor Clare's objets d'art makes a fine fictional parable about holy dying.

flicts of the much larger world from which it is seemingly isolated."

Hartley's *Facial Justice* (1960) is as interesting a novel about what the future may be as *1984* and *Brave New World*. I start with it because it presents his basic attitude toward life more explicitly than his other books. It differs from other good not-Utopias in its only superficial relationship to science fiction. ("I know nothing about science and couldn't even invent a bogus chemical formula," he has said.) It is, as he intended, "a sort of satire on present day trends in English life, set in the future." More specifically, it is about his central preoccupation: the difficulty of maintaining individuality in a society that impinges increasingly upon personal freedom and attempts to make us all identical.

The time of *Facial Justice* is long after the Third World War has driven the twenty million survivors into prepared caverns where they have become beasts with faint longings to become human. The story centers about Jael 97. She is among the braver half who have followed an ambiguously benevolent dictator, "The Voice," out onto the denuded British earth (where the climate is "perpetual March") after the danger of fallout has disappeared. Jael 97 begins as an Alpha, which means that she is one of the relatively few who have not been Beatified by substituting, for their own, *the* face that pleases everyone and that a panel of psychologists has chosen. Her gradual development into the leader of rebellion involves her in an accident, and she becomes Beatified without her consent while in a hospital. But she is never brainwashed by the hidden persuaders; she remains an individual revolted by and revolting against the dictatorship which apparently tries to abolish pain, love, idealism, and the right to know and become oneself. Finally the dictator— who perhaps felt, like Dostoevsky's Grand Inquisitor, that it was necessary to treat men and women like indistinguishable children because they could not govern themselves—is defeated and life in Britain returns to chaos. Significantly the dictator's last works, and this is the first time God has entered the book, are "God bless you all." Michael, a human counterpart of

Milton's angel, who has, like Jael 97, developed into the freedom of responsibility, is left alone with her, hoping for a future. The implication is that after living with their sentience carefully concealed in the Eden that "The Voice" invented, they are to emerge into a world where a continual struggle for existence is as necessary as it appears to be in the Old Testament, that they will ultimately find and help others find freedom within responsibility.

Within this framework most of Hartley's preoccupations appear. "The Voice" is a good-bad woman who has more hope for than trust in human nature and who sometimes seems like the voice of the people that is the voice of God. In the imperfect society that she "benevolently" dictates to, only horizontal aspiration is commendable. Vicarious and counterfeit emotions are safer than real ones. Although it is sometimes allowed, the exercise of free will is discouraged by making it a risk to one's life. To get out aggressions and make things peaceful, all countries (and one never travels) are made to seem beatific and the people are encouraged to make jokes and cartoons that satirize their dictator. Partly because of the after-effects of fallout, the natural is discouraged or absent. Love is a pleasant sexual twitch. Real flowers rarely grow and, when they do, they are considered inferior to artificial ones, which last longer. The means is Voluntary Persuasion, a technique comparable to the subliminal advertisements we've heard were tried on television. The entertainments are as sedating as most London and Broadway plays and most best sellers. If a change in standards is necessary the advised maxim is: "It is easier to lower a standard than to raise one." Individuality is this society's most serious virus with the exception of the infrequent appearance of excellence. The attitude towards excellence is masterfully parodied in a review Jael writes about the performance of an inexpert pianist, whose performance followed that of an exceptionally gifted one who had left the audience stunned to quietness. Jael 97's parody is altogether in keeping with the society's ideas about language, as represented in *The Daily Leveler,* which aims to "standardize the language . . . so that no one shall be better at writing than anybody else."

Nevertheless the impulse toward individuality, toward real feeling, toward "goodness," toward the realizations of responsible freedom persists in Jael 97, Michael, and some others. The conclusion of the book makes it evident that the dictator herself has constructed this unbrave new world because, like the Bolsheviks after the Russian Revolution, she believed dictatorship the only way to overcome the inherent bestiality that life in the caverns had accentuated. Actually, she wants her "subjects" to dare free will as they do when they risk their lives in the motor expeditions to the Western Tower[3] of Ely Cathedral, which survived the holocaust of World War III. She fears and hopes that people will bet on themselves rather than try to better themselves. She fails, as Hartley perhaps believes all rulers must. Often here, and in Hartley's other books, human nature seems fated to be mangled by conflict between the desire to be oneself and the fear that to be oneself is to violate either God's arcane mandates or what society pretends God demands. How to distinguish which is which, a few of the characters in Hartley's novels learn no more easily than we can.

*Facial Justice* and the other novels show that Hartley is an immensely gifted, stumbling Christian whose characters, like himself, fear and tremble because it is difficult to discriminate between their own wishes and those God ordained. Like Milton (but more awarely) he seems to be as often on Satan's side as on God's. At least, it is the tension between the apparently Satanic will to self-expression and the apparently Godlike force that impedes self-expression, that induces the conflicts in his novels from *Simonetta Perkins* to *Facial Justice*. "I never thought," Simonetta Perkins says in Hartley's first novel, "that one result of wrong doing was to ease the temper. I feel like an angel." But she is never more sure of salvation than a religious existentialist. Appropriately her moment of ecstasy passes into tears. It seems likely that Jael 97 and Michael felt much the same at the conclusion of *Facial Justice*. Indeed all

---

[3] The Western Tower appears in Hartley's three most recent novels. It is a clear reminder of his Christian belief in immortality as well as an effectively recurring symbol.

of Hartley's characters in all of his novels ultimately feel both ecstasy and anxiety about the human situation in which one is alone, sometimes guided, sometimes looking up at the sky and seeing a blank blue. Hartley's view of humanity was affected by World War I quite as much as that of the other authors considered here; Richard emphasizes this in both *The Brickfield* and *The Betrayal:* "It wasn't until the 1914 War that I began to have doubts about human nature. . . . You can have no idea . . . of the feeling of security there was at that time."

The plots that convey Hartley's meaning in a style that does not call attention to itself are of course important to a consideration of his novels. Except in *A Perfect Woman,* too patly planned, *The Hireling,* too melodramatically closed, and *The Betrayal,* too packed with incidents, the plots are always tense vehicles of meaning and the characters, round or flat, control the action rather than the other way around. Except for the most intense moments his style is appropriate rather than extraordinary. A typical example of his writing from one of his less successful novels, *A Perfect Woman,* reads:

> Suddenly, from the midst of the flatness at her feet, a long billow began to form. Fascinated, she watched it mounting up, a hump of green water, marbled with foam, moving slowly towards her. Gradually it curved inwards, till it was as tall and hollow as a wave in a Japanese print. Then a crest began to form and the whole mass toppled forwards.

Here, the use of "hump," of "marbled," of the comparison to "a wave in a Japanese print," stand out if one examines the passage out of context. Read in context—and this is generally true—the style of the passage is a transparent vehicle through which we see characters in actions that constitute a criticism of life.

The novels themselves have the unity in variety that Winckelmann thought was the primary requirement of any work of art. Hartley's primary preoccupation is with the efforts of men and women to realize themselves without offending God more than is human and without offending society more than is necessary. Naturally this involves the desire to please oneself and others without being overwhelmed by guilt or impelled to punish others or oneself. It is interesting to notice that these preoccupations are obsessive in both Christianity deeply felt and the depth psychology of Freud and his followers whom Hartley understands, though he has not read them.

Viewed from this vantage point one can say oversimply that his novels as a whole form a progressing variety within a modified but fundamentally unchanging unity. *Simonetta Perkins* is the story of a repressed young woman's short "affair" with a Venetian gondolier. The conflict is mainly interior (though her mother and her memory of her past are almost an external conflicting force). Both depth psychology and Christianity are involved in the internal conflict. Simonetta has rejected four suitors who pleased her mother. Her repressed sexuality is clear in expressions of anger and meanness that she disapproves though they give her a sense of release. Her "brief encounter" with the gondolier is even prepared for by a dream in which "she was going down a tunnel that grew smaller and smaller." She purposely shocks her mother by quoting a "vulgar" passage from the Bible about "the whoredoms of thy mother Jezebel." Always shame follows her outbursts. She feels the theological point that the will to do is the same as doing and thinks of herself as like Hester Prynne.[4] Yet at the same time she wishes that Hawthorne's heroine had lived in some place like Venice. At the end of the book it is left open to the reader to decide whether she has come to terms with both her wishes and God's, which she understands only partially (like all theists and agnostics).

The trilogy that followed after nineteen years of almost silence is a fictional account of how one becomes like Simonetta Perkins. Eustace, the shrimp who is almost devoured by the anemone, Hilda, is a frail boy, whose relationship with other children is always "tinged with a fearful joy," altogether unlike his sister's apparent intolerance and hostility. During his childhood every assertion of himself is followed by the feeling

---

[4] Hawthorne, James, and, latterly, Sir Thomas Browne apparently are Hartley's favorite writers—an interesting fact when one considers the tension between hope of heaven and one's own unworthiness, a significant aesthetic factor in the success of his novels.

that he must perform an act of expiation, which is usually formulated by Hilda. He admires, fears, loves and sometimes wishes dead his sister because she asks so much of him that he can think of no one who would suit her requirements "but God or Jesus." The frantic ingenuity of his neurasthenia is partly ameliorated by Miss Fothergill who believes "It's a great mistake not to feel pleased when you have the chance." Throughout his later life at school, at Oxford, in Venice, and in the days that precede his death—his best days because he comes to terms with himself—his will to enjoy is alternately encouraged by someone like Miss Fothergill and discouraged by Hilda or someone like her. He is never able to take the advice of the hedonist, Stephen:

> I wish you would not worry yourself about the Moral Law: Marx undermined it and Freud has exploded it. You cannot have any personal responsibility for your actions if your whole thought is conditioned by the class of society in which you were brought up, still less if your mind was infected by an Oedipus complex before it had attained to self-consciousness.

Eustace's trouble is that of the very sensitive man we too often denigratorily call neurotic. He wants both "to be pleased by pleasing" and to be like the saints in the West Window of the cathedral at Frontisham. His death wish for "a womb-like, tomb-like state" and his wish to experience everything and get it down on paper while living like an angel are almost exactly balanced against each other until the conclusion. The counterpointing conflict between Eustace and Hilda that represents every man's conflict is resolved in a tragic ecstasy only when Hilda agrees that the passage he recalls from the *Apocrypha* is correct:

> But the souls of the righteous are in the hand of God, and there shall no torment touch them. . . . And having been a little chastised, they shall be greatly rewarded: for God proved them and found them worthy for Himself.

My account of *Eustace and Hilda* emphasizes Eustace's conflict with and victory over his neurotic tendencies, but the novel nowhere resembles a case history. Eustace is fully and movingly drawn in both his small and his large moments: one sees and feels with him his delight with the coast town of Anchorstone, with Venice, hears and feels his pleasure at the gay and penetrating conversation in Venice and Oxford. His last day, when with weary determination he proves that he can be both himself and thoughtful of others, is a triumph one finds only in tragedy.

Though she is seen primarily through Eustace's only partially comprehending vision, Hilda becomes a fully drawn and sympathetic character. Within the limits of her temperament and of her imposed duty to take the place of Eustace's dead mother, she means and does well. The other characters, some forty of them, are rememberable and in proportion. Minney, the indulgent nurse; Nancy Steptoe, pretty and newly rich; Dick Staveley, a minor T. E. Lawrence, venturesome and insecure; Stephen Hilliard, a wit who hides his seriousness as he can; Lady Nelly, Miss Fothergill, the gondolier Silvestro— all of these are important in themselves and for the way they function in the development of Eustace.

Because it presents both on the surface and in depth a family, a social group, and a character who masters neurosis, *Eustace and Hilda* is both an excellent novel and a demonstration of the unrealistic parsimony of those who think the hero must be so well-adjusted that all his troubles are with circumstances and with others. The neurotic personalities of our time—as Proust, Malraux, Mann, Kafka, Auden, and L. P. Hartley in *Eustace and Hilda* demonstrate—are not to be ignored or denigrated. Rather they should be understood as people who are as capable of conquering themselves as are those presumed normal, who are frequently too little troubled to become interesting.

*Eustace and Hilda* shows dramatically the possibility of individual salvation. *The Boat* is concerned with a larger problem: the relationship of a sensitive and confused humanist to his country in a time of war as it is represented by his attempt to preserve "the right and duty of each human being to treat another as an end in himself, not as a flag or a coloured shirt or a sinner," to have "freedom of access to another's heart."

The action in *The Boat* is Timothy's private war to row his boat on a river that the established upper-class residents reserve exclusively for fishing. For Timothy boating is symbolic and representative (like Henry's dive into the river in *A Farewell to Arms*) of both a "release" and a "renewal." Timothy's effort to obtain boating rights is dramatized so skillfully that it does, as the rector of the small village that microcosmically represents the macrocosm, says, "involve the whole relationship of the individual to society." The feelings of the many from every class and caste who become involved in the struggle about Timothy's boat are intensified because the action takes place during World War II, in which Timothy does not serve. Among the many characters who influence Timothy are Magda and Vera, communists who feel that boating is a proletarian pastime preferable to fishing, the carefully guarded privilege of the rich. For them, and for Timothy as he planned it, successful rebellion against the conservative residents is paradoxically a victory both for communism and for individualism. Another friend, Esther, a plausible mixture of aesthete and patriot, understands better than Timothy the community's stand against him. She says, "In one way or another, though with such differing results, the war had taken possession of their minds, crowding out the he and she." The most powerful influence upon Timothy, at least ultimately, is Tyro, who changes from humanist to tolerant theist during the course of the action. Toward the beginning of the book he says:

> Ever since 1914 I have loathed the spectacle of humanity in collective action; they are homicides to a man, and what is nationalism, or patriotism, or whatever you choose to call it, but an excuse for legalizing and sanctifying the homicidal impulse. The State is man's greatest enemy . . . and The State disguised as "my country" is the most hateful form of the disease.

Tyro's early beliefs coincide sufficiently with those of Magda and Vera to make Timothy feel justified in flying both a Red and a British flag on his boat when he defies the solid citizens of the community by rowing down the river. He has come to believe that the failure of his life at Upton has been

> because I never had the courage to put my boat on the river. I was afraid of all sorts of things, public opinion, hurting people's feelings, being unpopular, breaking the law . . . and

> I was snobbish too; I wanted to make friends with the "gentry"
> and I knew I never could, if I insisted on using my boat.

He even thinks of himself as an heroic Chamberlain fighting a war-mad mob, as Eustace no doubt would have, in his middle period, if it had occurred at the time of Munich.

But the increasingly influential and theistic Tyro who had advised against the boat ride ( ' "A little patience, a little forbearance, a little understanding, a little laughter, *gentle* laughter . . . and all will be well" ' ) combines with Esther to convince Timothy that "Christian values are essential for the preservation of the species." After his rescue "by the very people he had set out to destroy," he feels he can "once more trust in the innate benevolence of man and in the greater benevolence of the Power that watched over them." Ultimately he accepts Tyro's evaluation—that his "excellent intentions" are "stultified by that fatal desire to be a general favorite." The conclusion of Esther and Tyro both universalizes the episode of the boat and restores Timothy to as balanced a humanity as Hartley believes one can achieve. Timothy hates to think of Mrs. Purbright and Vera as comparable enemies of individualism.

> "Which do you want to think of?" interrupted Tyro . . . with a
> loud guffaw. "One, you say, was an angel; the other—well!
> But remember *you* are just an ordinary sinner."
> Timothy frowned and again appealed to Esther.
> "But, Timothy, we went over all that. . . ." She stopped and
> Tyro supplied the missing words.
> "Mental astigmatism."
> "And you were only a little to blame for what happened to
> them, not more than—." She waited for Tyro to prompt her.
> "A negro might be for the people who get themselves crushed
> to death watching him lynched."
> "Thank you. What we mean is, *they* weren't in the boat."
> "I know," said Timothy. "And yet—." He left the sentence
> unfinished. Whether it was weariness, or the comfort of feeling
> that Esther and Tyro were beside him . . ., or whether to be
> out of Upton was to be in safety—who can say? But he did not
> notice the next milestone. He was asleep.

It is difficult to say which novel is an author's best because of the variety in unity that characterizes any good artist's work.

*Eustace and Hilda* goes deepest into the process of the maturing of the individual; *Simonetta Perkins* best reveals the effect of repressing the subconscious; *The Boat* interprets the interrelationship of the individual and society with the most balance; *A Perfect Woman* is unique both in its representation of a quadrangle and in its presentation of a conventional man who is believable and likeable; *My Fellow Devils* shows better than any of the others how sex may be identified with sin and still lead to salvation; *The Hireling* represents most movingly the relationship between the "upper" and the "lower" class; *Facial Justice* dramatizes most completely Hartley's quarrel with post-Edwardian civilization. The duology, *The Brickfield* and *The Betrayal*, shows best the consequences of an exaggerated feeling of guilt (that *has* some foundation in both Richard's life and human nature). Because it includes almost all of Hartley's varied preoccupations in intense unity, *The Go-Between* seems to me his best novel.

*The Go-Between* begins with the sentence, "The past is a foreign country: they do things differently there." The time is the turn of the century and Leo is twelve going on thirteen during the summer in which the main action takes place. Like all of Hartley's protagonists, Leo Colston hopes for more than can possibly occur. He believes the coming century will be "a realization on the part of the whole world, of the hopes that [he] was entertaining for" himself. He sees himself as Robin Hood and his friend Marcus's sister as Maid Marian, despite the fact that Marian is above him in class, appears angelic, and is undoubtedly the cause of his unrecognized sexual dreams about flying. He expects them to march purely together through their lives into a twentieth century totally different from and infinitely better than that *Facial Justice* presents. This is his dream world (and in dreams begin both revelations and responsibility?). In the actual world he worships Lord Trimingham, hopes and believes it proper that Marian will marry him, and acts as the go-between in the love affair between Marian and Ted Hughes, an apparently self-sufficient "lower class" tenant against whom he feels he should be prejudiced and with whom he empathizes because, on the subconscious level, he and

Ted are nearly identical. The actual world conquers the world of dream when he discovers that Marian has been charming to him so that she could use him as a messenger to Ted and when, a little later, he discovers her, his angel, and Ted, with whom he identifies most strongly, on the ground in the act of sexual intercourse—"the virgin and the Water-Carrier, two bodies moving like one." Ted's subsequent suicide completes the dissipation of his fantasy about the world. Looking back upon the experience—for the whole story is told from the point of view of an older man tracing back the reason that he is "a foreigner in the world of the emotions, ignorant of their language, but compelled to listen to it"—the happiest conclusion to which he can come (and the unhappiest conclusion in all of the novels) is that "the life of facts proves no bad substitute for the facts of life." It does not let one down.

An intensely personal novel, *The Go-Between* is also a parable of how the twentieth century deteriorated into what it has become. Leo and his experiences are a symbol of what Hartley in his darkest hour feels that modern man is. Class and caste still do exist (*The Hireling*); "normal" men like Trimingham are involved in triangles if not in quadrangles (*A Perfect Woman*); to a degree all men are our fellow devils; war is what begins on the personal level and is translated to the international level. Leo's realization—that "most people mind being laughed at more than anything else. What causes wars, what makes them drag on so interminably, but the fear of losing face?"—is a major theme in *The Boat*.

Hartley has said explicitly that one of the things that troubles him most is the "devaluation of the individual" so that the individual "can't expect the same interest and sympathy that he could in the nineteenth cenury." His duology does not provide a more hopeful answer to the constant human situation than Leo Colston's evaluation of our century when he is in his sixties:

> "Has the twentieth century," I should ask, "done so much better than I have? When you leave this room [this novel as it unfolds], which I admit is dull and cheerless and take the last bus to your home in the past, if you haven't missed it—ask

yourself whether you found everything so radiant as you
imagined it. Ask yourself whether it has fulfilled your hopes.
You were vanquished, Colston, you were vanquished, and so
is your century, your precious century that you hoped so
much of."

No, there is still the West Window at Frontisham for the
humanist, the theist, or the reverent agnostic, the West Window
that symbolizes the minimum of hope, a symbol that recurs
in all the novels, even in *Facial Justice* as the West Window of
Ely toward which Jael 97 dares to travel.

With what I hope is relative objectivity, I consider Hartley
one of the varyingly distinguished novelists of our century,
think that he has as good a chance of survival as "the psychological novelists" of Leon Edel, as the other differingly similar
novelists I write about. I believe even that Hartley in his "conventional" way penetrates the depths and explores the width
of man and his universe as deeply and as broadly as Joyce
and Lawrence, much more so than Woolf or Dorothy Richardson, almost as much as Faulkner.

Of course he has limits. He is never in any startling way a
technical innovator. He is never as bitter-hopefully amusing as
Rose Macaulay, though in all his novels there is comic relief
(to which I have not called attention). He does not have the
knowingness of Huxley. He cannot make a few characters in
a country village into a microcosm as well as Ivy Compton-
Burnett and Jane Austen can nor give the tragic purgation Miss
Compton-Burnett achieves at her best. He cannot make the
temporary horrible into a part of the continuous Catholic crisis
of existence as Graham Greene can nor make us rejoice with
minimal fearfulness as Joyce Cary does in his finest novels. He
is not at home in the corridors of power as C. P. Snow is nor
as capable as Snow of accepting the world as it is without
complacence. Though he comes close to empathy with the
working class—I have never known anyone more grieved than
he was at the death of his chauffeur who was his friend—he is
not at home inside the working-class mind and heart as are
Walter Allen and Alan Sillitoe. He is himself, his books are very
good, and they are unlike those of any other.

How long his best work will endure neither I nor anyone knows. To me now it seems that he can take his chance with the Fielding who wrote *Amelia* and the Thackeray who wrote *Vanity Fair*. But such speculation is ultimately foolish. For those who believe it important to understand twentieth-century man in both his mistakes and his potentiality, for those who want to know how novels that *make* nothing happen can cause us to be more aware and less likely to make our world a mess than our predecessors did, the best of L. P. Hartley is required reading for survival.

## Chapter Ten

# C. P. Snow: Scientific Humanist

OF ALL THE NOVELISTS I have discussed so far, Lord Charles Snow (who prefers to be called C. P. Snow) *is* the most traditional contemporary British novelist with a claim to representative eminence. He is traditional because he emphasizes substance and structure and engagement over form and texture and disengagement with the temporal (if one can agree on the meaning of any of these abstractions), in his sometimes pedestrian style, even in his use of headings for each chapter. He does not experiment with time-space, as Aldous Huxley and Lawrence Durrell do; with dialogue, as Evelyn Waugh and Henry Green and Ivy Compton-Burnett do; with cinematographic technique, as Graham Greene often does; with point of view, as Conrad and Joyce Cary do when they are at their best; with mixing satire and sympathy, like Rose Macaulay and Muriel Spark; with depth psychology, like L. P. Hartley and William Golding. Certainly he does not follow the manner or matter of the psychological novelists he deplores or has said sometimes he deplores: Dorothy Richardson, Virginia Woolf, Joyce, Lawrence.

It can be said—indeed it has been—that his work signals a return to the "lesser" fiction of the eighteenth, nineteenth, and early twentieth century, to the engaged and "hopeful" work of Trollope, Disraeli, and the early Bulwer-Lytton, to the "propagandistic" or "surface" realism one finds in the novels of Bennett, Galsworthy, and Wells. Although Snow published one first-rate novel during the thirties and had published four of the eleven projected novels in the *Strangers and Brothers* series by 1951, he did not become very well known in any country until 1957, when Queen Elizabeth knighted him for his distinguished work as a Civil Service Commissioner. I doubt that his reputation (or notoriety) was established firmly until the time of publication of *The Conscience of the Rich* in 1958 and of the Rede lectures, *The Two Cultures,* in 1959.

But his engagement as a critic, as a scientist, as a don, as a civil servant, as a man of conviction, as a reputable novelist, did give him considerable influence much earlier. Like the "lesser" novelists Disraeli and Wells, and the more important novelists Defoe, Smollett, Fielding, Dickens, Thackeray, George Eliot, and Hardy, he is and has been deeply engaged in the thought and action of his time. He never could have spoken of World War I as a distraction from his work, written that human nature changed about December 1910, or trusted intuition wherever it led him. He has plumped for the traditional novel and has become a rallying point for the good and bad novelists who prefer to use relatively conventional technique in fiction and for those who believe that novelists must be engaged both as writers and as persons with the perplexing problems of the modern period.

To a great extent since 1959, persistently since Dr. F. R. Leavis's attack in *The Spectator* in 1962, few days pass without an attack on or a defense of Snow's unsought eminence. He has been attacked as a member of the "Establishment," a position that seems to make him responsible for nuclear fission, the Conservative Party, bad writing, Suez, Eden, Harold Wilson, Sir Alec Douglas-Home, education in the humanities as well as in the natural and social sciences, the decline of the British Empire, an attitude that would encourage both the United States and the Soviet Union to get soft towards each other. He has also been defended for many of his attitudes towards all these responsibilities by people as eminent as Dame Edith Sitwell and Professor Bernal of the "Establishment," although there remains some confusion about whether the establishment stands for good or bad writing and a considerable perplexity about how he can be for both Harold Wilson and Sir Alec Douglas-Home, particularly now that he is Lord Snow and has been a member of the Labor Cabinet.

"On or about December 1910 human nature changed," Virginia Woolf said, carefully dating her intentional overstatement at the time of the first London Exhibition of Post-Impressionist paintings. Before that time British writers mainly had examined "the fabric of things": how men look and act; their relationships with each other, with society, with the overwhelmingness of environment. As the novels of Galsworthy and Bennett demonstrated, most British novelists were materialists, concerned with the body, not the spirit; in their preoccupation with how things looked and worked, they neglected the flux of sensibility men really are:

> Life is a luminous halo, a semi-transparent envelope surrounding us from the beginning of consciousness to the end. Is it not the task of the novelist to convey this varying, this unknown and uncircumscribed spirit, whatever aberration or complexity it may display, with as little mixture of the alien and external as possible?

However well Virginia Woolf exemplified the conviction her moderate query implies, whatever gains English fiction owes to the writers from Joyce to Elizabeth Bowen who have added another dimension to the portrayal of human beings, the practice of recording merely or mainly "the atoms as they fall upon the mind" has resulted in evil as well as good. The body and the body politic have tended to disappear in an excess of zeal about showing the inner depths. Sometimes *The Waves* and *The Years* (though not *To the Lighthouse* and *Mrs. Dalloway*) present us with only the dubious delights of the psychoanalyst listening to the patient on the couch, while large sections of *Ulysses,* most of *Finnegan's Wake,* nearly all of Dorothy Richardson's *Pilgrimage,* and the whole of the most meticulous imitators of all of these, convince us that there were, after all, virtues in the traditional English novel.

Important losses accompany the gains of this uncovering of a stratum of human consciousness. The virtues of Wells, Bennett, and Galsworthy tend to be ignored by a generation that is rarely unfashionable enough to read them. Only the academic critic (old-style) pays much attention to the eighteenth- and nineteenth-century novels everyone used to know, but dozens of books longer than *Ulysses* and more precious than anything the writer of *The Common Reader* could have written about herself, have made it nearly impossible (or unnecessary) to read with pleasure the excellent best work of Joyce and Virginia Woolf. And since the newest New Critics prefer solving erudite puzzles to the fundamental critical acts of mediation and stimulation, too much criticism of modern writers who defy the fashion of abstrusity seems designed to keep you from reading the writer himself. To too great an extent, our age has divided readers into an elite who read half a dozen authors and half a hundred critics, and a hoi-polloi who read the books that advertisements recommend into best selling.

For the novelist who puts matter before fashionable manner this dichotomy has been disastrous. The death of the novel is proclaimed periodically by those who see no innovators like the old innovators they revere. The different kind of originality one finds in Ivy Compton-Burnett, Henry Green, and P. H. Newby is given short shrift. The novelists I dare call representative (if daring can be diffident, mine is) are passed by or passed over lightly because they dare obvious intelligibility. So it is possible for as intelligent a critic as Leon Edel to write a book about the psychological novel (excellent within its prescribed limits) that concentrates upon "the most characteristic aspect of twentieth-century fiction; its inward-turning to convey the flow of mental experience." So it is that the most fashionable books on the novel deprecate or mention only briefly modern English writers other than James, Conrad, Dorothy Richardson, Virginia Woolf, Lawrence, Forster (the exception to test the rule?), and Joyce. So it was that C. P. Snow, in an essay that may become as important to the second half of the twentieth century as "Mr. Bennett and Mrs. Brown" was for the first, felt it necessary to condemn the "experimental" novel in the *New York Times Book Review* because "from about 1925–45 the sensibility novel was taken for granted, not only as the best kind of novel but as the only one. . . ." Yet, Snow continues:

> The novel only breathes freely when it has its roots in society.
> . . . sensibility is not enough; the novels of the near future . . .
> will make a new attack on the relations of men to their environ-
> ment. The environment will be the labyrinthine and highly

articulated complex of our technological society, but the problem is the constant one, the problem of what has been called the ecology of man.

As his own practice and other statements he has made show, Snow, like Virginia Woolf, overstates for effect. The "sensibility novel" has helped make good both his own novels and other contemporary novels he admires; its harmful influence is not the fault of Joyce or Virginia Woolf but of those who have imitated them too slavishly or praised them too lavishly. It is good that they gave the novel another dimension, sad that their over-sanctification has meant the neglect of excellent modern novelists who have returned in their own original ways to the tradition of the English novel that was vital and valid before Henry James and Joyce improved and constricted it.

It is dangerous and possible to argue that the novel of sensibility was the consequence of the limited lives of its creators, that they concentrated upon their inner lives because they had little to do with society as a whole. Virginia Woolf was as successful with Septimus Small as with Mrs. Dalloway, Joyce more successful with Leopold and Molly Bloom than with Stephen Dedalus, James nearly as good with his revolutionaries and businessmen as with the sensitive heroes and heroines he himself resembled. Yet it is true that all these novelists wandered along the streets *looking,* like young Stephen in *A Portrait of the Artist,* never speaking to the man in the street whose interests and activities they did not share. Often their imaginations bridged the gap, but they were primarily intellectuals living and talking with other intellectuals. Except for Joyce, who knew enough about the ordinary affairs of life to dislike and (when he could) avoid them, all these writers had independent incomes and had only the most platonic connections with business, politics, and science. Doubtless their disassociation helped them to develop their special qualities; perhaps it enabled them to see life more steadily and more whole than more engaged participants; certainly it limited the scope of their achievements. It is interesting that their most frequent interpreters enjoy the relative security of a university, that their interpreters often write more aloofly and for a smaller public than the somewhat isolated writers they interpret for a small public.

The defense of both writers and critics could be that disassociation is inevitable for the sensitive and well-educated in our time, that surely it is better than angry participation that leads to intemperate books. But is it *necessarily* true that they who touch pitch are defiled? Joyce Cary, Ernest Hemingway, André Malraux, Theodore Dreiser, Sherwood Anderson—I don't know how many others—have been active participants for large portions of their lives and their art has not suffered. Of course it would be ridiculous to say that Robert Browning's wealth or Dickens's poverty helped or hurt their writings, that Leonardo's many-sidedness or Giotto's asceticism made or harmed their art. It *is* certain that their differing experiences and gifts greatly affected what they did. Given talent, it is probable that a variety of experience will help the artist more than dealing and talking only with his peers.

Among modern writers no one has had the advantage of varied experience more than C. P. Snow. His parents were poor, only moderately educated, provincial, somewhat like the parents of Miles in *The Search* (1934) and those of Lewis Eliot in *Time of Hope* (1949). Scholarships took him to two very different schools: University College, Leicester (not then recognized as part of the higher education hierarchy though it prepared one for an "external" degree from the University of London), and Cambridge. By the time he was twenty-five he had been elected Fellow of Christ's College, Cambridge, because of his reputation as a physicist. At twenty-six he published his first novel, *Death under Sail* (1932), a still readable mystery. While he continued his scientific work at Cambridge, he published two more novels: *New Lives for Old* (1933) and *The Search* (1934), the latter a better novel about scientists than Lewis's *Arrowsmith*. In 1935 he became a tutor at Christ's College and began to plan his Lewis Eliot novels, the most ambitious series of linked novels anyone apart from Proust, DuGard, Mann, Romains, Dos Passos, and Anthony Powell has undertaken in our century. When World War II began he became chief of scientific personnel for the Ministry of Labour and, in the next year, published *Strangers and Brothers,* the first of the Lewis Eliot series, which Snow will name after its first volume. Until recently he was primarily active as a minister in the Labour government, but he remains active as a publicist for the coherence of the humanities with the natural and social sciences in our culture, as a lecturer in English, Scotch, Soviet, and American universities. He left the government to complete the last of the eleven novels that will comprise a linked panorama and interpretation of British life from 1914 to the present.

This bare listing by no means exhausts Snow's activities, interests and achievements. He has been editor of the Cambridge Library of Modern Science and chief fiction reviewer for *The London Sunday Times.* He has been physicist director of the English Electric Company, has travelled widely, loves cricket. In 1943 he was made Commander of the British Empire; in 1957 he was knighted; now he is a lord. He has received honorary degrees in Britain, the United States, and the Soviet Union; with his wife, the distinguished novelist Pamela Hansford Johnson, he continues to entertain and learn from and about all kinds and conditions of men and women, and he is, in his sixties, as active as one can imagine he ever was, despite a serious impairment of his eyesight. "If the arts and the scientist are to be brought nearer together," said *The London Sunday Times,* "he is one of the men who can do it." Administrator, teacher, practical man of science, he has a broader basis in experience than any other contemporary novelist, and it is as a novelist that he prefers and has preferred to be known since he was very young.

Reading his novels again, remembering what one knows of his public life, one finds it natural and appropriate that C. P. Snow's talk about "The Corridors of Power" headed the April 1957 number of BBC's *The Listener* and is the title of the ninth of the *Strangers and Brothers* series of novels. Even in *Death under Sail,* his first novel and a murder mystery, the struggle for power or prestige, interlocked as they usually are in his novels, is important in both the characterization and the action. Roger, the murderee, is both a personal and a public imperialist; he has taken credit for another's scientific discoveries and tries to dominate the private lives of those he knows. All the suspects and the two who solve the murder are power-prestige conscious, with beneficence, malevolence, or (most usually) with a combination of the two. In its preoccupation with power and in the amateur detective Finbow's unostentatious application of scientific principles, *Death under Sail* anticipates the better novels that have followed. Indeed, comparable complexities, greatly subtilized, recur in *Corridors of Power.* One wonders whether this may not be part of Snow's conscious attempt to bring his entire work into unity, since the main character in the latter novel is Roger Quaife, a minister who would like to stop nuclear escalation, and he resembles the murderee of *Death under Sail* in both name and fate, for his career as minister is murdered by his refusal to be supinely politic in either his public or his private life.

"When I was a young man," Lewis Eliot says in *Homecomings* (1956),

> too poor to give much thought to anything but getting out of poverty, I had dreamed of great success at the Bar; since then I kept an interest in success and power which was, to many of my friends, forbiddingly intense. And, of course, they were not wrong; if a man spends half of his time discussing basketball, thinking of basketball, examining with passionate curiosity the intricacies of basketball, it is not unreasonable to suspect him of a somewhat excessive interest in the subject.

Eliot is the speaker, but it does not seem unreasonable to suppose that here, as in many other places, he speaks for Snow. Snow himself has been preoccupied with success and power honorably, has achieved both, has used his personal and vicarious experience to illuminate "the official world, the corridors of power, the dilemmas of conscience and egotism" that have assumed paramount importance in the modern world. As sensibility has obsessed the experimental novelists and violence the naturalists, so the natural and perverted will to success-power-prestige has obsessed Snow. This will has never assumed psychotic proportions (no more did Hemingway's or James's obsessions); it has become the cohering center of both Snow's thought and his imaginative projections of it. Managers, a more pleasantly neutral word for the wielders of power we have and need, are the fuses and controllers of violence, the permitters or suppressors of sensibility. As Snow said in the essay "The Corridors of Power" in 1957 and makes emotionally evident in his novels, managers must be balanced and checked, feared when they talk too amiably about your or another's good. A necessary good-and-evil, they must be humanely educated, made aware that power let loose corrupts, recognize that they enjoy making people and things serve "useful" ends. Always they must be made to remember, to quote again from "The Corridors of Power," that "it is dangerous for anyone, it doesn't matter who he is, to have any power at all," as is shown of George Passant in private relations, too, in *The Sleep of Reason* (1968).

But I would not suggest that Snow's preoccupation with power-prestige is the only theme of his novels, especially if one thinks the search for power-prestige is confined to public life. What he somewhere calls "personal imperialism" shows up in the most private and obscure lives. There is, for example, Lewis Eliot's first wife, Sheila, who dominates by helping lame-ducks such as R. S. Robinson, himself a little magazine imperialist who demonstrates his "cleverness" by exploiting new talents; Mrs. Beauchamp, the landlady who shows her "ability" by finding out more about her tenants than they know of themselves; Eliot's mother and the women who resemble her, like Caro in *Corridors of Power,* who try to make up for lacks in their own lives by impelling their sons or lovers or husbands to act out what they couldn't. The list of public and private imperialists could be extended to include nearly all of Snow's characters, though some of them, such as Roy Calvert and Winslow, are defined more by their will against than by their will to power and all of his people are far more complex in their inner and outer lives than my crude generalization makes apparent.

Crude generalization is the necessary vice of the critic, the unpardonable vice in a novelist. Here Snow's knowledge of himself, his knowledge of others who are strangers and brothers, his assimilation of the scientific outlook, and his artistic talent, enable him to create a world that is both peculiarly his and recognizably our own. There is an annunciation of the last two qualities in his first novel. The narrator Ian (who, one is tempted to say, fuses with Finbow to become Lewis Eliot, who is confirmed and counterpointed by Francis Getliffe) detests "generalizations about types and sexes and everything else." Finbow, one solver of the mystery and the representative of the scientific outlook, says of our crude evaluation of people:

> We like to give them a label; and when we've given them a label we expect them always to act up to it. In writing, that process is known as keeping up with the tradition of the English novel.

Although some of the characters who seem to speak for Snow in the early novels can be labeled, most of the time Snow avoids this "tradition of the English novel." He uses the knowledge he has assimilated from wide reading in psychology, philosophy, history, and literature to help him present the people in his books understandingly without succumbing to the ostentation of scientific jargon. What he has learned from books, modern and classic, and what he has learned by insight and outsight, coalesce to enrich his interpretation of men and society, as the complex and integrated Lewis Eliot novels best demonstrate.

Where you begin does not matter as much as it does in Romains's *Men of Good Will,* Martin Du Gard's *The World of the Thibaults,* Mann's Joseph series, Dos Passos's *USA,* or Anthony Powell's *The Music of Time,* linked novels that Snow's can be compared with. I say this because I began my own reading of Snow with *The New Men* (1954) and enjoyed it as a single entity as I could not have enjoyed, say, *Within a Budding Grove* or *1919,* had I read them out of their proper place in the wholes of which they are parts. From what I have learned from others, however, I surmise that mine is an uncommon experience: each of Snow's novels is best appreciated as a portion of a more significant, larger entity. The separate novels are held together by character, place, theme, and time, as Proust's are, and there is the same intricate shuttling back and forth one finds in *Remembrance of Things Past.* One's appreciation increases if one begins with the first and title volume, *Strangers and Brothers,* and reads the rest in the order in which they were published; yet most of these novels stand firmly on their own, like trees that are part of a forest.

The time so far included in *Strangers and Brothers* is roughly from 1914 to 1963 (the last novel probably will stretch into the late sixties). The places, though there are relevant excursions to the continent, are mostly Cambridge and London and a Midland town like Leicester. The characters so far presented are most usually upper middle class, aristocrats, or people from the lower middle class who are on their way up or have "arrived." Since Snow's deepest experience has been in Leicester and Cambridge and London, and his nescient experience hardly can date from before the age of nine (1914), the choice of time and places is natural. His selection of characters calls for more accounting.

Certainly Snow is, as far as scientific disinterestedness permits, more sympathetic personally with the ideals of the working and lower middle class than with those of any other. The reason for his choice of characters would seem to go back to his preoccupation with the corridors of power which only recently have been occupied by those who retain their "lower" class affiliations and convictions. Perhaps the last novel of the *Strangers and Brothers* series will concentrate upon workers and Labour leaders who have tried for or obtained power. Since *Corridors of Power* brings the conservative politician of integrity to a point of no return in his effort to bring about moderated practical idealism, it did not seem implausible that the last two novels might turn towards working-class activity, until the appearance of *The Sleep of Reason* (1968). After reading it and Snow's remarks about "Last Things," his tentative title for the concluding novel, I find that I had wishfully thought stronger hope into the series than I now find there. It now seems to me that *Strangers and Brothers* will have as its unifying theme the maturing of Lewis Eliot and his sometimes wiser wife and friends to the realization that our century's "liberal illusion" that permissiveness leads to an earthly paradise is "idiot hope," that, though we must act as if the grace of a better world may occur, we must remember that if reason sleeps, horror is let loose.

Lewis Eliot, the "I" of *Strangers and Brothers,* is both interesting in himself and a means of making the entire series cohere. Apart from the fact that he is trained as a lawyer rather than as a physicist and that the events in his life are different, he resembles closely Finbow in the first novel, Miles in *The Search* and, increasingly, Snow himself. Like Miles and Snow, he enjoys "human intricacies . . . for their own sake," honors both the aberrant and the normal, and acts as if "humanism and social democracy" may work, though he considers over-idealized the interpretation of human beings propounded by many who share the liberal faith that has become only a liberal hope for him: "They were ineffectual because their human beings were ideal. . . . our human beings must at least be real." Successively a poor boy with nothing but natural endowment and "idiot hope," a clerk in an education office, a law student, a barrister, a don, a civil service administrator, Eliot pursues both his own career and his search for "the truth about human beings" without sentimentalizing or making inhumane either himself or the others he grows to understand. (This fact does not preclude a difficulty for the reader in adjusting to the omniprescence of Eliot, who is always in the right place at the right time. One must suspend disbelief about this omnipresence just as one does about the constant use of coincidence in Hardy and Dickens and the unrestraint of Molly Bloom in her stream of consciousness at the end of *Ulysses.*)

Though two of the novels, *Time of Hope* (1949) and *Homecomings* (1956), largely concern Eliot's career and the recollection of things past that conditioned it, though Eliot often refers to Proust, it would be difficult to conceive of two characters less alike than Proust's and Snow's main characters. Eliot's inner life—his childhood driven by mother worship and resentment, his gradual growth from extreme naïveté to maturity that includes bondage to a woman who cannot love him—suggests with important differences the difficulties of Proust's hero, as do the psychosomatic illnesses that sometimes occur in critical situations. But Eliot's suffering as a boy shaped by an insular community that rubs his nose in his father's inadequacy, his adjustment to the success his mother helped will him to, and his final escape from neurotic bondage to women too like or unlike his mother, have no Proustian parallels. Nor does Eliot detail the past because it is precious for its own sake; rather he relives it because reliving helps him understand the present that leads to the future, because his own experience with success and suffering enables him to understand more fully the strangers and brothers who interest him as much as himself. Proust retired to a cork-lined chamber that shut out the sounds and smells of the present; Eliot, like Snow, remains active in the corridors of power—doing, reflecting, seeing with unsentimental sympathy.

The style of C. P. Snow is as different from that of Proust as their two worlds. Walled away from the distractions of things present, Proust constructed the beautiful, intricate sentences that wind around time past until it seems time present. Snow's characteristically short chapters and sentences involve us in time becoming and coming. His prose is not elegant, nor should it be; usually bare of metaphor, rarely parenthetical, it marches, yet never with such rapidity that the generalizations about man's mixed nature, his essential aloneness, his public and private anguish, may not bring it appropriately to meditative rests that grow naturally from the action and illumine it. The progress of public lives that are also private, or of private lives that condition the public face, is carried on by a style that suits Snow's world of activity.

The sixty or so characters seen in the round in the *Strangers and Brothers* series are as varied a group as one can find in modern fiction. Predominant, and this at first seems curious, are the relative failures. George Passant—a sensual man who disapproves of sensuality, a Socrates who corrupts youth into independent thoughtfulness, a man made for greatness who persistently defeats himself, a believer in a Utopia no one will ever see or should want to, an active man whose shrewd introspection detects the self-deceit he continues to practice when he can—dominates the first novel that gives the series its title, recurs importantly or peripherally in most of the rest; in *The Sleep of Reason,* he recognizes the failure of his permissive philosophy, though he thinks still it should work—in Copenhagen, perhaps. He resembles, interestingly and coheringly, the successful Roger Quaife, the minister who dominates *Corridors of Power.* Quaife too seems to have every quality needed for success; his wife is wealthy, he is well-friended, he is able. He is even favored by chance when the Suez crisis makes his rise to eminence possible. Yet he fails, divorces his wealthy wife, and is, at the book's end, "reconciled" to a small life, though he retains a slight hope that he will come to power again and be able to lead those who would like to moderate nuclear escalation.

Roy Calvert, endowed with the charm, sensitivity, intelligence, and means that should ensure success, is both incorrigibly honest and innately melancholy. With none of Eliot's "idiot hope" (though he is glad Eliot has it and tries helplessly to find it in himself), Calvert compulsively helps the spiritually lame, sometimes causes suffering, is, except in manic periods that recur less and less frequently, the reluctant sufferer who finally becomes his own executioner. He is the chief character in *The Light and the Dark* (1947) and nearly dominates every scene in the other novels where he plays a part. Characters almost as complex and quite as well portrayed who "fail" can only be named: Mr. Knight, who was "so arrogant and so diffident" he didn't even attempt to succeed; Jago, the chief character in *The Masters* (1951); Martin Eliot, Lewis's brother and the most memorable of the atomic physicists in *The New Men* (1954); Sheila, Lewis Eliot's first wife and Snow's most fully characterized woman, who nearly takes the center away from the more important characters in *Time of Hope* and *Homecomings;* Tom Orbell, the inefficient radical who is hated so much that the reader of *The Affair* (1960) grows to hope against reasonable hope that he will become both a success and likeable; Mr. March, the integral Jew of *The Conscience of the Rich* (1958) who one wishes could have his silly unrealizable hopes for stasis fulfilled.

Perhaps (again I hesitate into psychology) the importance given these "failures" is the consequence of the deep feeling that one might have failed shared by most who, like Eliot (perhaps Snow), emerge from a lower class into eminence, who are mother-driven. Whether this is aesthetic appropriateness, as it surely is, alone, or the distillation of the author's life that is always somewhere in the best fiction, is not of fundamental importance. The artistic virtue of these portraits of failure is that they point up the limitations of a society led by men who (necessarily or unfortunately or both) walk the corridors of power and affect our private lives. Passant is a better man (more sensitively humane and human) than Eden, the employer who won't promote him, than Sir Herbert Rose, who keeps his eminence as a civil servant when Passant loses his. Roy Calvert is superior as scholar and man to the "great" Sir Culstone Lyall, though Roy compulsively persists in indiscretions that Sir Culstone, who steals the archaeological discoveries of a dead man to become "great," would not think of committing. Martin Eliot, who retires to the relative obscurity of a university as a protest against the inhumanity of atom-bombing, is the superior of the engineer Pearson and the essential functionary Drawbell, both of whom maintain public position because they do not feel even the need to protest. Comparably, Roger Quaife is the best and most sensible of all the ministers who surround him just as Sheila is a good deal more valuable than the more normal women, such as Daphne and Rosalind, who get along.

Especially in *Corridors of Power* (1964) and *The Sleep of Reason* (1968), novels that leave us looking without confidence or "idiot hope" towards the unpredictable future, one wonders if Lewis Eliot, who increasingly resembles Snow, may not be approaching the position of Francis Getliffe, who has "given up" to the dominion of numerical power in a "democratic" society. Eliot's wife, Margaret, we learn in the closing pages of *Corridors of Power*, "was not giving up" nor will she let her husband. Still the book's final grim sentence, like the grim talk about man's condition in *The Sleep of Reason,* makes those who remember the many times of hope in the earlier novels wonder if the tone will change further in the volume to come:

> We talked as though the future were easy and secure, and as though their [the children's] lives would bring us joy.

*Strangers and Brothers* may be the cause of indignation in others, but Snow himself usually eschews indignation, particularly if it is colored by righteousness. "It has often seemed to me strange that men should be so brazen with their moral indignation," Lewis Eliot says in *Time of Hope.* "Were they so utterly cut off from their own experience that they could utter these loud, resounding moral brays and not be forced to look within?" Here, I am confident, Eliot speaks for Snow. In all these linked novels (his early books could be included too), there are few characterizations marked by indignation: that of Sir Culstone Lyall, the archaeologist who rises to distinction dishonestly, that of Nightingale, the incompetent scientist whose delusions of grandeur operate malignantly, and that of Brodzinski, the nuclear "politician" whose unreasoning hatred would permit him to sacrifice all of humanity. The moving "failures" are never portrayed so that the luxury of indignation appears, or would appear natural. The reasons they do not succeed are evident to both character and reader. "Whatever I have done in my life, I claim to be responsible for it all. No one else and nothing else was responsible for what I have done," George Passant says, before he deteriorates. Sheila, Martin, Roy Calvert, and Jago implicitly or explicitly agree. Not able to take the same objective interest in the success of "inferior" men that Lewis Eliot does, they accept the inevitability that enables such men to walk the corridors of power in apparent ease as they act out their self- and other-fated fates. If Snow idealizes his "failures," it is not because he makes them blameless but because he makes them too discerningly fair about their responsibility for and to themselves.

In Snow's gallery of successes, the most fully realized, the most complex, and the most ambivalent in his attitude towards power-prestige is Lewis Eliot himself. The others in the gallery are almost as impressive. Herbert Getliffe, the barrister who employs and exploits Eliot, is the most fully developed among them. Though he uses the ideas and briefs of his juniors unabashedly, bullies and promises recognition and money he does not give, one not only grows to see his usefulness but to feel affection for him. Getliffe's is a troubled mind, wishing for but not daring integrity, as one sees best in his defense of George Passant, where he expresses publicly his admiration for him as a Socrates who corrupts youth and for Martineau, a Christian so literal-minded that he admits he lies. One realizes that Getliffe, unlike the pathetically righteous Porson, who would twist truth to put Passant in jail, knows himself and has cried in the night, that he recognizes superiorities in those who fail. "For most kinds of success, intelligence is a very minor gift," Eliot comments after he "saves" Passant. The other men who get on illustrate this generalization with no loss of artistic plausibility: the master in *The Light and the Dark* and *The Masters,* and Crawford, who succeeds him in the latter book; the minister Beville in *The New Men* and *Homecomings;* Lufkin and Sir Horace, the two civil service administrators who play significant parts in the series so far. Collingwood and Monty Cave, simple-minded, integral, and dedicated, are politicians who illustrate this in *Corridors of Power.*

None of them are, to refer again to the essay "The Corridors of Power," given to much meditation about the value of what they're doing, but they like to see things get done and "are considerably more competent than the rest of us." So Getliffe wins his cases, the master controls his college, Crawford defeats his more brilliant competitor to succeed the master, who "like so many managers . . . died in full career," Lufkin and Sir Horace succeed in business, Beville prevents disastrous mismanagement and disagreement in the atomic project he knows little about, Collingwood and Monty Cave continue as ministers and will preserve the ministry's necessary function, perhaps until a Roger Quaife or his better comes along who will help mankind out of the "hideous trap of nuclear escalation" by using "courage and intelligence and a little luck." All of them do what seems socially good to them and, when they harm, do so without malice. One grows to understand and like the lot of them even if one does not identify with any of them (except Francis Getliffe), as one does with the "failures" and the intermediate characters who fall into none of the categories a critic's simplification requires.

These others who must be mentioned too sparsely and too fast are Martineau, who prefers practicing Christianity to enjoying security and is as plausible as Graham Greene's priest in *The Power and the Glory;* Lord Boscastle, the snobbish aristocrat whose occupation is gone; his wife, an aged but unrepentant pagan who is antifascist when Franco and Chamberlain are fashionable; Jack Cottery, an amorist and a cook and a likeable fellow; Gay, the old don who lives the sagas he writes about; Margaret Davidson, who seems an effective counterbalance to Eliot's tendency towards too much hope or despair, who becomes his wife; Ann March, the likeable communist; Walter Luke, the naïve genius; Douglas Osbaldiston, the best of ministers, perseverant as a statesman although he knows the wife he loves is dying painfully; Charles, Eliot's son, whose "time of hope" in *The Sleep of Reason* seems more wisely rational than his father's. It would be an impossible strain to fit these disparate characters neatly into my simplifications, although they are essential parts of Snow's world and enliven it and make it real. Nor is it untrue to say, though I won't try to prove this, that they are all connected with (not tied to) the power-prestige, reason-permissiveness motifs that give *Strangers and Brothers* ideological unity, and that they are all engaged in the conflicts of personal and public imperialisms that give the series dramatic force.

These conflicts can be given only in general outline. Lewis Eliot's struggle for personal prestige, for the happiness and success of his friends, for a satisfactory life no woman's imperialism dominates, is the persistent personal drama throughout. But each novel has its conflict that meshes with the private and public conflicts of Eliot, that makes the series as a whole both an ideological and a dramatic unity. George Passant opposes the smug conventionalism of a middling Midland town in the title volume; in *The Light and the Dark,* Roy Calvert defies the hypocrisy and careful-mindedness of a Cambridge college and of the archaeologist's hierarchy; in *Time of Hope,* Eliot combats the rigid class structure of the Midland town that defeated Passant and the rigid professional structure of the legal profession; in *The Masters,* Jago and his multimotivated advocates try to defeat the traditional middle-browedness of the Cambridge college that disapproved of Roy Calvert; in *The New Men,* Martin Eliot and Luke try to disintegrate both the atom and the fatuity that sees the atom-bomb as a practical necessity; in *Homecomings,* the most complex novel Snow has written, Eliot nearly defeats "the disciplined conformity" of civil servants, and does adjust his own neurotic compulsions when he marries Margaret and has a son; in the *Conscience of the Rich,* the intricacies of a Jewish family are defeated by the will of a Jew who makes those he loves suffer so that he can feel the joy of freedom that makes achievement possible; in *The Affair,* Tom Orbell's dubiously valuable "victory" asserts the possibility of justice overcoming political and academic unreasonableness; in *Corridors of Power,* sanity in international affairs is postponed by Roger Quaife's fallibility and the bad luck of external circumstance, though it is not shown to be impossible; in *The Sleep of Reason,* Eliot, his wife, his son, and his brother see the reduction to horror of Passant's belief in permissiveness as they participate in and observe the trial of Cora Ross and Kitty Pateman, who tortured and killed an eight-year-old boy.

As only a reading of the novels can show, my exposition is too simple. Snow is never just an "abstractionist." His interweaving of characters in action and reflection, of themes related to the central theme, of place, heredity, and time in their effect on characters from whose action the themes grow, shows an admirable and of course imperfect skill no modern novelist of comparable scope has surpassed. In the more than three thousand pages Snow has completed, there are few inconsistencies, but rather, arranged complexities; there is no sentimental psychologizing; except in very minor characters, no blandly simple interpretation. All his characters are plausibly enough noble-and-ignoble to illustrate Miles's statement of a probable psychological truth in *The Search:*

> We can no more avoid jealousy of a friend's success than happiness at our own. And to pretend that it is not there, or to regret it, is a sentimentality; just as it is a sentimentality to pretend that the jealousy is all we feel, to disguise the generous pleasure with which it is mixed.

This statement and the actions of Snow's characters imply an undogmatic morality that has been called scientific humanism. There is no rule of thumb here, no nose-thumbing either. Sometimes defying, rarely flouting conventions, all his most sympathetic characters would agree with the generalization of Finbow in *Death under Sail* (that is, as far as intelligent people can agree with any generalization):

> I . . . firmly believe that conventions are made only to be broken—except the codes of manners and of honesty between friends, without which any unconventionality becomes merely a coarse and sordid caricature of decent living.

These two statements *Strangers and Brothers* vivifies. They represent, I think, the realism, the respect for reasonableness that must underlie change, and the belief that one must act as if "progress" is possible, that characterize the scientific humanism in which Snow believes, the philosophy that gives to his novels their peculiar distinction. Snow's scientific humanism, as all the novels show, as *Corridors of Power* and *The Sleep of Reason* show most formidably, allows room for the possibility of a fatal outcome of all man's social efforts that no reasonable man desires. As Francis Getliffe, who has always resembled and counterpointed the Snow we know from what he has published apart from his novels, implies appropriately in all the novels in which he appears, as Margaret, Charles, and Martin do in the penultimate novel, one must act as if man will prevail, but not assume that he will automatically. It is especially significant that Getliffe says fairly early in *Corridors of Power:*

> Sometimes I can't helping thinking that people won't see sense in time. I don't mean that people are wicked. I don't

even mean they're stupid. But we're all in a mad bus, and the only thing we're all agreed on is to prevent anyone getting to the wheel.

The subject under discussion is nuclear escalation and control, but Getliffe's comments upon people and the human situation in the fifties are appropriate enough for most of the action that has occurred in the public and private corridors of power diversely occupied and dominated from the "time of hope" that stretched from 1914 to 1933 (when Eliot and Getliffe were about the same age) to the time of scarcely moderated despair dramatized in Snow's latest novel.

It is appropriate that *Corridors of Power* concludes with Francis Getliffe and Lewis and Margaret Eliot together after Roger Quaife, the minister for moderation, has been defeated. Eliot, sustained by Margaret, now as meaningful a partner in the dialectic of meaning as he is—"she was not giving up, nor letting him"—is happy, though less spontaneously than when he and Getliffe had been fellow scientists conjoined emphatically by social and scientific hope. The novel ends movingly:

> We talked a little, the three of us, of the college and Cambridge. We went to the end of the balcony. Over the garden, over the rooftops, shone the misty, vivid night life of London, the diffused recognition of all those lives. . . . The memory of the struggle [over nuclear power], even the reason for it, dimmed down. We talked of the children, and were happy. . . .
> Under the town's resplendent sky we talked of the children and their future. We talked as though the future were easy and secure, and as though their lives would bring us joy.

Perhaps the close of *The Sleep of Reason*, with Martin and Lewis discussing the marriage of Martin's son to Roy Calvert's daughter, is even more pertinent:

> We were back in the flow of things. It mightn't be very grand: there was the splendid, of which we had seen a little, there was the hideous, of which we had seen enough: yet this was neither, it was what we lived in, in order to endure.

Quite obviously I think Snow's novels important. A lot I like in them, and some things that I do not I haven't mentioned, nor have I tried to say which novels *exactly* are best as novels. I have not attempted to place him precisely among his contemporaries nor among the dead great. I have not predicted posterity's opinion of his work.

Let me avoid or dodge part of my presumed function. I know no absolutes that measure novels, do not know how exactly to place any but the valueless novels of our time, do not, as I write, recall the "great" novels of the past with sufficient immediacy to give my opinion of Snow's probable place in the hierarchy in which he will ultimately find his proper position. Like most writers about reading, first I have an impression, a feeling, a stimulation, an illumination (perhaps all of these indescribably combined) that impels me to read more of and more closely in a poet or novelist I admire. That is what happened when I read *The New Men* in 1954, what excited me to read his other twelve novels. I do not pretend that my reactions have been any more constant than my psychophysical system. Ultimately I accepted or ignored even those qualities in Snow's novels that annoyed me, just as I have accepted Wolfe's rhetoric, Mann's excess of detail, Thackeray's moralizing, and the commonplace minutiae of Defoe. If I knew what perfection is I might judge each book impeccably. As it is, all I can do and all I can believe other critics do, is to justify judgments that several and not dissimilar reactions have left with me.

Snow's best work (*The Search* and the series to be entitled *Strangers and Brothers*) I consider very good. No earlier novelist has so effectively applied dramatic talent and the scientific outlook to power as it is exercised privately and publicly. Wells's impulsive jump to conclusions is the antithesis of this outlook; Aldous Huxley's great scientific knowledge too often is made mystifying by mysticism. There is unique value in Snow's application to fiction of the scientific outlook: as it is made meaningful by his artistic talent, it judges and evaluates by understanding; it discourages self-righteous indignation; it shows us the complexity that simplicity conceals; it encourages discriminating tolerance; it helps to adjust man to the "real" universe.

Of further, perhaps greater, importance is the fact that Snow, by his work and in his person, undogmatically encourages those writers who recognize life as an interplay of the life within and the life without, who see the atoms as they fall but know they are important both in themselves and as a part of a larger entity. Since the Second World War and its cold aftermath, the understandable dead end for many novelists has been the retreat into the womb that no longer is safe either. Talent has gone into many of their novels and illumination of a limited kind has come out. But, if one believes that hope for hope is desirable and that fiction is more than a refuge for despairing hours, can one not anticipate more than the talented novels of Capote and the brilliant, esoteric pessimism of Beckett? The not foolishly (I trust) hopeful younger and older novelists Snow has encouraged by example and praise, though they often express their hope by an Orwellian examination of the worst consequences possible, are devoted to a sympathetic, unsoft presentation of the man within who may help the world without. Perhaps all this is useless and we should console ourselves with beautiful expressions of unecstatic isolation. I like to think not and to believe that C. P. Snow and others like him will help man's persistence and be remembered in the centuries that still may ensue.

## Chapter Eleven

# War, Cold

THE TRAUMA ENDED; its effects did not. In the twenties writers and readers alike (of course I allow for many exceptions) were bitter and disenchanted because the tea was no longer there at Grantchester, because neither the war nor the peace seemed worth its loss. The brief time of hope and depression ended at Munich has not reappeared in England (or elsewhere in the West) since, except sporadically in individuals and years. There were no war writers, no strenuous hopers for lasting peace even among those who of course supported the United Nations. Queuing and getting angry about it, hoping against hope, dim-viewing, concentrating on individual sensations (Beatlism), or salvation, looking back in nostalgic wonder—all these became the order of the day after 1938 (except for most politicians everyone knew the war would come), and the habit after 1946, March 5, Winston Churchill's Fulton, Missouri speech, the convenient date for the start of the Cold War Russia anticipated.

I exaggerate slightly. But what have been the good dates and events? The Nuremberg Trials and the first meeting of the United Nations? Punishment of the wicked and planned internationalism (most recently scuttled in the Arab-Israeli crisis)? Population explosion or the Commonwealth displacing the British Empire? The American dominance—well-intended naïveté leading to Korea and Vietnam—met or incited by a variety of powers comparable to those that have resented irresistible force since history has been recorded? A more democratic Russia? A China like the Soviet Union after the Revolution? The French Third Force? The excluding Common Market? A succession of public figures characterized by their equal incompetence—yes, Truman and Bevan had a flair, Kennedy complimented Khrushchev for his statesmanlike con-

duct in abandoning Cuba? NATO? Joe Louis? *The Stranger?*
*The Plague?* LSD?

England, still one of the best places to live if not to hope
in, felt quiescence it thought foreboded doom. Again, there were
hopeful "moments." The Angry Young Men flailing at everything. Plays in factories (*Chips with Everything*); Pope John
XXIII. Relaxation of censorship, of cruelty to homosexuals,
prostitutes; less religious dogma (Jehovah's Witnesses excepted)
No-God could believe. Ironic points of light in unexpected
places. Civil Righters. Peace Crusaders. Some who recognize
stupid abstractions: Nigger, Communist, Catholic. But the best
have little conviction, the worst simulate intensity.

Too many young resemble Olivia Manning's Anna in "Growing
Up" (1951), who marvelled at the beliefs of the "absurdly
young" older people since she knew "we can't expect much from
the future." Coexistence. Containment. "Security." Less poverty. Universal conscription. Threats of extinction we're
*practically* sure are threats only (on all twenty sides). There's lots
of talent, used too quickly, too often, or too vehemently. (Olivia
Manning is a good novelist and so are a hundred I won't name;
Benjamin Britten's *War Requiem* is so tragically probable we'd
die listening to it if its aesthetic beauty didn't make it unbelievable.) But count the novels since 1938 that exceed
pleasant competence—not the fashionable for a while. Exceptions
allowed, most of them have been by the eight who learned how
to cope with the queasy ball-room floor between 1914 and 1938.

The "failure" (unevenness or part realization) of those who
began after 1938 is to be noted, not blamed. So is the failure
to continue to mature of those as good as any I've written of:
Rebecca West, May Sinclair, R. C. Hutchinson, James Hanley,
Henry Green, Christopher Isherwood, Anthony Powell, others.
In a trough of history it is hard to mature further, harder to
grow up, even though one knows troughs lead to peaks. No
wonder that Osborne looks back and around in anger, that
Philip Larkin dwells on the ruined church, that Phillip Toynbee
and Durrell give up quest and "content" themselves with
multiplying relativity in pleasing novels—*Tea at Mrs. Goodwin's*
(1947), *The Alexandria Quartet* (1960)—that P. H. Newby has

not realized the promise of *Journey into the Interior* (1945), though *Barbary Light* (1962) comes close.

What new and old writers (those who matured and those who were diverted from it) feel as a too ponderable weight about to fall, J. B. Priestley, the gifted journalist who started to become a good novelist, wrote about in *The New Statesmen* in the fall of 1957:

> We [Britain] ended the war high in the world's regard. We could have taken over its moral leadership, spoken and acted for what remained of its conscience; but we chose to act otherwise. . . . It has been said we cannot send our Ministers naked to the conference table. But the sight of a naked Minister might bring to the conference some sense of our human situation.

Poetry (or fiction) *makes* nothing happen. Auden's words are accurate and relevant. But such writing does not satisfy as well as Tennyson's confrontation of nature red in tooth and claw (however little we can agree with his poetic solution) or even Hardy's acceptance of an Immanent Will that might fashion all things fair sometime. With unconstraining voices all serious writers would like to persuade us to rejoice. Today they cannot, except minusculy. Most novelists who have become properly prominent since World War II have the virtue of anger and the ability to dramatize it for a time. But, except for those who have humanist or religious faith, they write novels that decreasingly repay our reading of them. Kingsley Amis and Iris Murdoch, the best of the miscalled Angries, delighted and appeared to be advancing on meaning in *Lucky Jim* (1953), *That Uncertain Feeling* (1955), *Under the Net* (1954), *Flight from the Enchanter* (1956). Since these novels they've written good novels, but there's not enough new in the later Amis, only delightful philosophic pirouettes in Iris Murdoch's yearly novels. Vaguely like them but better is Malcolm Bradbury. In *Eating People Is Wrong* (1959), Treece, a university teacher a little like Lionel Trilling's teacher in "Of This Time, That Place," becomes "terribly tired" of what is "terribly interesting" and asks if the round of homosexual bars the imperturbable sociologist Jenkins has taken him through hasn't been "enough discontent" for one night. A "poor little liberal humanist" in a fragmented world with "no Utopia in sight," Treece immerses himself in the destructive element, hoping to rise and to raise others to a new world that believes in "civilized and respectful contacts, deep personal relationships, honesty and integrity of motive, recognition of the individuality of persons." Bradbury presents his serious point with comic skill as he does again in *Stepping Westward* (1965), where the most sympathetic character wants to show that one cannot live "in the ethically flabby belief that the world is good and innocent," that "deeper connections had to be made" between men and men, man and the universe.

Angus Wilson's novels, which explore the nightmare "truth" of the unreconciled existence of instinctive and puritanical imperatives that he sees deep in the English character, are flaggingly interesting. None of them is as good as the brilliant short stories that started with *The Wrong Set* (1949), which devastate hypocrisy, but they "bombard" readers with "distortions and caricatures" of life now and in the future he sees, in a way more skillful and likely to succeed than, say, the unrelieved nihilism of Beckett and Genet.

The contemporary novelists with varied faiths who do not overlook the destructive element, I prefer. Though William Golding's work is uneven (*Free Fall, Pincher Martin,* and *The Inheritors* seem interesting only), all his novels celebrate paradoxical triumphs—as he believes tragedy does. Using the novel as a means of philosophic exploration, as Iris Murdoch does, he wishes "to discover whether there is that in man which makes him do what he does," whether fall or rise is free, in other words. Against the grain of most criticism I feel that it is triumph he writes about in *Lord of the Flies* (1954), of Ralph and Piggy's endurances by cowardice and cunning until the return of the reign of law that keeps us civilized. *The Spire* (1964) I like best. Jocelin, who raises the spire that still stands incredibly on an insecure foundation, recognizes, as rulers, the led, writers, and readers must, that ambition's achievement is the consequence of horrifying *Hubris* that causes death and unhappiness, that it is the flouting and following of what we think is God's will that kills as it makes beauty.

What William Golding does for the exceptional man in the extreme situation, Pamela Hansford Johnson does in the best of her uneven good novels for "the majority of lives" that "fade gently away without a noticeable peroration." She does this best in her recent novels *An Error of Judgment* (1962) and *The Humbler Creation* (1959). Maurice in the latter novel "thought that a man like himself, so much more obviously of the humbler creation, was a small creation . . . that what he had to offer was little enough," but his giving up Alice to return to Libby—his cold, self-martyring wife—is a little like Thomas Hawkes's striking or "clapping" his hands "three times together," rejoicing at his death (reported in Foxe's *Book of Martyrs*). Maurice follows the "moral law" for a reason as good and inexplicable as any proof of the existence of God:

> Well, he thought, I have just about managed to heave one hand out of the fire.
> The smell of the smoke had not quite gone, it lingered in the corners of the room and in the creases of his palms.
> And I can only hope, God being with me, to keep it there.

Although she had (till *The Mandelbaum Gate*, 1965) too much the trick of giving her novels a Catholic "twist" at the end, probably Muriel Spark is the most accomplished British novelist to grow up since World War II. Her novels hustle us so rapidly from event to event that we do not recognize the high seriousness of the whole until we have finished and thought and thought about it. Her novels have the virtue of conveying grave gaiety, even her novel of old people crowing about their friends' preceding them in death, *Memento Mori* (1959). This grave gaiety is suggested by the conclusion of *The Ballad of Peckham Rye* (1960), after Humphrey learns sadly that Dixie feels as if two hours of marriage had been twenty years:

> But it was a sunny day for November, and, as he drove swiftly past the Rye, he saw the children playing there and the women coming home from work with their shopping bags,

the Rye for an instant looking like a cloud of green and gold, the people seeming to ride upon it, as you might say there was another world than this.

Alan Sillitoe, still in his forties, with two good, two fair novels published already, is less expert technically than Muriel Spark, but he seems to dramatize what I guess to be the ordinary man's seen truth in the quiescence after the trauma. His most eloquent work of fiction is "The Loneliness of the Long Distance Runner." A Borstal boy, running his long distance for his jailer, who thinks he uses him kindly, thinks:

> For when the governor told me to be honest it was meant to be in his way not mine, and if I kept on being honest in the way he wanted and won my race for him he'd see I got the cushiest six months still left to run; but in my own way, well, it's not allowed, and if I find a way of doing it such as I've got now then I'll get what-for in every mean trick he can set his mind to. And if you look at it in my way, who can blame him? For this is war—and ain't I said so?

Sillitoe faces the fact that it's a battlefield for most men still, though they work hard as crooks or blokes for a weekend of uneasy pleasure. It's different, worse, than it was as Joyce Cary and John Dos Passos, Jack Conroy and C. P. Snow, Robert Cantwell and Graham Greene saw and dramatized it in the thirties (there was more "idiot hope" then).

But it's not too bad, this life, even if it's all of it, as Arthur thinks in *Saturday Night and Sunday Morning*, 1958 (note how different and similar these thoughts are to Robert Jordan's, dying, in *For Whom the Bell Tolls*, 1941):

> Born drunk and married blind, misbegotten into a strange and crazy world, dragged-up through the dole and into the war with a gas-mask on your clock, and the sirens rattling into you every night while you rot with scabies in an air-raid shelter. Slung into khaki at eighteen, and when they let you out, you sweat again in a factory, grabbing for an extra pint, doing women at the weekend and getting to know whose husbands are on the nightshift, working with rotten guts and an aching spine, and nothing for it but money to drag you back there every Monday morning.

Well, it's a good life and a good world, all said and done, if
you don't weaken, and if you know that the big wide world
hasn't heard from you yet, no, not by a long way. . . . it
won't be long now.

Walter Allen, best known as a critic but a good novelist in
*Innocence Is Drowned* (1938) and *Dead Man over All* (1950),
dramatizes most accurately the feel of English society now in
*Three Score and Ten* (1959). Through the recollection of
Billy Ashted—seventy-six, a not unusual workingman, a gifted
questor, writing his memoirs while benevolently "imprisoned"
by one of his two sons, both of whom are among the leaders
of England—one gets the picture, felt now, of England before
and after the trauma. He thinks of his approaching death:

> And yet man still exists in the realm of the natural. It
> remains the basis of his being, and he cannot escape from
> it, and the longer he lives the more he is subject to the tyranny
> of the natural, whose law is decay and death. The process
> may be stayed; it cannot be put off forever; and fear of it . . .
> means only that a man becomes life's show and grovels under
> the dominance of nature, which he himself has made omnipo-
> tent. For nature is omnipotent only if a man allows it to be.

The distinction of Walter Allen—who matured later than the
proletarian novelists of the thirties, is older than Alan Sillitoe,
less committed than Pamela Hansford Johnson and Muriel
Spark—is that he sees and presents with barely biased clarity
the human condition we see after the trauma, what the others,
more ideologically involved, distort artistically. The age his
novel looks towards recognizes the worst one must see to get
to the better. Perhaps *Three Score and Ten*, and others I
don't know among novels flooding from the presses each year,
will help us all to a better Georgian age, with more tea and
not just at Grantchester.

# Index